# SCHUBERT

## SOLO PIANO LITERATURE


Edited by

**Carolyn Maxwell**

Reviewers

**Eileen Cline**

**Gayle Kliever**

**Marti Epstein**

**Geraldine Gant Luethi**

Assistant Editor

**Geraldine Gant Luethi**

**ACKNOWLEDGMENTS**

Geraldine Gant Luethi--Foreword, Biography,
Prefaces, and Critiques of the Sonatas
Elizabeth Harris--Cover Design
Kenneth Andrus--Production

Contributors
F.E. Luethi
Russell Miller
Ruth Wood

Published by Maxwell Music Evaluation Books
1245 Kalmia, Boulder, Colorado 80302

First printing, 1986



Printed in the United States of America

ISBN 0-912531-03-7

# TABLE OF CONTENTS

# FOREWORD

MAXWELL MUSIC EVALUATION BOOKS proudly presents Schubert: Solo Piano Literature for the purpose of recognizing this composer's immense contribution to keyboard literature. The piano works of Franz Schubert are numerous, with only a small portion to be found in published multi-composer collections. This book lists and reviews all available pieces for keyboard, with hopes that the entire body of Schubert's works will gain a more appreciated status in the minds of teachers, performers, and audiences.

This book contains a brief biography of Schubert and some pertinent information on published sources. Critiques of each work follow, arranged in groups and catalogued by the numbering system of Otto E. Deutsch; opus numbers are included when available. Each review is accompanied by a thematic or incipit for recognition purposes, and published sources are listed for each piece. A summary section gives tempo, length, and technique requirements for every work. We have used the G. Henle Verlag editions as our definitive source, recognizing obvious differences in notation and tempo markings. The technique is based on significant challenges presented by each piece. Grade levels included are based on technical, rhythmical, and musical content. Measure numbers refer only to the number of printed bars, including second endings; repeats and da capos are not considered.

Our subjective "performance" recommendations apply to any type of performance--recitals, auditions, and concerts. We found many pieces in this category that are not included in popular collections and we hope these comments will broaden the scope of choices.

The sections in the back of the book are as follows:

- Three complete indices:
  - Primary: Title index in order of appearance in the book.
  - Secondary: index in chronological D. (Deutsch) numbers.
  - Key Index: keys listed, starting with A Major, then presented with category names.
- Glossary: defines the terms used in the "technique" section.
- Grade Leveling: brief list of criteria used.
- Sources: list of collections devoted to Schubert used in this book.
- Bibliography: rather than using footnotes, all the sources of quotes are listed.

## BIOGRAPHICAL NOTES

For many, the man who was Schubert is an artificial figure, made unreal by cliche and myth. The image is often that of a lovable, awkward hero, immersed in the bohemian life of wine and song, scribbling songs on napkins, and leaving unfinished his most significant symphony. Early biographies of Schubert did not entirely separate fact from fiction; several were colored by reminiscences of friends who romanticized or even dreamed up stories about him. The culmination of such fantasies is the shadowy figure immortalized in film and operetta, while the real triumphs and tragedies of the composer's life remain hidden.

There are several recent biographies that present the man clothed in reality. They reveal some facts that will be discussed briefly, perhaps inspiring readers to search deeper for themselves.

Schubert was rarely penniless or starving. He was born into a family of peasant stock, but his father was an educated man who eventually owned his own school in the suburbs of Vienna. Franz received a decent elementary education and private musical training. Because of his obvious abilities, he was admitted into the prestigious school at the Imperial Court Chapel and later into the Imperial Royal City Seminary, the foremost boarding school in Vienna. The musical education he obtained there was the finest available. His teachers, including Salieri of "Amadeus" fame, singled him out for special attention. Later criticisms of inadequate training in basic rudiments and counterpoint were unjust. Schubert chose his own directions, moving away from classic and contrapuntal techniques into more innovative and personal melodic statements.

The financial struggles of his mature years were somewhat self-imposed. His first position was as a qualified teacher in his father's school, a career he could have pursued at any time. His musical training would have allowed him a living as a private teacher. He spent two summers tutoring the daughters of Count

Karl Esterazy and composed elegant pianoforte duets for them, but there is no further record of private instruction. He was a talented pianist, violinist, and singer, and perhaps could have attained a career as a professional concert artist. His lack of interest or his inability in performing limited his acceptance with the publishers of his day; fame was the key to publication and Schubert's obscurity was a definite handicap.

Schubert's choice to compose, with no fixed income nor financial security, left the world a staggering number of compositions during his brief career, and left him as an unrecognized genius except in his own circle of friends and supporters. He was not a total failure as a composer. About half of his major works were published in his lifetime, although he was paid shamefully for them. His music received favorable reviews in Vienna, Leipzig, and other cities, but publication beyond the provincial limits was denied. There was enough recognition and financial success to keep his hopes alive, and his friends and family supported him when times were bad.

There were uncontrollable factors that worked against Schubert's success in composition. His working career began at a time of severe ecomonic depression and political repression. Napoleon demanded harsh levies from the Austrian government, leaving the court without the means to support the arts as in the past. Fear of revolution led to the development of a "police state" under Prince Metternich, who curtailed individual and social freedoms with abusive force. The young lawyers, writers, and artists in Schubert's circle were particularly suspect. Schubert was arrested while in a friend's apartment. The friend was exiled and Schubert was released, but the record remained. Two of his songs were banned because of unacceptable poetry. His political "disfavor" destroyed any possibility of court patronage, and Schubert's dislike of priests precluded any support from the church.

Support of the arts became the prerogative of the growing middle class. The Viennese tried to forget the oppressive political climate with evenings of singing and dancing that became Schubert's arena of expression. The lovely compositions that he generously shared became the basis of his fame. Publishers clamored for these works, especially in the years between 1820 and 1823, when the "Schubertiads" were at their height. Publication fees paid the rent, but the public demand was for easy pieces, to be sung and played by the amateur. Schubert's larger works, revealing the true depths of his instrumental genius, were never accepted. There is one public concert on record in March of 1828, featuring Schubert's songs and chamber works. The crowd's joyful acceptance of his music was almost ignored by the critics, whose attention was focused on a performance by Paganini the following evening. His support came from civil servants, professional men, and merchants who could not afford private string quartets or orchestras. Schubert never heard his mature orchestral works performed.

The overwhelming tragedy in Schubert's life struck in 1822, when he contracted syphilis. He withdrew from society for almost two years, facing the certainty of social deprivation and death. He continued to compose, but his career suffered serious setbacks. His remaining years were marked by alternating periods of optimism and creative energy, and total despair and stagnation. His death in 1828 is attributed to typhoid fever. His family paid the funeral expenses but were later reimbursed through publication royalties. Schubert was buried near Beethoven's grave in a cemetery now called "Schubert Park." The bodies of both composers were later moved to the Grove of Honor in the Central Cemetery of Vienna.

Schubert's older brother, Ferdinand, retained careful custody of the composer's manuscripts and worked tirelessly at getting them published. Interest was minimal, and after 1830 both composer and works were almost forgotten. Ferdinand eventually sold all his manuscripts to Diabelli, who published them intermittently through the nineteenth and into the twentieth centuries. About eighty remain unpublished.

A revival of interest in Schubert's music began in the 1860's, with performances of several chamber works and the Unfinished Symphony. The era of radio broadcasting began to extend the orchestral repertoire, and Schubert's symphonies become part of that renaissance. Artur Schnable was largely responsible for the awakening of interest in the Schubert piano works, especially the sonatas.

The dream of any musicologist is to find an unknown composition by any great composer. With the manuscripts of Schubert, that would seem a definite possibility. He was incredibly careless with his autographs. He would give them to friends and forget to whom. He would send them to publishers, neglecting to insist on their return. Many were misplaced or lost. Many compositions are unpublished due to lack of interest. There are probably some in private collections that are unknown to both scholars and publishers. The possibility of new discoveries is tantalizing.

In the latter half of the nineteenth century, an interest in Schubert's music was reawakened. It resulted in the publication of the "Critically Revised Complete Edition" of Schubert's works in 1895, with an additional supplement appearing in 1897. This set of thirty-nine volumes, published by Brietkopf and Hartel (with Brahms as a consulting editor) revealed the astounding outpouring of Schubert's genius. The sheer number of published works proves that, though careless and impractical, the composer worked with a feverish, irreproachable discipline. A statement by the most recent biographer, George Marek, gives brief insight:

"Of 603 songs, fewer than a tenth are in general usage. Of his symphonies, only 2 form a part of the orchestral repertoire. Of his fourteen extant string quartets, four or five are regularly played. Of his fifteen completed piano sonatas, 5 or 6 alone are frequently presented. His 15 operas lay buried, and to hear a live performance of one of his masses is an exceptional event."

Chronological catalogue of Schubert's works has been extremely difficult. The first edition of Grove's Dictionary of Music lists 1,131 compositions with some dates that have since proved questionable. Later editions used the Brietkopf and Hartel listings, also faulty. The most careful study of chronology was done by Otto E. Deutsch, who completed a chronological thematic catalogue in 1951 that is considered authoritative. New editions list all Schubert works by D (Deutsch) number, representing their probable order of composition. In 1967 the International Schubert Gesellshaft was founded in Tubingen, with its chief objective being the preparation of the Neue Schubert Ausgabe, a complete and authentic edition of the composer's work to be published by Barenreiter. It consists of series of classified works and includes biographical information and thematic cataloguing by Deutsch. The volumes were printed in the late 1960's, through the efforts of senior editors including Walter Durr, Arnold Feil, Christa Landon, and many other Schubert scholars. There may be editions of the future, with works not presently known. This poem by George Eliot is provocative:

> Schubert, too, wrote for silence; half his works
> Lay like a frozen Rhine till summer came
> And warmed the grass above him.
>
> even so,
> His music lives now with a mighty youth.

# I. DANCES

The Schubert dances, grouped in Ecossaises, Galopps, German Dances, Landlers, Minuets, Waltzes, and a single Cotillon, present to the modern performer an appealing microcosm of the composer's genius. They are of uneven quality, but many seem to be prototypes of the dance movements of the larger piano works, revealing subtleties of melody, harmony, and rhythm that express Schubert's individuality.

These miniatures are rooted in the Viennese and Austrian folk culture. In their original context, they were intended to accompany dancing. At various social events the composer would sit at the keyboard for hours, improvising these short tunes for waltz-happy friends. As the composer wrote them down, they became a loose succession of melodies, generally divided into two eight-measure sections and often containing motifs of musical phrase or rhythm integrating them as a set. Because they were easy and accessible, the publishers accepted them with enthusiasm but often transposed or regrouped them, probably with the composer's knowledge, into easier keys or more workable pairings.

The majority of the dances are in triple meter, with the distinction between lander, German dances, and waltzes difficult to define. The landler is a very old peasant dance which probably originated in lower Austria. It seems to be a little slower than a waltz, with well accented pulses that enhance the swaying motion of the action. Without physical dance steps delineating the differences, these compositions retain significant similarities in sound.

The ecossaises and galopps are in 2/4 time. The term ecossaise comes from the French language and means "Scottish"; there is a correlation between it and the German name "Schottisch." Modern scholars feel that both dances reflect what French and German composers felt a Scottish dance ought to be, rather than a true ethnic transplant of music form. It is a species of contredanse, which probably originated in England in

1848, known as the German polka. The name was known in France from the early 18th century. There are approximately 382 of these short, delightful dances, offering a source of moderately easy pieces that are largely neglected in the collections of Schubert's smaller works. We have used as the primary source Samtliche Tanze, edited by Paul Mies (G. Henle Verlag), which contains all of the dances in two volumes.

## ECOSSAISES, D. 145 (Op. 18)

Note: All of D. 145 may be found in:

MIES, Paul: Schubert--Samtliche Tanze, Band I
(G. Henle Verlag 74).

No. 1, Ab Major <u>Early Intermediate</u>

AGAY, Denes: An Anthology, The Romantic Period, Vol. III (Yorktown).
ALFRED (Publisher): Schubert--21 of his Easiest Piano Selections.
CLARK and GOSS: Piano Literature, Book 5b (Summy-Birchard).
DEXTER, Harry: Selected Piano Works--Schubert (Hansen).
HANSEN (Publisher): Schubert--A Highlight Collection.
HERRMANN, Kurt: Easy Schubert, Schumann, and Weber (Kalmus 9541/Belwin-Mills).
HUGHES, Edwin: Master Series--Schubert (G. Schirmer).
MOTCHANE, Marthe M.: An Introduction to Pianistic Styles, Book 3, Romantic (Bourne/G. Schirmer).
NIEMANN, Walter: Schubert Dances (Peters No.150).
SCHIRMER (Publisher): Schubert Dances (Vol. 1537).
WILLS, Vera: The Purple Book #1 (G. Schirmer 3449).

The first six measures of this ecossaise are identical to those in D. 299, No. 1 (Opus 33). Notes and ties have been added and the rhythm has been changed in the last section of D. 145.

This familiar dance has an accessible homophonic sound and texture. There are contrasting detached and slurred notes which are notated differently in the various editions, as are the tempo markings. The scoring for the left hand includes an alternating intervallic pattern in the first eight measures, and a strong descending octave line in the second half. Alfred, Hughes, and Wills have changed the octaves to single notes.

Tempo: Varies in editions
Length: 16 measures
Technique: staccato, octaves

No. 2, Ab Major — Intermediate

A quiet, music-box sound is evoked by the light, high-register melody. The left hand jump bass is played with a leggiero touch in keeping with the overall dynamics. High melodic notes often receive an "fp" emphasis. Wide right hand intervals employ a smooth hand expansion and contraction.

Length: 16 measures
Technique: high leger lines, jump bass

No. 3, B Minor — Intermediate

AGAY, Denes: More Easy Classics to Moderns, Vol. 27 (Consolidated).
ALFRED (Publisher): Schubert--21 of his Easiest Piano Selections.
DEXTER, Harry: Selected Piano Works--Schubert (Hansen).

GRANT, Lawrence: More Classic to Contemporary Piano Music (Ashley).
HANSEN (Publisher): Schubert--A Highlight Collection.
LANNING, Russell: Music by the Masters (Musicord/Belwin-Mills EL2543).
MOTCHANE, Marthe M.: An Introduction to Pianistic Styles, Book 3, Romantic (Bourne).
NAHUM, WOLFE, KOSAKOFF: Piano Classic (J. Fischer/Belwin-Mills).
NIEMANN, Walter: Schubert Dances (Peters No.150).
SCHIRMER (Publisher): Schubert Dances (Vol. 1537).

This familiar ecossaise presents an attractive and appealing contrast in harmonies and dynamics. The first phrase in B Minor is "p" and has a bass clef reach of a ninth that can be shared by the right hand. The second phrase in D Major employs considerable strength and power at the fortissimo level. Pedal point harmonies are an excellent complement to the repeated chords. First and second endings are marked.

Tempo: Alfred - Allegro moderato
Grant - Allegretto
Nahum - Allegro con Espressivo
Length: 18 measures
Technique: repeated chords

No. 4, G Major, or "Scottish Dance" — Advancing Elementary

AGAY, Denes: Easy Classics to Moderns, Vol. 17 (Consolidated).
AGAY, Denes: From Bach to Bartok, Volume C (Warner).
ALFRED (Publisher): Schubert--21 of his Easiest Piano Pieces.

DEXTER, Harry: Selected Piano Works--Schubert (Hansen).
GRANT, Lawrence: Piano Music by the Great Masters (Ashley).
HALFORD, Margery: Schubert--An Introduction to his Piano Works (Alfred).
HALFORD, Margery: Schubert--The First Book (Alfred).
HANSEN (Publisher): Schubert--A Highlight Collection.
HERRMANN, Kurt: Easy Schubert, Schumann, and Weber (Kalmus 9541/Belwin-Mills).
HUGHES, Edwin: Master Series--Schubert (G. Schirmer).
LANNING, Russell: Music by the Masters (Musicord/Belwin-Mills EL2543).
NIEMANN, Walter: Schubert Dances (Peters No.150).
ROYAL CONSERVATORY OF MUSIC: Piano Examination Repertoire 2 (Frederick Harris).
SCHIRMER (Publisher): Schubert Dances (Vol. 1537).
SHEALY, Alexander: Schubert--his greatest Piano Solos (Ashley).
VOLGER, Heinz: Schubert--Easiest Piano Pieces (Peters No. 5015).
WILLS, Vera: The Purple Book #1 (G. Schirmer 3449).

A steady rhythmic pulse propels this familiar and accessible ecossaise. The opening two measures, because of embellishments, have a tendency to be much slower than the rest of the piece. Although editions differ in phrase markings, the phrasing is more effective if grouped in 4+4+2+2+4 measure sections. The varying figures in the right hand have a chordal accompaniment in the left hand. The use of secondary dominants in the sequences, measures 9-12, can be of instructive value. This piece appears in a different form as D. 529, No. 3.

Tempo: Agay - Allegretto
Hughes - Presto
Length: 16 measures
Technique: broken octaves, 8th note scalar passages, ornaments

No. 5, B Major Early Intermediate

AGAY, Denes: Classics to Moderns, Intermediate, Vol. 37 (Consolidated).
DEXTER, Harry: Selected Piano Works--Schubert (Hansen).
HANSEN (Publisher): Schubert--A Highlight Collection.
NIEMANN, Walter: Schubert Dances (Peters No.150).
SCHIRMER (Publisher): Schubert Dances (Vol. 1537).
SHEALY, Alexander: Schubert--his greatest Piano Solos (Ashley).

Classical harmonies and technical challenges demanding coordination in both hands characterize this dance. Broken and blocked octaves and sustained and moving notes provide the challenge. This ecossaise could be played quickly, but should not get out of control. Ecossaise D.421, No.1 in Ab Major is similar to this one.

Length: 16 measures
Technique: wide interval leaps, sustained and moving notes, octaves, jump bass, 8th note passage work, high leger lines

No. 6, Ab Major Intermediate

AGAY, Denes: Easy Classics to Moderns, Vol. 17 (Consolidated).
DEXTER, Harry: Selected Piano Works--Schubert (Hansen).

HALFORD, Margery: Schubert--An Introduction to his Piano Works (Alfred).
HALFORD, Margery: Schubert--The First Book (Alfred).
HANSEN (Publisher): Schubert--A Highlight Collection.
HERRMANN, Kurt: Easy Schubert, Schumann, and Weber (Kalmus 9541/Belwin-Mills).
NEIMANN, Walter: Schubert Dances (Peters No.150).
SCHIRMER (Publisher): Schubert Dances (Vol. 1537).
VOLGER, Heinz: Schubert--Easiest Piano Pieces (Peters No. 5015).

A charming melody and well-balanced structure are revealed in this ecossaise. Some hand coordination is necessary for the two right hand voices. Melodic embellishments keep the character light and give the rhythm momentum. Measures 9-12 offer an excellent contrast of texture and mood. Mies and Agay present these measures in a simpler fashion. Ecossaise, D.697, No.5 in Ab Major is similar to this one.

Length: 16 measures
Technique: sustained and moving notes, jump bass, broken octaves, ornaments

No. 7, B Major — Advancing Intermediate

AGAY, Denes: Classics to Moderns, Intermediate, Vol. 37 (Consolidated).
SHEALY, Alexander: Schubert--his greatest Piano Solos (Ashley).

This ecossaise has an unusual unpredictability in its harmonic and dynamic schemes. The augmented 6th chord (with an altered spelling) in measure 4 has a subdominant function which also anticipates the sudden key change to C Major. "fp","fz","ff", and "pp" dynamics and accents are fairly abrupt and very effective.

Length: 8 measures

Technique: sustained and moving notes, broken octaves and octave chords, jump bass, 16th note passage work

No. 8, B Minor <u>Intermediate</u>

AGAY, Denes: Classics to Moderns, Intermediate, Vol. 37 (Consolidated).
HALFORD, Margery: Schubert--An Introduction to his Piano Works (Alfred).
HALFORD, Margery: Schubert--The First Book (Alfred).
NAHUM, WOLFE, KOSAKOFF: Piano Classic (J. Fischer/Belwin-Mills).
SHEALY, Alexander: Schubert--his Greatest Piano Solos (Ashley).

Lovely minor pedal point harmonies and the intriguing countermelodies give much promise to the opening of this ecossaise, but the ending in D Major is mundane. The Nahum, Wolfe, Kosakoff edition rewrites the rhythm by doubling the time values.

Length: 8 measures

Technique: jump bass, octaves, octave chords, sustained and moving notes

No. 9, G Major <u>Intermediate</u>

AGAY, Denes: Classics to Moderns, Intermediate, Vol. 37 (Consolidated).
ALFRED (Publisher): Schubert--21 of his Easiest Piano Selections.
HALFORD, Margery: Schubert--An Introduction to his Piano Works (Alfred).
HUGHES, Edwin: Master Series--Schubert (G. Schirmer).
SHEALY, Alexander: Schubert--his greatest Piano Solos (Ashley).

Ornamentation, trills, and leaping appoggiaturas, add grace to this otherwise uninspiring ecossaise. Full advantage should be taken of the distinct dynamic changes. The primary triad harmonization adds a bit of spice in measure six.

Tempo: Halford - molto moderato
Length: 8 measures
Technique: sustained and moving notes, jump bass, ornamentation

**ECOSSAISE,** D Minor, D. 158 <u>Early Intermediate</u>

MIES, Paul: Schubert--Samtliche Tanze, Band I (G. Henle Verlag 74).
STEINER, Eric: Dances by the Great Composers (Boston).

WEINMANN/KANN: Schubert--Landler, Ecossaisen, Menuette (Wiener 50064).

This ecossaise is surprisingly turbulent and intense for such a short work. Its tonality is rather ambiguous, starting in D Minor and ending in F Major. However, the majority of the piece has a dark D Minor sound. This dance sounds more difficult to play than it is, although accidentals may cause some reading problems.

Length: 16 measures
Technique: sustained and moving notes, 16th note passage work, octaves, accidentals

## **ECOSSAISES**, D. 299 (Op. 33)

Note: All of D. 299 may be found in:

MIES, Paul: Schubert--Samtliche Tanze, Band I (G. Henle Verlag 74).
WEINMANN/KANN: Schubert--Landler, Ecossaisen, Menuette (Wiener 50064).

No. 1, Ab Major <u>Intermediate</u>

HERRMANN, Kurt: Easy Schubert, Schumann, and Weber (Kalmus 9541/Belwin-Mills).
SHEALY, Alexander: Schubert--his greatest Piano Solos (Ashley).
VOLGER, Heinz: Schubert--Easiest Piano Pieces (Peters No. 5015).

Almost bombastic in its musical gaiety, this familiar ecossaise has a very homophonic sound and texture which is quite accessible. Observing the dynamics is crucial as they add style and zest to this already attractive piece. Most of the chords are detached, although there are some slurs across the bar line. Harmonically, Schubert uses a sequence similar to many ecossaises which is appealing and also creates some necessary harmonic contrasts to the main tonality. There is a marked resemblance to D. 145, No. 1 (Op. 18), particularly in the first six measures and the descending octaves.

Length: 17 measures
Technique: double 3rds, 6ths, and octaves, ties across the bar, sustained and moving notes

No. 2, Eb Major <u>Intermediate</u>

AGAY, Denes: An Anthology, The Romantic Period, Vol. III (Yorktown).
AGAY, Denes: Classics to Moderns, Intermediate, Vol. 37 (Consolidated).
SHEALY, Alexander: Schubert--his Greatest Piano Solos (Ashley).

In this set of ecossaises, Schubert indicates with a D.C. notation that they are to be paired in a minuet and trio fashion. This piece is quite a pleasant and fitting companion to D. 299 No. 1, as it has an attractive dance-like interlude quality. Various double notes are used along with some subtleties of detached and legato touches.

Length: 16 measures
Technique: double 3rds, scalar figures, ties across the bar

No. 3, E Major <u>Intermediate</u>

AGAY, Denes: An Anthology, The Romantic Period, Vol. III (Yorktown).

This accessible ecossaise is subtle and charming, with clearly defined dynamic contrast. The patterns are largely double 6ths and octaves with challenging half-step alterations.

Tempo: Agay-Poco piu mosso
Length: 16 measures
Technique: double 6ths and octaves, sustained and moving notes, trills, accidentals

No. 4, A Major <u>Intermediate</u>

AGAY, Denes: An Anthology, The Romantic Period, Vol. III (Yorktown).
BARRATT, Carol: Chester's Concert Pieces, Volume Two (Chester JWC 55197).

This ecossaise is characterized by light leaping triplet figures in the right hand. It provides an excellent contrast in its pairing with No. 3.

Tempo: Agay - Allegretto comodo
Length: 16 measures
Technique: broken chords, leaps, jump bass, high leger lines

No. 5, Db Major — Intermediate

AGAY, Denes: An Anthology, The Romantic Period, Vol. III (Yorktown).
HERRMANN, Kurt: Easy Schubert, Schumann, and Weber (Kalmus 9541/Belwin-Mills).

This expressive piece is both beautiful and flowing, with a constant gentle eighth note pattern. The left hand has a Db pedal point in the first section while the second half is characterized by a broken interval sequence. This sequential treatment is lovely and produces some effective harmonies. The right hand also has pedal points in its broken interval construction and will benefit greatly from melodic voicing.

Length: 16 measures
Technique: sustained and moving notes, slow Alberti bass, broken intervals

No. 6, Ab Major — Intermediate

A smooth legato sound is created by pedal points simultaneously in both hands. The first half of the piece is in a higher register at a soft dynamic level, making the fortissimo marking in the second section startlingly effective. This ecossaise is meant to be played as a trio section to D. 299, No. 5.

Length: 16 measures
Technique: sustained and moving notes, broken chords, octave chords, high leger lines

No. 7, E Major <u>Intermediate</u>

This wonderful work is light and delicate, almost flowery. Sensitive cross-phrasing between hands enhances the character. The second half contains a lovely sequence involving contrary motion between right and left hands, which creates some gorgeous and surprising harmonies. The E Major tonality of this piece contrasts effectively with the C major tonality of D. 299, No. 8.

Length: 16 measures
Technique: broken chords, important rests, clef changes

No. 8, C Major <u>Intermediate</u>

BARRATT, Carol: Chester's Concert Pieces, Volume One (Chester JWC55145).
SZAVAI/VESZPREMI: Piano Music, Book 1 (Belwin-Mills).

In this elegant ecossaise the C Major tonality contrasts beautifully with the E Major tonality of D. 299, No. 7, its intended pairing. There are many opportunities for echo dynamics. Both hands share in the melodic motive which involves frequent clef changes.

Tempo: Szavai/Veszpremi - Allegretto
Length: 16 measures
Technique: scalar figures, broken chords, sustained and moving notes, clef changes

No. 9, F Major — Intermediate

This boldly dynamic dance has a driving rhythmic quality. The expressive performer will present the bravura qualities within a leggiero touch. A quick tempo will insure its success.

Length: 16 measures
Technique: broken intervals, double notes, octave chords, ties across the bar, finger facility

No. 10, Bb Major — Intermediate

Right hand octaves provide this ecossaise with a colorful, bright character which goes well with its counterpart, D. 299, No. 9. The first eight measures have a chordal accompaniment. The second half contains left hand passing tones which would benefit from a dramatic crescendo.

Length: 16 measures
Technique: octaves, chords

No. 11, Ab Major <u>Intermediate</u>

This charming ecossaise sounds very much like the familiar folk song "Ah, vous dirai-je, Maman," otherwise known as "Twinkle, Twinkle." It is spiced up with lovely articulations and dynamics. Paired with No. 12, this would be a wonderful performance selection.

Length: 16 measures
Technique: leaps, octave chords, voicing, 8th note passage work

No. 12, F Minor <u>Intermediate</u>

WEINMANN/KANN: Schubert--Landler, Ecossaisen, Menuette (Wiener 50064).

This gentle dance with its minor/major harmonies contrasts beautifully with D. 299. The first half contains quiet blocked chords while the second half has an Alberti hass and is marked at an "mf" dynamic level.

Length: 16 measures
Technique: chords, tonal balance, slurs, ties across the bar, sustained and moving notes

## ECOSSAISES, D. 421

Note: All of D. 421 may be found in:

MIES, Paul: Schubert--Samtliche Tanze, Band II
(G. Henle Verlag 76).

### No. 1, Ab Major — Advancing Intermediate

BANOWETZ, Joseph: The Pianist's Book of Classic Treasures (GWM/Kjos).

A vigorous octave statement introduces this ecossaise, appearing initially in the right hand and later imitated in the left. The first section ends with a long series of broken intervals. A cleverly contrasted second section opens with a bright tune, treated in sequential fashion. A very similar setting appears in B Major in D. 145, No. 1.

Length: 16 measures
Technique: octaves, 8th note passage work, sustained and moving notes

### No. 2, F Minor — Intermediate

BANOWETZ, Joseph: The Pianist's Book of Classic Treasures (GWM/Kjos).

The rhythm, key, melody, and harmonies of this ecossaise are intricately linked to D. 421, No. 1. This dance begins in F Minor and with several alterations (such as diminished seventh chords) ends in A Major.

Tempo: Banowetz - Allegro vivace
Length: 16 measures
Technique: octave chords, sustained and moving notes, broken chords and intervals

No. 3, Eb Major — Advancing Intermediate

Double thirds, octave chords, leger lines, and accidentals present reading and technical challenges in this ecossaise. Secondary dominant sevenths modulating to the key of Bb give a fascinating twist to the harmony. The two sections contrast in mood and dynamic levels.

Length: 16 measures
Technique: octave chords, double 3rds, clef changes, double grace notes, wide dynamic range

No. 4, Bb Major — Intermediate

This short dance has a romantic Schumannesque sound and technique with a large dynamic range. Broken chord figurations occur throughout. The use of the tonic inversion at the ending suggests an immediate continuation into D. 421, No. 5.

Length: 16 measures
Technique: broken intervals and chords

No. 5, Eb Major <u>Intermediate</u>

The homophonic sound of this ecossaise creates a light overall mood. Right hand figurations cover a wide range quickly and need careful fingering. Position changes of the sequences are challenging but the work is pianistic.

Length: 16 measures
Technique: repeated chords, 8th note passage work, clef changes

No. 6, Ab Major <u>Advancing Intermediate</u>

A melody in octaves, accompanied by broken triads, provides the first section of this ecossaise with a full sound. The second half utilizes the triads in blocks, moving in a series of secondary dominants to the Ab Major ending. These six ecossaises of D. 421 work beautifully as a set for performance.

Length: 16 measures
Technique: octaves and octave chords, sustained and moving notes, 2-note phrases

**ECOSSAISE**, D. 511, Eb Major — Intermediate

MIES, Paul: Samtliche Tanze, Band II
(G. Henle Verlag 76).

Reminiscent of a yodelled folk song, this ecossaise is spirited and gay. The first section is built of moving eighth notes with wide interval leaps. The second section opens with a right hand duet featuring a dotted note turn, and ends with a reprise of the intitial eighth note melody.

Length: 16 measures
Technique: 8th note passage work, jump bass, high leger lines, 32nd notes.

**ECOSSAISES**, D. 529

Note: All of D. 529 may be found in:

MIES, Paul: Schubert--Samtliche Tanze, Band II
(G. Henle Verlag 76).

No. 1, D Major — Intermediate

In the fanfare-like opening of this dance both hands use octave chords, but the harmonic sound is static even with the right hand altered tones. The chromaticism in the second section is an appealing contrast.

Length: 16 measures
Technique: octave chords, clef changes, 8th note passage work

No. 2, D Major — Intermediate

AGAY, Denes: Piano Recital (AMSCO).
AGAY, Denes: From Bach to Bartok, Vol. C (Warner).
VOLGER, Heinz: Schubert--Easiest Piano Pieces (Peters No. 5015).

This "circus music" dance is light and happy. However, the staid repeated chords could become too heavy, detracting from the engaging grace note patterns.

Tempo: Agay - Allegretto
Length: 16 measures
Technique: octaves and octave chords, single and double grace notes

No. 3, G Major — Intermediate

VOLGER, Heinz: Schubert--Easiest Piano Pieces (Peters No. 5015).

Double grace notes give a gentle lift to the opening eighth note motive of this ecossaise. The scalar passage, ending in broken octaves, appears in both sections. Straightforward simplicity adds a folk-like character to this bright dance, which bears a striking resemblance to D. 145, No. 4.

Length: 16 measures

Technique: 8th note scalar patterns, broken octaves, repeated chords, clef changes

No. 4, D Major — Early Intermediate

HERA and SARMAI: Easy Piano Music from the Period of Romanticism (Musica Budapest/Boosey & Hawkes Z.12.409).

Simple rhythms and harmonies in this "music box" ecossaise are unvaried and rather mundane. Right hand facility is needed for the running eighth notes in the first section. The treble clef changes to broken chords in the second section.

Length: 16 measures

Technique: octaves, 8th note passage work

No. 5, D Major — Early Intermediate

HERA and SARMAI: Easy Piano Music from the Period of Romanticism (Musica Budapest/Boosey & Hawkes Z.12.409).

WEINMANN/KANN: Schubert--Landler, Ecossaisen, Menuette (Wiener 50064).

This harmonically static piece is of similar construction to D. 529, No. 4, offering little interest. It is built on right hand broken chords.

Length: 16 measures

Technique: 8th note passage work, melody and accompaniment in same hand

No. 6, D Major — Intermediate

This processional march has a full sound. Both hands begin with double notes and move into octave chords and octaves. This rather mundane ecossaise will gain from an assured and vigorous performance.

Length: 16 measures

Technique: double 3rds, 5ths, and octaves, octave chords, clef changes

No. 7, D Major — Intermediate

HERA and SARMAI: Easy Piano Music from the Period of Romanticism (Musica Budapest/Boosey & Hawkes Z.12.409).

This ecossaise has extremely static classical harmonies combined with an uninspiring melody. The right hand has many repeated figures and broken octave chords accompanied by a chordal left hand.

Length: 16 measures
Technique: changing fingers on repeated notes, broken octave chords

No. 8, D Major Intermediate

BERINGER, Oscar: Beringer's School of Easy Classics--Schubert (Galaxy).
GRANT, Lawrence: More Classic to Contemporary Piano Music (Ashley).
VOLGER, Heinz: Schubert--Easiest Piano Pieces (Peters No. 5015).

In this dance the same simple and unsophisticated harmonies are present as in the other seven. All have a folk-dance orientation and are easier for the level than other sets. Schubert has provided no dynamic markings. The Urtext scores of this ecossaise notate the repeated measures of the first section.

Tempo: Grant - Allegretto
Length: 24 measures
Technique: jump bass, repeated chords, clef changes

**ECOSSAISE,** Db Major, D. 643 Advancing Intermediate

MIES, Paul: Schubert--Samtliche Tanze, Band II (G. Henle Verlag 76).

This short ecossaise is paired with a German dance (D. 643) in C# Minor. The opening sequence is lovely and relates to the major/minor fluctuations that occur in the preceding German dance. This attractive piece could be used as an early double note etude. The overall character flows smoothly.

Length: 16 measures
Technique: double 3rds, leaps, 8th note passage work

## **ECOSSAISES**, D. 697

Note: All of D. 697 may be found in:

MIES, Paul: Schubert--Samtliche Tanze, Band II (G. Henle Verlag 76).

No. 1, Ab Major — Advancing Intermediate

A vigorous dance with important dynamic changes, this ecossaise builds around a phrase of wide broken intervals with interspersed repeated chords. The material in the first eight measures focuses on the right hand, but in the last eight measures the intervallic phrase is imitated between the hands. This is a vibrant opening piece for the set of dances.

Length: 16 measures
Technique: jump bass, 8th note passage work, octave chords

No. 2, Ab Major

Advancing Intermediate

Beginning on the dominant seventh chord in the first section and the subdominant in the second, this is complete, but serves well as a continuation of D. 697, No. 1. Both sections open with a four-measure statement that is repeated an octave higher. The thematic phrase builds around eighth note triplets, but the first section adds a zesty rhythmic motive. The left hand accompanies predominantly with a jump bass.

Length: 16 measures
Technique: scalar patterns, jump bass, clef changes, high leger lines

No. 3, Ab Major

Early Advanced

As with D. 697, No. 2, this dance begins on the dominant seventh chord in the first section and the subdominant in the second. It also utilizes a four-measure statement with an echo. The left hand jump bass accompanies constantly moving eighth notes in the right hand, producing a gentle flowing effect. A more subtle romantic flavor comes from the narrow dynamic changes.

Length: 16 measures
Technique: jump bass, 8th note passage work, wide interval leaps, high leger lines, sustained and moving notes

No. 4, Ab Major <u>Intermediate</u>

This sturdy dance builds on detached repeated chords and sharply percussive dynamic effects. It contrasts beautifully with D. 697, No. 3. The straightforward chordal construction is more accesible than those of the companion dances of this set.

Length: 16 measures
Technique: repeated chords, grace notes, sustained and moving notes

No. 5, Ab Major <u>Early Advanced</u>

A fanfare opens this dance, calling for abrupt dynamic effects and dramatic intensity. The last phrase of the first section changes the character, and is carried through as the motive of the second section. It is lighter in mood, with constantly moving eighth notes and frequent ornamentation. This ecossaise has varied material within the patterns. These five contrasting ecossaises would make an excellent performance choice.

Length: 17 measures
Technique: broken chords, 8th note passage work, octaves, clef changes, ornamentation

## ECOSSAISES, D. 734 (Op. 67)

Note: All of D. 734 may be found in:

MIES, Paul: Schubert--Samtliche Tanze, Band II
(G. Henle Verlag 76).

No. 1, A Minor Intermediate

DEXTER, Harry: Selected Piano Works--Schubert (Hansen).
HANSEN (Publisher): Schubert--A Highlight Collection.
KING-ORDEN, Esther: 100 Classics for Young Pianists (Shattinger/Hansen 0111).
WEINMANN/KANN: Schubert--Landler, Ecossaisen, Menuette (Wiener 50064).

The right hand in this ecossaise is largely an octave melody with alternating slurs, staccatos, and accents. The left hand jump-bass features chords tied across the bar. There are brief modulations to the relative major.

Length: 16 measures
Technique: jump bass, octaves

No. 2, A Major Intermediate

DEXTER, Harry: Selected Piano Works--Schubert (Hansen).
HANSEN (Publisher): Schubert--A Highlight Collection.

KING-ORDEN, Esther: 100 Classics for Young Pianists (Shattinger/Hansen 0111).
WEINMANN/KANN: Schubert--Landler, Ecossaisen, Menuette (Wiener 50064).

The right hand in this dance has clever sequential patterns plus broken octaves and chords. The left hand has chordal patterns with a descending stepwise octave line. There is a brief modulation to E Major. D. 734, Op. 67 also includes 16 landler.

Length: 16 measures
Technique: octaves, 8th note passage work

## **ECOSSAISES**, D. 735 (Op. 49)

Note: All of D. 735 (Op. 49) may be found in:

MIES, Paul: Schubert--Samtliche Tanze, Band II (G. Henle Verlag 76).

GALOPP, G Major — Advancing Intermediate

SHEALY, Alexander: Schubert--his greatest Piano Solos (Ashley).

This folk sounding galopp and trio depends heavily on a brisk, animated tempo and a light touch for its charm. Harmonies, melodies, and rhythms are typical of Schubert's short dances. Both consist of sixteen bars with a double bar after the first eight measures. An ABA form is created by repeating the Galopp (D.C. al fine). The high register of much of the piece necessitates many leger lines.

Length: 33 measures
Technique: wide interval leaps, repeated chords, double 3rds, clef changes, jump bass

No. 1, G Major Intermediate

ALFRED (Publisher): Schubert--21 of his Easiest Piano Selections.
SHEALY, Alexander: Schubert--his greatest Piano Solos (Ashley).

A vigorous fanfare opens and closes this short ecossaise. The strong, crisp character and the quick position changes are a challenge. Patterns and texture indicate two-measure phrase groupings. Imaginative harmonies include diminished seventh chords and a modulation to the mediant. Dynamics contrast widely and abruptly in this and all other dances in this set.

Tempo: Alfred - Molto moderato
Length: 8 measures
Technique: 16th note passage work, octave chords

No. 2, E Minor Intermediate

ALFRED (Publisher): Schubert--21 of his Easiest Piano Selections.
SHEALY, Alexander: Schubert--his greatest Piano Solos (Ashley).

Accents and articulations have much importance in this E Minor ecossaise. The touches and the material employ hand independence and quick hand shifts. The left hand is quite varied and imitates the right hand in the second section. The minor key is a fine complement and contrast in its relative position in the set. The sequential diversion after the double bar contributes to a fine overall sound.

Length: 8 measures
Technique: staccato vs. legato, 8th and 16th note passage work, register changes

No. 3, D Major <u>Intermediate</u>

There are several similarities between this and the first of the set (G Major), including rhythmic motives, solid and broken chord material, and a fanfare-like sound. This dance has a more subdued character and a less extended hand position.

Length: 9 measures
Technique: repeated chords, jump bass, 16th note passage work

No. 4, Bb Major <u>Intermediate</u>

A light-hearted, almost circus-like character pervades this bouncy ecossaise. The technical demands of the right hand should not obscure the essential light and even pulse. The left hand jump bass remains detached from the busy right hand.

Length: 8 measures
Technique: staccato vs. legato, jump bass, sustained and moving notes

No. 5, Eb Major — Advancing Intermediate

The variety of textures found in this ecossaise provide a fine overall technical etude within eight measures. The double thirds that flow downward lend a romantic, Schubertian sound.

Length: 8 measures
Technique: double 3rds, important rests and phrasing, jump bass, clef changes

No. 6, Eb Major — Intermediate

AGAY, Denes: From Bach to Bartok, Vol. C (Warner).

The articulation of this accessible dance gives it a light and airy feel. The left hand is a consistent detached jump bass and the melodic downbeat is always emphasized by either a triplet or a trill. The last two bars use 8va for a high register ending that is typical of this set. In the Agay edition everything is doubled in time value making it sixteen measures instead of eight. There is also no 8va indication at the ending.

Tempo: Agay - Scherzando
Length: 8 measures
Technique: jump bass, 16th note passage work, important phrasing and rests

No. 7, Eb Major — Advancing Intermediate

The octaves in this ecossaise are challenging, outlining chords at a moderately fast tempo. The jump bass covers wide leaps. The last section contains a dramatic change to C Minor, with an abrupt alteration back to Eb Major that is too brief to be convincing. Although it contains some excellent octave work, the difficulties are almost more than the music merits.

Length: 12 measures
Technique: octaves and octave chords, jump bass, wide intervals

No. 8, Ab Major — Intermediate

This final ecossaise of the set seems to be a continuation of No. 7. It uses the same formal scheme, with a two-measure modulation after the double bar, and an abrupt ending cadence. The contrast between the quiet, discreet first section and the forthright, outspoken second section is highly original. This is a creative ending piece to this delightful set of performance caliber.

Length: 8 measures
Technique: 8th and 16th note passage work, jump bass, wide interval leaps

## **ECOSSAISES,** D. 781

Note: All of D. 781 may be found in:

MIES, Paul: Schubert--Samtliche Tanze, Band II (G. Henle Verlag 76).
WEINMANN/KANN: Schubert--Landler, Ecossaisen, Menuette (Wiener 50064).

No. 1, Gb Major <u>Intermediate</u>

HALFORD, Margery: Schubert--An Introduction to his Piano Works (Alfred).
HALFORD, Margery: Schubert--The First Book (Alfred).

In the first section of this ecossaise the left hand pedal point is in sustained half notes under an off-beat pattern, giving a unique harmonic flavor. The right hand has a beautiful melodic line, moving in double thirds and sixths. The wide dynamic range and poignant harmonies create a fine performance piece.

Length: 16 measures
Technique: sustained and moving notes, double 3rds, 6ths, and octaves, wide dynamic range (p-ff)

No. 2, D Major Advancing Intermediate

HALFORD, Margery: Schubert--An Introduction to his Piano Works (Alfred).
HALFORD, Margery: Schubert--The First Book (Alfred).

This bright dance has jump bass chords in the first section. The second section features the same bass figuration moving in a downward chromatic pattern. The right hand is notated in contrary motion, giving a unique harmonic effect. Although the rhythm is simple, quickly changing chord positions and wide keyboard range are more difficult than they seem at first glance.

Length: 16 measures
Technique: sustained and moving notes, jump bass, wide dynamic range (p-ff)

No. 3, Gb Major Intermediate

Dynamics and accents (p, fp, f, fz) are important to the expression of this ecossaise. The two eight-measure phrases are well-contrasted; the first is quiet and lyrical, the second full and accented. The attractive harmonies add to the pleasure of performing this piece.

Length: 18 measures
Technique: jump bass, octaves, sustained and moving notes, important rests, accents, and dynamics

No. 4, Eb Major <u>Intermediate</u>

This ecossaise is delightful, filled with textural, stylistic, and rhythmic contrasts. Harmonic and rhythmic aspects are attractive, with a question and answer format. Combining this with a group of complementary dances would assure a charming performance choice.

Length: 16 measures
Technique: jump bass with a wide interval span, octaves and octave chords

No. 5, Ab Major <u>Intermediate</u>

The key, contrast of material, and rhythmic accents of this ecossaise fit well in a pairing with No. 4. The creative parallel construction of the phrase line in the second section piques the imagination of the performer.

Length: 16 measures
Technique: octaves and octave chords, jump bass, important dynamic contrasts

No. 6, Bb Major <u>Intermediate</u>

The detached rhythm and the cluster-like chords lend an air of a march to this ecossaise. The clever chord progressions and increasing dynamic intensity build to an assured finale.

Length: 16 measures
Technique: jump bass, full chords, wide dynamic range, important rests

No. 7, B Minor — Advancing Intermediate

An expansive, strong performance is needed for this dramatic dance. It opens with a tritone movement that is unusual and startling. This strange and interesting piece uses sudden accents and dynamic changes, chords, and octaves.

Length: 19 measures
Technique: octaves and octave chords, sustained and moving notes, important dynamic changes, accidentals

No. 8, D Major — Intermediate

A light-hearted opening is contrasted by a dramatic ending with "fz," crescendo, and a chromatically rising octave bass. The left hand has the most interest, with sustained and moving notes in the first section and the octave bass in the second. A sense of drama is needed to perform this dance effectively.

Length: 16 measures
Technique: sustained and moving notes, octaves

No. 9, B Major <u>Advancing Intermediate</u>

Harmonies and inner voice melodies in this ecossaise are challenging. Right hand coordination is needed to control the "pp" and to bring out the melody in the inner voice. Altered harmonies are original, but the ending is banal. This piece would pair well with D. 781, No. 10.

Length: 16 measures
Technique: sustained and moving notes, jump bass, accidentals

No. 10, G# Minor/B Major <u>Advancing Intermediate</u>

The prevailing dotted rhythm could create a light sound, but if it is really snapped, the short-long pattern makes the character of this ecossaise brisk and vigorous. The left hand bass is interrupted by one section of octaves which outline the B Major chord. The G# Minor section uses double sharps.

Length: 16 measures
Technique: octaves and octave chords, jump bass, accidentals, Scotch snap rhythm

No. 11, D Major <u>Advancing Intermediate</u>

Schumann's "Important Event" is brought to mind in this bombastic ecossaise. Large, strong hands are needed to span the ninths and the rolled tenths. The right hand is a study in chord inversions and tonal balance. The left hand has a simple octave accompaniment.

Length: 16 measures
Technique: octaves, octave chords, rolled chords, wide intervals, sustained and moving notes

**ECOSSAISE,** D Major, D. 782 <u>Advancing Intermediate</u>

MIES, Paul: Schubert--Samtliche Tanze, Band II (G. Henle Verlag 76).

These sixteen measures open and close with predictable I, IV, V harmonies, with a brief respite in measures 9-12. Left hand leaps and jumps are large and challenging. The right hand carries the melody and harmony in sustained and moving notes.

Length: 16 measures
Technique: octaves, octave chords, jump bass, sustained and moving notes

## ECOSSAISES, D. 783 (Op. 33)

Note: All of D. 783 may be found in:

MIES, Paul: Schubert--Samtliche Tanze, Band II (G. Henle Verlag 76).

No. 1, B Minor <u>Advancing Elementary</u>

BERINGER, Oscar: Beringer's School of Easy Classics--Schubert (Galaxy).
DEXTER, Harry: Selected Piano Works--Schubert (Hansen T366).
HALFORD, Margery: Schubert--An Introduction to his Piano Works (Alfred).
HALFORD, Margery: Schubert--The First Book (Alfred).
HANSEN (Publisher): Schubert--A Highlight Collection.
HERRMANN, Kurt: Easy Schubert, Schumann, and Weber (Kalmus 9541/Belwin-Mills).
INTERNATIONAL LIBRARY OF PIANO MUSIC, Album Four (University Society)
KALMUS (Publisher): Schubert--An Easy Album for Piano Solo (Belwin-Mills).
KING-ORDEN, Esther: 100 Classics for Young Pianists (Shattinger/Hansen 0111).
MOTCHANE, Marthe M.: An Introduction to Pianistic Styles, Book 3, Romantic (Bourne/G.Schirmer).
NAHUM, WOLFE, KOSAKOFF: Piano Classics (J. Fischer/Belwin-Mills).
NIEMANN, Walter: Schubert Dances (Peters No.150).
ROWLEY, Alec: The Easiest Original Schubert (Hinrichsen No. 6/Peters).
SCHIRMER (Publisher): Schubert Dances (Vol. 1537).
SHEFTEL, Paul: Classics - Romantics - Moderns - Solos for the Intermediate Pianist (C. Fischer ATF102).

WEISMANN, Wilhelm: Romantic Masters (Peters No. 5033).

In the first section of this sprightly ecossaise there is an Alberti bass accompanying a short two-note phrase motive in the right hand. An unusual dissonance occurs between the right hand "E" and the left hand "E#." Both hands take up the two-note phrase in the second section, ending with a filigree of eighth notes.

Tempo: Beringer - Allegretto
Rowley - Con moto
Herrmann - Allegretto
Kalmus - Con moto
Weismann - Allegro
Nahum - Allegro con espressivo

Length: 16 measures

Technique: 8th note passage work, octaves, important rests and dynamics

No. 2, B Minor — Advancing Elementary

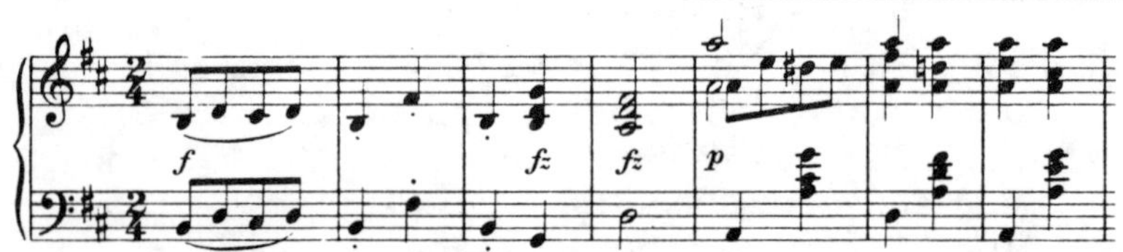


BERINGER, Oscar: Beringer's School of Easy Classics--Schubert (Galaxy).

DEXTER, Harry: Selected Piano Works--Schubert (Hansen T366).

HALFORD, Margery: Schubert--An Introduction to his Piano Works (Alfred).

HALFORD, Margery: Schubert--The First Book (Alfred).

HANSEN (Publisher): Schubert--A Highlight Collection.

HERRMANN, Kurt: Easy Schubert, Schumann, and Weber (Kalmus 9541/Belwin-Mills).

INTERNATIONAL LIBRARY OF PIANO MUSIC, Album Four (University Society)

KALMUS (Publisher): Schubert--An Easy Album for Piano Solo (Belwin-Mills).

KING-ORDEN, Esther: 100 Classics for Young Pianists (Shattinger-Hansen 0111).
NEIMANN, Walter: Schubert Dances (Peters No.150).
ROWLEY, Alec: The Easiest Original Schubert (Hinrichsen No. 6/Peters).
SCHIRMER (Publisher): Schubert Dances (Vol. 1537).
SHEFTEL, Paul: Classics, Romantics, Moderns, Solos for the Intermediate Pianist (C. Fischer ATF102).
WEISMANN, Wilhelm: Romantic Masters (Peters No. 5033).

Utilizing the same key and two note motivic idea this ecossaise is light and cheery and is an excellent companion piece to D. 783, No. 1. The changing clefs and sustaining harmony notes give it its individuality. D. 783 also has sixteen German dances. (Weekly and Arganbright have written authentic duet arrangements of this opus (German Dances and Ecossaises, Op. 33), which is published by Kjos West, WP97.)

Tempo: Beringer - Allegretto
Rowley - Con moto
Herrmann - Allegro risoluto
Kalmus - Con moto
Weismann - Allegro
Length: 16 measures
Technique: jump bass, clef changes, sustained and moving notes

## ECOSSAISES, D. 816

Note: All of D. 816 may be found in:

MIES, Paul: Schubert--Samtliche Tanze, Band II (G. Henle Verlag 76).
WEINMANN/KANN: Schubert--Landler, Ecossaisen, Menuette (Wiener 50064).

No. 1, D Major <u>Intermediate</u>

Romantic harmonies enhance the lyrical opening of this dance, as well as the fuller, more dynamic second half. The undesignated tempo can be taken slowly, with a legato touch, or fast with a bouncy character. If played slowly with careful dynamics, this piece will express a vivid musical drama.

Length: 16 measures
Technique: octaves and broken chords, sustained and moving notes, 8th note passage work

No. 2, D Major <u>Intermediate</u>

This ecossaise features varied ideas and a left hand that does much more than just accompany. Textures and range change often within the short sixteen-measure span, with both hands using sustained and moving notes and detached and legato touches.

Length: 16 measures
Technique: sustained and moving notes, 8th note passage work

No. 3, Bb Major <u>Intermediate</u>

This martial piece features right hand chords accompanied by left hand octaves, with contrasting dynamics (p-ff). This set sounds more romantic than many of the others. Its length and accessibility make it a fine choice to learn and play as a group.

Length: 16 measures

Technique: octaves and octave chords, wide dynamic range

## ECOSSAISES, D. 977

Note: All of D. 977 may be found in:

HERRMANN, Kurt: Easy Schubert, Schumann, and Weber (Kalmus 9541/Belwin-Mills).

MIES, Paul: Schubert--Samtliche Tanze, Band II (G. Henle Verlag 76).

No. 1, Db Major <u>Intermediate</u>

Reminiscent of a folk dance, this ecossaise is composed around the tonic, subdominant, and dominant seventh harmonies with simple thematic writing. The opening phrase of the first section provides the motive for the second section, employing even eighth and quarter notes. The left hand accompanies both sections with a jump bass.

Tempo: Herrmann - Allegretto grazioso
Length: 16 measures
Technique: jump bass, 8th note passage work, ornamentation (Herrmann notates this)

No. 2, Db Major <u>Intermediate</u>

The simple chord progressions of D. 977, No. 1 are retained in the opening bars of this dance, but the second section provides surprising complex harmonic alterations. The two-voice writing in the right hand pairs with a left hand jump bass in the first section, changing to solid octave chords in the second. The simple beginning effectively contrasts with the harmonic creativity of the ending.

Length: 16 measures
Technique: sustained and moving notes, jump bass, octave chords

No. 3, Ab Major <u>Advancing Intermediate</u>

This bouncy dance changes in tonality, but retains the folk character of the first two pieces of the set. It gains a vigorous flavor with the dotted rhythms, important rests, and sharp accents. The left hand accompanies with repeated chords in the first half, but gains more complex status in the second half.

Length: 16 measures
Technique: complex rhythmic subdivision, octave chords, sustained and moving notes, clef changes

No. 4, B Major Intermediate

Featuring the abrupt change to B Major and more complex writing, this dance is a delightful contrast to its companions. The flowing motions of constantly moving eighth notes accompanied by repeated chords is rhythmically straightforward. The second half is particularly effective, with descending left hand chord spelling and similar outlining in the right hand.

Length: 16 measures
Technique: sustained and moving notes, 8th note passage work, clef changes, repeated chords

No. 5, D Major Early Intermediate

With a simple melody and accompanying chords, this dance and No. 6 are easier than the others in this set. The change to B Minor in the last three measures seems to lead into the next piece, which is in the same key signature and similar compositional style.

Length: 16 measures
Technique: octave chords, 8th note passage work

No. 6, D Major <u>Early Intermediate</u>

Written in the same style and key as No. 5, this dance is straightforward and easily learned. There is a music box quality to the eighth note melody accompanied by repeated triads and two-note phrases. The entire piece is in the treble clef.

Length: 16 measures
Technique: 8th note passage work, octave chords

No. 7, Bb Major <u>Intermediate</u>

HERA and SARMAI: Easy Piano Music from the Period of Romanticism (Musica Budapest/Boosey & Hawkes Z.12.409).

The short two-measure motive in the first section of this dance is amplified to four measures in the second section. Both halves are well-contrasted, with an accompaniment of repeated chords changing to a jump bass. The simple rhythmic structure is given added spice with important rests and accents, to create a piece which sounds more difficult than it is.

Length: 16 measures
Technique: 8th note passage work, jump bass, clef changes

No. 8, D Minor

Early Intermediate

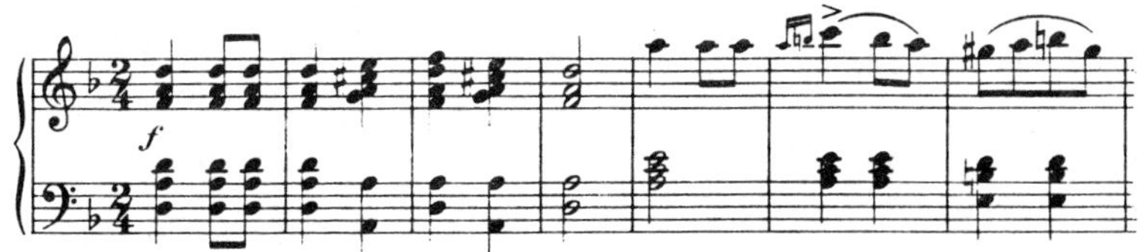

The opening tonic, dominant chords give a vigorous character to the ending dance of this set. There is a unique momentum to the piece as a result of its changing tonalities in the first section, which moves from D Minor to A Minor. The second section alters abruptly to F Major and its character becomes more melodic, with its eighth note motive reflecting the ending of the first half. There is creative thematic and harmonic writing within this short piece, and it becomes an effective ending to this set of eight ecossaises. In the Hera-Sarmai edition there is a D.C. al fine instruction to go back to No. 7. These ecossaises (D. 977) are an excellent performance set.

Length: 19 measures

Technique: octave chords, 8th note passage work, jump bass, grace notes

## GERMAN DANCES, D. 128

Note: All of D. 128 may be found in:

MIES, Paul: Schubert--Samtliche Tanze, Band I (G. Henle Verlag 74).

No. 1, F Major — Intermediate

ANTHONY, George Walter: Schubert to Shostakovich (Presser) German Dance only.
HEINRICHSHOFEN/PETERS (Publisher): Schubert--Easier Favorites (N. 4051).

This German dance has an eleven-measure introduction which ends on the dominant. This provides the general character and tone for the entire set. The odd number of measures is also indicative of things to come.

A light bouncy feeling is projected throughout by the agile right hand melody. Four measures of contrasting material create an ABA form, offering a dramatic contrast with the fanfare sound that is such an integral part of this set. The forte dynamics of the middle section is a sudden change from the overall quiet mood. The Anthony version does not have the introduction and is called "Waltz."

Tempo: Anthony - Moderato
Length: introduction - 11 measures
D. 128, No. 1 - 20 measures
Technique: octaves, 8th note passage work, sustained and moving notes

No. 2, C Major, or "Viennese Dance" Intermediate

The odd phrase structure characteristic of this set is taken to an extreme in this dance. The 32 measures are divided into varying phrase lengths (2-6-4; 4-4-4-8). Quite a variety of material is used, including static chords, sequences, leaping melodic figures, appoggiaturas, and sustained and moving notes in both hands. Abundant nonharmonic tones have melodic and harmonic significance throughout.

Length: 32 measures
Technique: 8th note passage work, sustained and moving notes, clef changes, grace notes

No. 3, Ab Major Intermediate

Both texture and melodic content of this lovely piece are reminiscent of string quartet writing. The sound is classical, somewhat predictable, but appealing. The ABA form consists of three 12-measure groups. The A sections have a melody of chord outlining with quiet, rocking inner figures. The B section is more robust, with octave chords.

Length: 36 measures
Technique: sustained and moving notes, octaves and octave chords, short appoggiaturas

No. 4, E Major, or "Viennese Dance" Intermediate

An attractive opening fanfare utilizes large octave chords interspersed with scales. These contrasting patterns create an effective balance with appealing harmonies, modulations, and interesting hemiolas. The opening eight measures also close the piece, but upon the repetition, the textural intensity is reduced and the ending is very quiet.

Length: 28 measures
Technique: octave chords, scalar passages

No. 5, C Major, or "Viennese Dance" Intermediate

The opening rhythms and textures of this fifth dance are much like the beginning of No. 4. Other similarities are the contrast of material and dynamics. Technically, this is the easier, but harmonies are not quite as attractive. Changes in dynamics are numerous, with a quiet ending.

Length: 32 measures
Technique: octaves and octave chords, sustained and moving notes, 8th note scalar patterns and passage work

No. 6, C Minor, or "Viennese Dance" Intermediate

This dramatic dance has a large and impressive sound that appears to the listener to be quite difficult. However, the technique is pianistic and much easier than it sounds. A successful performance needs an assured, bombastic approach. Dynamic discretion is left to the performer within an "ff" range.

Length: 36 measures
Technique: 8th note scales, arpeggios, and passage work, octaves, octave chords

No. 7, F Major, or "Viennese Dance" Intermediate

HALFORD, Margery: Schubert--An Introduction to his Piano Works (Alfred).
HALFORD, Margery: Schubert--The First Book (Alfred).
HANSEN (Publisher): Franz Schubert--A Highlight Collection.
HEINRICHSHOFEN/PETERS (Publisher): Schubert Easier Favorites (No. 4051).
HERA and SARMAI: Easy Piano Music from the Period of Romanticism (Musica Budapest/Boosey & Hawkes Z.12.409).
HERRMANN, Kurt: Easy Schubert, Schumann, and Weber (Kalmus 9541/Belwin-Mills).
HUGHES, Edwin: Master Series--Schubert (G. Schirmer).

This charming dance is fairly easy. Melodic, dolce sections are alternated with forte octave material. A singing tone is needed for the melody, which should stand out clearly above the subdued inner figures. The octave technique is not difficult.

Length: 24 measures
Technique: sustained and moving notes, octaves, 8th note passage work

No. 8, Bb Major, or "Viennese Dance" <u>Intermediate</u>

ALFRED (Publisher): Schubert--21 of his Easiest Piano Selections.
HEINRICHSHOFEN/PETERS (Publisher): Schubert Easier Favorites (No. 4051).

A bouncy, folk-like theme is the basis of this short dance. The left hand is quite simple throughout and the right hand carries running eighth notes with appoggiaturas and chromatic scales. The sound is rather unsophisticated.

Tempo: Alfred - Allegro moderato
Length: 24 measures
Technique: sustained and moving notes, jump bass, 8th note passage work

No. 9, D Major, or "Viennese Dance" <u>Intermediate</u>

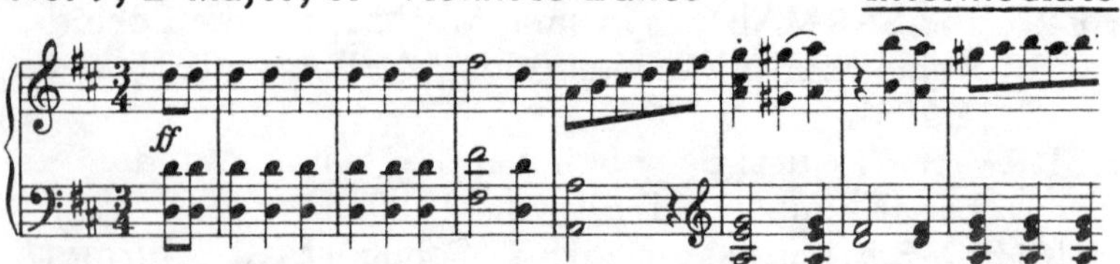


HEINRICHSHOFEN/PETERS (Publisher): Schubert Easier Favorites (No. 4051).

The brassy sound of a fanfare opens this bright dance. One almost expects the actors or singers to make their entrance. Solid octave and chord technique is needed to produce the impressive sound.

Length: 20 measures
Technique: sustained and moving notes, octaves, clef changes

No. 10, D Major, or "Viennese Dance" Intermediate

HEINRICHSHOFEN/PETERS (Publisher): Schubert Easier Favorites (No. 4051).

This comparatively lengthy piece gives the effect of an interlude. The opening fanfare octaves are followed by crashing dominant chords. In the last four measures, the left hand introduces a quiet horn call.

Length: 36 measures
Technique: octaves and octave chords, 8th note passage work

No. 11, D Major, or "Viennese Dance" Intermediate

ALFRED (Publisher): Schubert--21 of his Easiest Piano Selections.

HEINRICHSHOFEN/PETERS (Publisher): Schubert Easier Favorites (No. 4051).

This dance uses a variety of common thematic material and harmonies. The technique is pianistic and includes double notes and detached articulations. Overall, this piece is accessible and easy.

Length: 24 measures

Technique: sustained and moving notes, repeated octaves and chords, 8th note scalar passages

No. 12, F Major, Advancing Intermediate

HEINRICHSHOFEN/PETERS (Publisher): Schubert Easier Favorites (No. 4051).

This strong and forceful dance is comprised of repeated octaves, chords, and broken chords which function as both contrasting and accompanimental material.

Each of these "Viennese Dances" is fanfare like with an interludal quality. The repeated octave patterns tie them together as a set.

Length: 20 measures

Technique: octaves, octave chords, 8th note passage work

## GERMAN DANCES, D. 420

Note: All of D. 420 may be found in:

MIES, Paul: Schubert--Samtliche Tanze, Band I (G. Henle Verlag 74).

No. 1, D Major, or "Landler" Intermediate

BERINGER, Oscar: Beringer's School of Easy Classics--Schubert (Galaxy).
INTERNATIONAL LIBRARY OF PIANO MUSIC, Album Four (University Society)

Written almost entirely in harmonic thirds, sixths, and parallel octaves, a folk dance feeling is strong in this piece. These consonant sounds in the right hand are given some zest by the use of pedal points in the left hand accompaniment. The dramatic dynamic changes provide delightful contrasts.

Tempo: Beringer - Allegro moderato
Inter. Library - Allegro moderato
Length: 24 measures
Technique: double 3rds, octaves, sustained and moving notes

No. 2, A Major Early Intermediate

HERA and SARMAI: Easy Piano Music from the Period of Romanticism (Musica Budapest/Boosey & Hawkes Z.12.409).

An effective contrast to D. 420, No. 1, this dance has a delicate filigree of running notes accompanied by straightforward waltz rhythm. The tie over some downbeats in the first section gives a piquant touch to this charming short piece.

Length: 16 measures
Technique: 8th note passage work, sustained and moving notes

No. 3, D Major

Intermediate

Beginning with a rhythmic pattern reminiscent of D. 420, No. 1, this lovely waltz has an uncomplicated melody doubled in octaves in the first section. The harmonic interest is carried in the left hand, with effective chromatic voicing. The second section utilizes this type of harmonization in the right hand as well. The dynamic level is "pp" with few changes other than accent markings.

Length: 16 measures
Technique: octaves, sustained and moving notes

No. 4, A Major

Intermediate

The persistent tonic, dominant-seventh progressions result in some monotony, not much relieved by the highly sequential melody. Dynamic change provides the only contrast in the piece.

Length: 16 measures
Technique: 8th note broken chords, triple grace notes, waltz bass

No. 5, D Major — Early Intermediate

Tonic and dominant seventh chords predominate in this dance as they did in D. 420, No. 4, but the melodic line is somewhat more creative. The strong similarity between them seems to indicate pairing the two dances.

Length: 16 measures

Technique: jump bass, sustained and moving notes, 8th note passage work

No. 6, A Major — Intermediate

The use of secondary dominants in this dance relieve the static harmonies of D. 420, Nos. 4 and 5. Both the chord structures and the elongated phrases add complexity, but the writing is excessively sequential and rather redundant.

Length: 24 measures

Technique: double 3rds, 8th note passage work, clef changes

No. 7, E Major — Early Intermediate

Introduction of a triplet figure gives a welcome feeling of contrast to this dance. It has a rather delicate first section, with a dash of brilliance beginning the second. The ending returns to the beginning mood of quiet elegance.

Length: 16 measures
Technique: 8th note scalar patterns and passage work, jump bass

No. 8, A Major — Intermediate

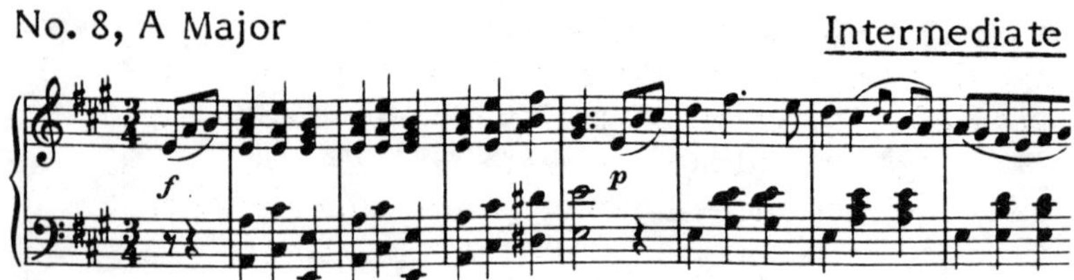


Almost a continuation of D. 420, No. 7, this dance utilizes the triplet figure but in a very solid, dramatically contrasted mood. Each section opens with a full fanfare sound, followed by a delicate waltz ending.

Length: 16 measures
Technique: octaves, scalar patterns

No. 9, D Major — Intermediate

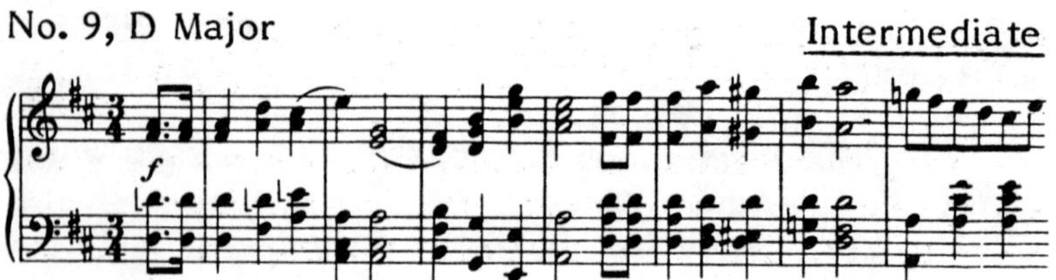


The fanfare-like character of D. 420, No. 8 is retained in this dance, although the rhythmic pattern is changed. Sturdy, solid chords and the "f" and "ff" dynamics produce a bombastic march flavor.

Length: 16 measures
Technique: octaves and octave chords

No. 10, A Major <u>Early Intermediate</u>

ALFRED (Publisher): Schubert--21 of his Easiest Piano Selections.

Open fifths and octaves in the left hand give a surprising contrast to the consonant thirds in the right hand of this dance. It relates in character to No. 9, retaining the almost march-like feeling. The "p" beginning and increasing dynamics produce a continuing crescendo of sound. This German Dance resembles Landler D. 679, No. 1, which is in Eb Major.

Length: 16 measures

Technique: octaves and octave chords, double 3rds

No. 11, D Major <u>Intermediate</u>

Very Schubertian in flavor, this dance has great charm and elegance. It has much musical impact, with a delightful usage of contrary motion, voicing, and climactic sequential progressions.

Length: 16 measures

Technique: sustained and moving notes, double 3rds, clef changes

No. 12 and Coda, A Major/D Major <u>Intermediate</u>

This dance has widely divergent thematic ideas in both sections and ends with a lengthy coda. Each section contains new material, but the coda reprises the preceding dances, especially D. 420, No. 9. When played as a group, this set of dances has a logical progression in material and mood. If played separately, the pieces are disjointed and incomplete. This factor, plus the nature of the coda, would seem to indicate performing D. 420 in its entirety, resulting in an integrated long work much like the Strauss waltzes of the later ninteenth century.

Length: 88 measures
Technique: 8th note passage work, double 3rds, octaves and octave chords

**GERMAN DANCE,** C# Minor, D. 643 <u>Advancing Intermediate</u>

MIES, Paul: Schubert--Samtliche Tanze, Band II (G. Henle Verlag 76).
WEINMANN/KANN: Schubert--Walzer und Deutsche Tanze (Wiener 50063) German dance only.

Chromatically altered leading tones are an integral part of the continuous melody of this German dance. In the A sections the right hand moves in constant eighth notes with an accompanying waltz bass. The hands switch material in the B section. The contrast between the two sections is quite dramatic. Major/minor mode figurations occur throughout but the ending is major. Schubert dedicates this single German dance to Herrn Josef Huttenbrenner. In the Mies edition a 16-measure ecossaise in Db Major is paired with this German dance.

Length: 17 measures

Technique: 8th note passage work, jump bass, octaves and octave chords

**GERMAN DANCE,** Gb Major, D. 722 — Advancing Intermediate

MIES, Paul: Schubert--Samtliche Tanze, Band II (G. Henle Verlag 76).

WEINMANN/KANN: Schubert--Walzer und Deutsche Tanze (Wiener 50063).

This lovely German dance has intriguing unbalanced phrases with opening and closing sections repeated. The difficult Gb Major key is harder than it sounds.

Length: 28 measures

Technique: sustained and moving notes, 8th note scalar passages, jump bass, broken octaves

## **GERMAN DANCES,** D. 769

Note: All of D. 769 may be found in:

MIES, Paul: Schubert--Samtliche Tanze, Band II (G. Henle Verlag 76).

No. 1, A Major <u>Intermediate</u>

The extremely soft dynamics and the "mit Verschiebung" (with delay) indication give an otherwise outspoken and direct German dance a sense of otherworldliness. A faraway effect may be created by the use of the una corda pedal and a subdued finger technique. Smooth legato thirds are the most demanding technical element. This dance requires musicianship and expressiveness.

Length: 16 measures
Technique: double 3rds, sustained and moving notes, double grace notes

No. 2, D Major, <u>Advancing Intermediate</u>

The second dance of this short set is also subdued, with an equal balance of important material in each hand. Moving lines, interesting rhythms, and unusual harmonies provide the lovely quality.

Length: 16 measures
Technique: octaves, 8th note passage work

## GERMAN DANCES, D. 783 (Op. 33)

Note: All of D. 783 may be found in :

HANSEN (Publisher): Schubert--A Highlight Collection.
MIES, Paul: Schubert--Samtliche Tanze, Band II (G. Henle Verlag 76).
NIEMANN, Walter: Schubert Dances (Peters No.150).
SCHIRMER (Publisher): Schubert Dances (Vol. 1537).
WEINMANN/KANN: Schubert--Walzer und Deutsche Tanze (Wiener 50063).

### No. 1, A Major — Early Advanced

KALMUS (Publisher): Schubert--An Easy Album for Piano Solo (Belwin-Mills).
ROWLEY, Alec: The Easiest Original Schubert (Hinrichsen No. 6/Peters).

This majestic dance begins with declamatory unison octaves. The treacherous leaping left hand octaves in the second section will determine the tempo. Grace notes, in keeping with the strong character, are dignified rather than flippant. An uncharacteristic decrescendo and piano dynamic level end the piece.

Length: 25 measures
Technique: octaves, chords, sustained and moving notes, varied dynamics, grace notes

### No. 2, D Major — Advancing Intermediate

HALFORD, Margery: Schubert--An Introduction to his Piano Works (Alfred).
HALFORD, Margery: Schubert--The First Book (Alfred).
HUGHES, Edwin: Master Series--Schubert (G. Schirmer).
KALMUS PIANO SERIES #9547: Masters for the Young - Weber and Schubert (Belwin-Mills).
KALMUS (Publisher): Schubert--An Easy Album for Piano Solo (Belwin-Mills).
ROWLEY, Alec: The Easiest Original Schumann (Hinrichsen No. 6/Peters).
VOLGER, Heinz: Schubert--Easiest Piano Pieces (Peters No. 5015).

The dolce sound of this German dance offers a fine contrast to the first of the set. Double dotted rhythms provide lift and buoyancy. The varying articulations include a graceful portato. A surprise cadence of the first section prepares for the relative minor but proceeds to the major.

Length: 16 measures
Technique: homophonic construction, intricate rhythms

No. 3, Bb Major — Advancing Intermediate

KALMUS (Publisher): Schubert--An Easy Album for Piano Solo (Belwin-Mills).
ROWLEY, Alec: The Easiest Original Schubert (Hinrichsen No. 6/Peters).

A light, quick tempo is appropriate for this charming dance. The right hand has some rather awkward jumps. The important rests give an implied accent to the downbeat that is later marked "fp" or "fz".

Length: 16 measures
Technique: jump bass, wide leaps, important rests

No. 4, G Major, or "Landler" <u>Early Advanced</u>

This engaging and vital waltz has a Viennese flow. The scalar flourishes of 5, 6, 7, and 8 notes create the spontaneous and lovely character. These should be in strict time with clear pulsation. The "fz" accents on the downbeat emphasize the goal of each scalar upbeat.

Length: 16 measures
Technique: quick scalar flourishes, jump bass, octaves

No. 5, D Major, or "Waltz" <u>Intermediate</u>

HUGHES, Edwin: Master Series--Schubert (G. Schirmer).
NEVIN, Mark: 50 Beloved Piano Solos, Bach to Bartok (Boston 14062).
VOLGER, Heinz: Schubert--Easiest Piano Pieces (Peters No. 5015).

This delicate lilting piece has a legato right hand supported by a waltz bass, with slight but unusual accents. The continuous eighth notes include many repeated notes.

Length: 16 measures
Technique: jump waltz bass, sustained and moving notes, 8th note passage work

No. 6, Bb Major — Advancing Intermediate

SMALL, Allan: Schubert Waltz Sampler (Alfred).

This grand fanfare-like allegro has large chords and octaves that fill both hands, which are predominantly homorhythmic. accents (fz, ffz, and fp) break the piece into one and two-measure groupings.

Length: 16 measures
Technique: octaves and octave chords, accidentals, accents

No. 7, Bb Major or "Waltz" — Intermediate

CLARK and GOSS: Piano Literature, Book 3 and Book 3-4a-4b (Summy-Birchard).
GLOVER, David Carr: Piano Repertoire, Level Six (Belwin-Mills).
HERRMANN, Kurt: Easy Schubert, Schumann, and Weber (Kalmus 9541/Belwin-Mills).
KALMUS (Publisher): Schubert--An Easy Album for Piano Solo (Belwin-Mills).
KREUTZER, Hilde B.: 42 Favorites for Piano, Book 3 (Brodt).

McGRAW, Cameron: Four Centuries of Keyboard Music, Book 3 (Boston).
MEDLEY, Bill and Pat: Standard Literature, Volume 2 (Hal Leonard HL00240902).
ROWLEY, Alec: The Easiest Original Schubert (Hinrichsen No. 6/Peters).
SHEFTEL, Paul: More Classics - Romantics - Moderns (C. Fischer ATZ103).
SMALL, Allan: Schubert Waltz Sampler (Alfred).
VOLGER, Heinz: Schubert--Easiest Piano Pieces (Peters No. 5015).

This familiar dance is found in many editions, with slight editorial differences. The urtext edition includes an indication under the first measures, "mit erhobener Dampfung" (with heightened dampening pedal) which may enhance the muted sound of the initial piano indication. The dynamics broaden in the second section.

Tempo: Glover - Allegretto
McGraw - Tempo di valse
Length: 16 measures
Technique: jump bass, octave chords

No. 8, Eb Major — Intermediate

This spirited dance calls for an assured but never forceful touch. "Fp" accents on the second beat should be controlled within the overall dynamic level where an mp-mf seems appropriate. In the second section dynamics are very specific. A wide variety of material offers excellent contrast in this short piece.

Length: 16 measures
Technique: octaves and octave chords, 8th note passage work, grace notes

No. 9, C Major, or "Landler" Intermediate

AGAY, Denes: An Anthology, The Romantic Period, Vol. III (Yorktown).
CLARK and GOSS: Piano Literature, Book 3 and Book 3-4a-5a (Summy-Birchard).
SMALL, Allan: Schubert Waltz Sampler (Alfred).

The thick repeated chords, slightly altered at each repetition, are challenging. A very attractive sound is generated by the interesting harmonies, particularly those in the second section which wander quickly through many keys that are never fully established. The hands share in the same rhythm and articulation throughout, with staccato indications. "Fp" accents in measures four and eight also have a tenuto indication. The Agay edition entitles this piece "Landler."

Tempo: Agay - Allegretto
Length: 17 measures
Technique: octaves, thick octave chords, accents

No. 10, A Minor, or "Landler" Intermediate

AGAY, Denes: An Anthology, The Romantic Period, Vol. III (Yorktown).
BANOWETZ, Joseph: The Pianist's Book of Classic Treasures (GWM/Kjos).
GLOVER, David Carr: Piano Repertoire, Level Six (Belwin-Mills).

NOONA, Walter and Carol: Classical Patterns B (Heritage).
PACE, Robert: Music for Piano, Book 6 (Roberts/Schirmer).
SHEFTEL, Paul: More Classics - Romantics - Moderns (C. Fischer ATF103).
SMALL, Allan: Schubert Waltz Sampler (Alfred).
VOLGER, Heinz: Schubert--Easiest Piano Pieces (Peters No. 5015).

A haunting melody and intriguing harmonies make this familiar dance a lovely choice for study and performance. Piquant augmented 6th chords are followed by a chromatic descending sequence that leads to the final cadence. Dynamics are generally very quiet, and expressive markings are explicit. The Agay edition calls this German dance "Landler," and Robert Pace entitles it "Valse Lente."

Tempo: Banowetz = Allegro
Glover = Moderato
Noona = Grazioso
Length: 24 measures
Technique: jump bass, double grace notes, octaves

No. 11, G Major — Advancing Intermediate

A very agile right hand is necessary to perform the yodel-like eighth note melody. Third beat "fz" accents highlight these leaping intervals. Although the majority of the piece is in G Major, it begins in E Minor. The initial reading is difficult due to left hand clef changes. Dynamics and musical expression marks are quite explicit.

Length: 16 measures
Technique: clef changes, jump bass, 8th note passage work

No. 12, C Major, or "Miniature" <u>Intermediate</u>

SHEALY, Alexander: Schubert--his greatest Piano Solos (Ashley).

This attractive German dance has a pleasant balance of contrasting material in a simple setting. Melodic, legato thirds are followed by detached solid chords. The two-note appoggiaturas and incisive articulations add a zesty character. Dynamics alternate every four measures between "p" and "f". The second section has a distinctive martial feeling that is due to the change in left hand figuration.

Length: 16 measures
Technique: double 3rds, octaves and octave chords, sustained and moving notes

No. 13, C Major, or "Miniature" <u>Intermediate</u>

SHEALY, Alexander: Schubert--his greatest Piano Solos (Ashley).

Third beat accents are the most distinctive element in an otherwise quiet dance. An almost berceuse-like quality is evoked by the dotted rhythm.

Length: 16 measures
Technique: thick octave chords, sustained and moving notes

No. 14, F Minor/F Major — Intermediate

BANOWETZ, Joseph: The Pianist's Book of Classics Treasures (GWM/Kjos).
SMALL, Allan: Schubert Waltz Sampler (Alfred).

Key scheme plays an important role in this German dance. It begins in F Minor, modulates to Ab Major, and then changes key signature to an abrupt F Major. The thematic material seems more at home in the minor mode. Quick trills amid running eighth notes are frequent.

Tempo: Banowetz - Allegro
Length: 16 measures
Technique: jump bass, 8th note passage work, trills

No. 15, Ab Major — Intermediate

BANOWETZ, Joseph: The Pianist's Book of Classics Treasures (GWM/Kjos).
CLARK and GOSS: Piano Literature, Book 6b (Summy-Birchard).
HALFORD, Margery: Schubert--An Introduction to his Piano Works (Alfred).

HALFORD, Margery: Schubert--The First Book (Alfred).
SMALL, Allan: Schubert Waltz Sampler (Alfred).

Minimal melodic movement and ties across the bar lines give this quiet dance a sustained feeling. The sparse melody moves to the inner voice in the second section. The key scheme vacillates between F Minor and Ab Major. A lovely sound is created by the subtle material in this dance.

Tempo: Banowetz - Allegro
Length: 16 measures
Technique: jump bass, ties across the bar, sustained and moving notes

No. 16, F Major, <u>Advancing Intermediate</u>

CLARK and GOSS: Piano Literture, Book 6b (Summy-Birchard).

In one of the more attractive dances in this set, Schubert combines large chords, octaves, lovely harmonic movement, and an occasional rhythmic surprise. An 8va is written above the first eight measures in the urtext (Weinmann/Kann). The second eight-measure phrase contains some intriguing harmonic changes. A forceful, assured touch will bring out the dynamic character. Because of the length of this set, a selected grouping would be effective in performance. D. 783 also contains two ecossaises.

Length: 16 measures
Technique: octaves, octave chords, sustained and moving notes

## GERMAN DANCES, D. 820

Note: All of D. 820 may be found in:

MIES, Paul: Schubert--Samtliche Tanze, Band II
(G. Henle Verlag 76).
WEINMANN/KANN: Schubert--Walzer und Deutsche
Tanze (Wiener 50063).

No. 1, Ab Major — Early Advanced

This high register dance has both hands in the treble clef. Phrasing, melodic shape, and clear direction are key elements to a coherent performance. The right hand is composed of broken octaves that often outline chords. The melodic material is shared between the hands. Nos. 2 and 3 both function as trio sections to be used in conjunction with this dance.

Length: 16 measures
Technique: broken octaves, accidentals,
sustained and moving notes

No. 2, Ab Major — Intermediate

The harmonic progression in the opening measures of this dance are almost contemporary in sound. The lovely delicate melody is accompanied by lush chords.

Length: 16 measures
Technique: 8th note passage work, 3 and 4-note chords

No. 3, Ab Major — Advancing Intermediate

This second trio to D. 820, No. 1 is similar in character to the first (D. 820, No. 2). The figuration is especially conducive to the dampened pianissimo sound. Right hand double notes and sustained and moving notes are supported by a basically chordal left hand. Musical indications are quite explicit and expressive, with echo effects and third beat accents. In the Mies edition, No. 1 is rewritten after both Nos. 2 and 3. In the Wienmann/Kann edition there is a D.C. al fine indication after both Nos. 2 and 3.

Length: 16 measures
Technique: sustained and moving notes, double 3rds, 3rd beat accents

No. 4, Bb Major — Advancing Intermediate

This bombastic dance gives few aural clues as to the 3/4 meter; frequent two-note groupings and accents suggest a 2/4 or 4/4 time signature. Large solid chords are found in a variety of detached, accented articulations. Dynamics are explicit and involve terraced or building effects. Two trios are indicated for this German dance (D. 820, Nos. 5 and 6).

Length: 24 measures

Technique: octaves and octave chords, varied articulations and dynamics, wide interval leaps

No. 5, Bb Major <u>Advancing Intermediate</u>

This short dance is much more accessible than D. 820, No. 4, but the three bracketed eighth notes are easily misread as triplets. The pulse is secure and the rhythmic figures are similar throughout. The first section is marked "pp," and the second section enlarges the pattern at an "ff" level. Varying accents and articulations are frequent throughout.

Length: 16 measures

Technique: broken octaves, octaves, octave chords, explicit dynamics and accents

No. 6, Bb Major, or "Waltz Legato and Staccato" <u>Advancing Intermediate</u>

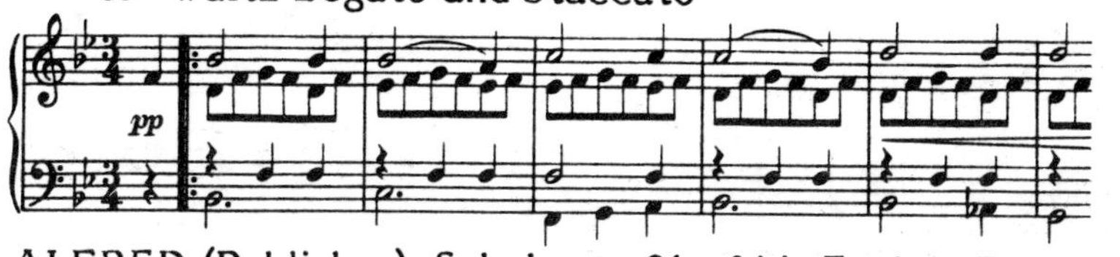


ALFRED (Publisher): Schubert--21 of his Easiest Piano Selections.

The four voice texture of this dance allows the soprano and bass to "sing" a duet while the inner voices accompany. This grouping would be a lovely performance choice.

Length: 25 measures

Technique: voicing, sustained and moving notes, "Spinning Song" accompaniment, 9ths

## GERMAN DANCES, D. 841

Note: All of D. 841 may be found in:

MIES, Paul: Schubert--Samtliche Tanze, Band II (G. Henle Verlag 76).

No. 1, F Major — Intermediate

The opening dotted-note motive of each section has lovely contrary motion voicing, giving a piquant flavor to this enjoyable short dance. The tie over the bar line adds to the creativity of the composition, as does the complex harmonic progressions.

Length: 16 measures

Technique: sustained and moving notes, octaves

No. 2, G Major — Intermediate

These two charming dances are very different, and as a set they are a delightful contrast for performance. This dance is simple and unsophisticated, with a definite folk character.

Length: 16 measures

Technique: broken chords, melody and accompaniment in the same hand, legato vs. staccato

## GERMAN DANCES, D. 970

Note: All of D. 970 may be found in:

MIES, Paul: Schubert--Samtliche Tanze, Band II (G. Henle Verlag 76).

No. 1, Eb Major <u>Intermediate</u>

The simple harmonic progressions of this dance are made doubly apparent by their outlining in the right hand melody. The opening of the second section provides an unprepared contrast of key, beginning in C Minor but returning to Eb Major in the closing measures.

Length: 16 measures

Technique: octaves, broken chords, jump bass

No. 2, Eb Major <u>Advancing Intermediate</u>

Beginning in Eb Major but changing abruptly to C Minor, this dance is similar to D. 970, No. 1. Its melody, doubled at the octave, has a step-wise thematic pattern accompanied by a typical waltz bass in the first section, with more sophisticated pedal point chords in the second. The ABA form is indicated by a repetition of the first eight measures.

Length: 16 measures
Technique: octave and octave chords, jump bass

No. 3, Ab Major — Advancing Intermediate

The folk idiom of this dance is strengthened by the repetitive tonic/dominant seventh progressions. The octave melody is sprightly, with occasional repeated eighths and quarters, lending a fanfare quality. The sequential patterns in the second section, with their altered passing tones, add zest to the rather redundant harmonic structure.

Length: 16 measures
Technique: octaves, jump bass

No. 4, Ab Major — Intermediate

The simplicity of D. 970, No. 3 is retained in this piece, although the tonic/dominant seventh harmonies are enriched by the subdominant in the second section. The melody has lilting broken chord triplets that add charm and grace to this folk dance.

Length: 16 measures
Technique: 8th note triplets, jump bass

No. 5, Db Major

Intermediate

This dance relates closely to D. 970, No. 4, retaining the triplets in its rhythmic scoring. The tonic/dominant seventh progressions abound in the waltz bass, but the melody has unusual twists. This creative touch adds elegance to the folk character of the piece.

Length: 16 measures
Technique: 8th note triplets, jump bass

No. 6, Db Major

Intermediate

D. 970, No. 6 ends the set beautifully, as it retains the folk character but adds complexity of rhythm and harmony in an elegant way. As in D. 970, No. 1, the melody outlines the chord structures, but in agile two-note phrases. The harmonic progressions of the second section are given heightened interest with a pedal point bass.

The German Dances of this set, listed as Landlers in Grove's Dictionary, are charming in their simplicity and grace.

Length: 16 measures
Technique: 2-note phrases, jump bass, ornamentation

## GERMAN DANCES, D. 971

Note: All of D. 971 may be found in:

MIES, Paul: Schubert--Samtliche Tanze, Band II (G. Henle Verlag 76).
WEINMANN/KANN: Schubert--Walzer und Deutsche Tanze (Wiener 50063).

No. 1, A Minor — Advancing Intermediate

A bravura technique will enhance this heavy pesante dance, which is scored in octave and ninth chords. The 3/4 pulse is slightly obscured in a most intriguing manner by accenting the second beat. Phrasing is in two-measure groups. The left hand is generally in octaves, with a pedal point in the first section.

Length: 17 measures
Technique: octaves, octave and 9th chords, sustained and moving notes, important accents

No. 2, A Major — Advancing Intermediate

HERA and SARMAI: Easy Piano Music from the Period of Romanticism (Musica Budapest/Boosey & Hawkes Z.12.409).

The light, floating quality of this second German dance offers excellent contrast between the two heavier dances of this attractive set. The leggiero character is basically due to the ascending scalar lines in a high register. These are in two beat groups over a simple waltz bass, creating a sophisticated rhythmic opposition. Dynamics are quiet, rising only to "mf". The three eight-measure phrases use the key scheme of A Major-C# Major-A Major.

Length: 24 measures
Technique: 8th note scalar passages, jump bass

No. 3, E Major Advancing Intermediate

The truncated phrases give this German Dance an asymmetrical feeling. Right hand octaves and large chords are supported by a varied left hand accompaniment. Accidentals are frequent and include double sharps. This rather odd piece offers an ambiguous finale to the set.

Length: 24 measures
Technique: octaves, octave chords,
accidentals, clef changes

## GERMAN DANCES, D. 972

Note: All of D. 972 may be found in:

MIES, Paul: Schubert--Samtliche Tanze, Band II (G. Henle Verlag 76).

No. 1, Db Major <u>Intermediate</u>

Opening with a fanfare on inverted triads and a pedal point bass, this dance has a vigorous, spirited quality. The remaining measures utilize eighth and quarter note broken chords with typical waltz accompaniment.

Length: 16 measures
Technique: octaves, 8th note passage work, jump bass

No. 2, Ab Major or "Waltz" <u>Intermediate</u>

GEEHL, Henry: Schubert--Compositions of Moderate Difficulty (Ashdown).

Bearing a resemblance to the first dance of D. 972, this piece utilizes the eighth note broken chords accompanied by the waltz bass. Subtle tonal balance could create a more lyrical melodic line.

Length: 16 measures
Technique: 8th note passage work, jump bass

No. 3, A Major, or "Waltz" <u>Intermediate</u>

AMSCO (Publisher): It's Easy to Play Classics.
BASTIEN, James: Easy Piano Classics (Kjos West).
HERA and SARMAI: Easy Piano Music from the Period of Romanticism (Musica Budapest/Boosey & Hawkes Z.12.409).

The alteration of the Ab Major key of No. 2 to A Major in No. 3 recalls the same tonal change utilized in the Adagio movement of the "Wanderer Fantasy." Schubert seemed fond of this "Neopolitan" relationship, which moves the tonic up one half step. This dance has more contrast than its companions, with scalar patterns interspersed with broken chords against the waltz patterns of the left hand. This set of dances has great charm and could be a delightful performance choice.

Tempo: AMSCO - Moderato
Bastien - Semplico
Length: 16 measures
Technique: jump bass, 8th note scalar patterns

## GERMAN DANCES, D. 973

Note: All of D. 973 may be found in:

MIES, Paul: Schubert--Samtliche Tanze, Band II (G. Henle Verlag 76).
WEINMANN/KANN: Schubert--Walzer und Deutsche Tanze (Wiener Urtext 50063).

No. 1, E Major — Intermediate

This rather sedate, courtly dance belies the snapped, dotted rhythms found in the opening. The octave leap in the first downbeat occurs in a dotted rhythm that is omitted on each subsequent appearance. This may be attributed to Schubert's quick and not always thorough sketching habits. The finished sound of this dance is pleasant but not overly exciting.

Length: 16 measures
Technique: octaves, sustained and moving notes, 8th note passage work

No. 2, E Major <u>Advancing Intermediate</u>

The first eight-measure phrase of this short piece has a quiet introductory effect. The second eight measures adds a waltz bass to the original thematic material, which relates closely to D. 973, No. 1. The performer should emphasize the contrast between the quiet introduction and the fuller, louder second section.

Length: 16 measures
Technique: jump bass, octave chords, sustained and moving notes

No. 3, Ab Major <u>Advancing Intermediate</u>

Both rhythm and key set this dance apart from the other two of the set. The rhythmic structure is disorienting, never seeming to establish either a duple or triple feeling. Abrupt dynamic changes, sudden unexpected accents, and important rests are not easily felt. The harmonic modulation in the last sections add a fresh touch.

Length: 16 measures
Technique: sustained and moving notes, illogical rhythm, important rests and accents

## GERMAN DANCES, D. 974

Note All of D. 974 may be found in:

MIES, Paul: Schubert--Samtliche Tanze, Band II (G. Henle Verlag 76).
SHEALY, Alexander: Schubert--his greatest Piano Solos (Ashley).
WEINMANN/KANN: Schubert--Walzer und Deutsche Tanze (Wiener 50063).

No. 1, Db Major — Advancing Intermediate

This large and elegant ballroom waltz flows with an assured sound and a quick tempo. Right hand keyboard range is quite wide with many leaps. Effective dynamic, register, and voicing changes occur in the second section. Harmonies are conventional.

Length: 16 measures
Technique: double 3rds, octave chords, jump bass, 8th note passage work

No. 2, Db Major — Advancing Intermediate

This flowing legato dance pairs well in key and harmonic scheme with the first of the set. It is more pianistic than the first, with fewer hand shifts and a smaller keyboard range. The double flats add zest to this conventional but lovely piece.

Length: 16 measures

Technique: jump bass, 8th note passage work

**GERMAN DANCE,** D Major, D. 975 — Advancing Intermediate

MIES, Paul: Schubert--Samtliche Tanze, Band II (G. Henle Verlag 76).

This beautiful short waltz deserves more attention than it has received from editors of piano collections. Its lilting, mazurka-like melody is rhythmically infectious. The creative opening chords, beginning on the submediant, are totally unexpected and very endearing. This is an excellent choice for study and performance.

Length: 16 measures

Technique: dotted rhythms, repeated chords, jump bass

## LANDLER, D. 145 (Op. 18)

Note: All of D. 145 may be found in:

MIES, Paul: Schubert--Samtliche Tanze, Band I (G. Henle Verlag 74).

No. 1, Eb Major <u>Intermediate</u>

SHEALY, Alexander: Schubert--his greatest Piano Solos (Ashley).

Harmonies and patterns of the accompanimental material are indicative of the simplicity of the landler and this set in particular. I, IV, and V harmonies are placed in a waltz bass setting. The melody is composed of broken chords with a folk-like sound. Occasional trills on the third beat add a light touch.

Length: 16 measures
Technique: ornaments, broken chords, jump bass, clef changes

No. 2, Eb Major, or "Country Dance" <u>Intermediate</u>

AGAY, Denes: Classics to Moderns, Intermediate, Vol. 37 (Consolidated).
GRANT, Lawrence: More Classic to Contemporary Piano Music (Ashley).
SHEALY, Alexander: Schubert--his greatest Piano Solos (Ashley).

An exaggeration of the dynamics in this piece will enhance the light and airy character. The ABA form is written out, the only one of the set to be so notated. Tonic and dominant harmonies predominate, with the B section firmly in the dominant key. Both sections use similar melodic material. This landler exudes a jolly spirit which is typical of Schubert's short dances.

Tempo: Agay - Allegretto
Grant - Allegretto
Length: 24 measures
Technique: sustained and moving notes, octaves, jump bass

No. 3, Ab Major, or "Country Dance" Intermediate

AGAY, Denes: Classics to Moderns, Intermediate, Vol. 37 (Consolidated).
GRANT, Lawrence: More Classics to Contemporary Piano Music (Ashley).
HUGHES, Edwin: Master Series--Schubert (G. Schirmer).
SHEALY, Alexander: Schubert--his greatest Piano Solos (Ashley).
WILLS, Vera: The Purple Book #2 (G. Schirmer 3450).

This good-humored dance is full of fun and frivolity. A common element in this set of landlers is the ornamental or rhythmic emphasis on the downbeat. The first beat triplets and light accents add sparkle to the right hand melody. The harmonies are kept simple, with a variety of articulations.

Tempo: Hughes - Allegro
Grant - Moderato
Length: 16 measures
Technique: 8th note triplets, jump bass

No. 4, Db Major Advancing Intermediate

SHEALY, Alexander: Schubert--his greatest Piano Solos (Ashley).
ZEITLIN, Poldi: Schubert Dances for Piano (Presser).

This quiet, gay dance requires technical agility. The wide leaps in the left hand waltz bass and high leger lines in the right hand may cause initial reading difficulties. The ornamentation on the upbeats enhances the pulse and light-hearted character.

Tempo: Zeitlin - Giocoso
Length: 16 measures
Technique: ornaments, jump bass with large leaps, 8th note triplets, high leger lines

No. 5, Db Major, or "Country Dance" Intermediate

HUGHES, Edwin: Master Series for the Young--Schubert (G. Schirmer Ed.1113).
SHEALY, Alexander: Schubert--his greatest Piano Solos (Ashley).
WILLS, Vera: The Purple Book #2 (G. Schirmer 3450).

The most attractive element of this landler is the major/minor fluctuation in the opening bars. After this intriguing opening, tonic/dominant harmonies in the major tonality take over and keep the mood quite serene. The downbeats vary from triplets to even eighth notes.

Tempo: Hughes - Allegro
Length: 16 measures
Technique: repeated notes, sustained and moving notes, jump bass, 8th note triplets

No. 6, Db Major — Intermediate

SHEALY, Alexander: Schubert--his greatest Piano Solos (Ashley).

The triplet downbeat and double dotted rhythms are characteristic of many Schubert landlers, producing a happy dance-like effect. These elements and the quiet dynamics help express the generally light character of this work. Leger lines and rhythms tend to make reading and learning more difficult than actual playing.

Length: 16 measures
Technique: 8th note triplets and double dotted rhythms, leger lines, sustained and moving notes, jump bass

No. 7, Db Major — Intermediate

SHEALY, Alexander: Schubert--his greatest Piano Solos (Ashley).

The extremely high register and dotted rhythms combine to give this landler a light and bouncy character. Schubert was explicit with his "fp" dynamics. All downbeats are trilled, giving this piece a dance-like nature. The pervasive tonic/dominant harmonies cause the occasional subdominant harmony to sound like a revelation.

Length: 16 measures

Technique: dotted rhythms, trills, jump bass, leaps

No. 8, Db Major <u>Advancing Intermediate</u>

SHEALY, Alexander: Schubert--his Greatest Piano Solos (Ashley).

The melodic broken octaves and the very high register give this dance a light music-box sound. The broken octaves are also one of the more difficult technical demands in this entire set. Some experimentation could be done with various touches on these octaves. The forte dynamic level contrasts with the previous piece.

Length: 16 measures

Technique: ornaments, broken octaves, high register, jump bass

No. 9, Db Major <u>Advancing Intermediate</u>

SHEALY, Alexander: Schubert--his greatest Piano Solos (Ashley).

The rhythm and ornamentation used in this landler is consistent with the others in this set. It radiates carefree joy and exuberance. Downbeats and double dotted notes are preceded by elaborate ornaments. Simple I-V harmonies are interrupted only once by a pleasant change to the subdominant.

Length: 16 measures
Technique: double 3rds, ornaments, leaps, jump bass, double dotted rhythms

No. 10, Db Major, or "Country Dance" <u>Intermediate</u>

AGAY, Denes: Dances--Baroque to Jazz (Warner).
AGAY, Denes: Classics to Moderns, Intermediate, Vol. 37 (Consolidated).
GRANT, Lawrence: More Classics to Contemporary Piano Music (Ashley).
HUGHES, Edwin: Master Series--Schubert (G. Schirmer).
SCHWERDTNER, Hans-George: Easy Piano Pieces and Sonatinas (Schott 6086 AP).
SHEALY, Alexander: Schubert--his greatest Piano Solos (Ashley).
WILLS, Vera: The Purple Book #2 (G. Schirmer 3450).

The melody harmonized in double notes creates an idiomatic landler sound. The triplet downbeat, which is so common to this set of landlers, is used again. Four-measure phrase groups are easily distinguishable by their similar melodic and textural content. The sudden dynamic changes within these four-measure groupings enhance the vitality of the dance. I, IV, and V harmonies contain an occasional nonharmonic tone which adds zest.

Tempo: Agay - Allegretto
Hughes - Allegro
Grant - Moderato
Length: 16 measures
Technique: sustained and moving notes, 8th note triplets, jump bass

No. 11, Db Major — Intermediate

SHEALY, Alexander: Schubert--his greatest Piano Solos (Ashley).

One of the more accessible and attractive of the group, this dance employs a smooth legato sound and occasional third beat accents. Phrases are made up of ascending lines which change in the second section, adding an element of surprise.

Length: 16 measures
Technique: 2-note slurs, jump bass, broken chords, ornaments, octaves

No. 12, Db Major — Advancing Intermediate

SHEALY, Alexander: Schubert--his greatest Piano Solos (Ashley).

The fanfare-like triplets which characterize this dance are used deftly to create both a light texture in the beginning and a heavy, forceful texture in the second section. The most distinctive part of this piece occurs in the second section where the dynamics are amplified in the relative minor.

Length: 16 measures
Technique: dotted scalar figures, leger lines, octaves and octave chords, jump bass, triplets

No. 13, A Major <u>Advancing Intermediate</u>

Much diverse material is contained within these sixteen measures. A left hand accompanimental pattern alternates a waltz bass with treble clef intervals for a beautiful musical effect. Both hands have quick leaps which will develop a familiarity with the keyboard topography.

Length: 16 measures
Technique: leaps, broken chords, jump bass

No. 14, D Major <u>Advancing Intermediate</u>

A quick tempo will enable scalar figures to soar and shimmer, creating the music box sound which is typical of Schubert's dances. Occasional trills and third beat accents lend rhythmic definition. This is a fine landler and an excellent scale etude.

Length: 16 measures
Technique: scales, ornaments, jump bass

No. 15, G Major, or "Miniature" <u>Intermediate</u>

SHEALY, Alexander: Schubert--his greatest Piano Solos (Ashley).

This landler is a contrast to many of the others in that it is not boisterous or exuberant. It is rather quiet and subdued in its calm beauty. The single note melody is pianistic and not difficult.

Length: 16 measures
Technique: sustained and moving notes, waltz bass, both hands in treble clef

No. 16, G Major <u>Intermediate</u>

SHEALY, Alexander: Schubert--his greatest Piano Solos (Ashley).

This light and delicate landler has quiet dynamics throughout. As with many of Schubert's dances, the broken chord melody is simple but needs a musical line and some direction to keep it moving. Occasional important rests in the melodic line add interest.

Length: 16 measures
Technique: broken chords, ornaments, jump bass

No. 17, D Major Advancing Intermediate

SHEALY, Alexander: Schubert--his greatest Piano Solos (Ashley).

The formal and harmonic structure of this landler is similar to that of the previous one, No. 16; they would be an effective performance pair. The right hand leaps are charming, but need careful consideration to create smooth overall motion.

Length: 16 measures
Technique: broken chords, leaps, 8th note scalar passages, jump bass

**FOUR LANDLER,** D Major, D. 354 Early Intermediate

MIES, Paul: Schubert--Samtliche Tanze, Band II (G. Henle Verlag 76).

These four landlers are included in the appendix of the Mies edition because they are sketches, probably intended for a small ensemble of instruments. All are written entirely in the treble clef, with the bass staff scored in two voices only. The top alternates with one and two voices, and the melodies are sprightly and creative. Many of Schubert's dances were originally composed in this form and later filled out for performance on the piano. These were never altered and would not be suitable for solo performance.

Length: 16 measures each
Technique: 8th note passage work, harmonic intervals, ornamentation

**EIGHT LANDLER,** F# Minor, D. 355

MIES, Paul: Schubert--Samtliche Tanze, Band II (G. Henle Verlag 76).

The eight landler of D. 355 are sketches, written on one staff and containing only a melody. The exception is No. 5, which adds a few treble clef harmonic intervals. All pieces in this set follow the same key pattern, with a rather melancholy first section in F# Minor, moving to a happier second section in A Major. Each of the eight dances contain two eight-bar sections, and all begin with a third beat pick-up, most often of two eighth notes. The symmetry is obvious and would seemingly result in a dreary "sameness," but the freshness of each folk-like melody is surprisingly delightful.

Length: 128 measures total
Technique: 8th note passage work, varying articulations, wide interval leaps, ornamentation

LANDLER, D. 366

Note: All of D. 366 may be found in:

MIES, Paul: Schubert--Samtliche Tanze, Band I (G. Henle Verlag 74).
WEINMANN/KANN: Schubert--Landler, Ecossaisen, Menuette (Wiener 50064).

No. 1, A Major <u>Advancing Intermediate</u>

BANOWETZ, Joseph: The Pianist's Book of Classic Treasures (GWM/Kjos).
NIEMANN, Walter: Schubert Dances (Peters No.150).
SCHIRMER (Publisher): Schubert Dances (Vol. 1537).
SHEALY, Alexander: Schubert--his greatest Piano Solos (Ashley).
SHEFTEL, Paul: Classics, Romantics, Moderns--Solos for the Intermediate Pianist (C. Fischer, ATF 102).

This landler is simple, gay, and charming. with unexpected harmonies. Right hand leaps and jumps, along with various light touches, require agility and coordination. Leger lines occasionally cause difficulties in reading. The indication D.C. al fine produces an ABA form that gives the piece symmetry.

Tempo: Banowetz - Allegro moderato
Length: 24 measures
Technique: leger lines, jump bass, 8th note scalar patterns and passage work

No. 2, A Major <u>Intermediate</u>

NIEMANN, Walter: Schubert Dances (Peters No.150).
SCHIRMER (Publisher): Schubert Dances (Vol. 1537).
SHEFTEL, Paul: Classics, Romantics, Moderns--Solos for the Intermediate Pianist (C. Fischer ATF 102).
VOLGER, Heinz: Schubert--Easiest Piano Pieces (Peters No. 5015).

A light, quick tempo will capture the delicate character of this quaint and charming dance. It has left hand accompanimental figures that jump between the treble and bass staves. The second phrase of the dance provides interesting harmonic and textural contrast.

Length: 16 measures
Technique: LH countermelody, jump bass

No. 3, A Minor <u>Intermediate</u>

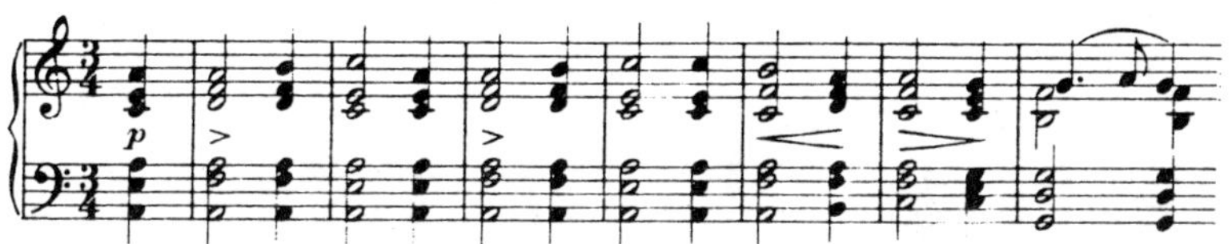

BANOWETZ, Joseph: The Pianist's Book of Classic Treasures (GWM/Kjos).
GLOVER, David Carr: Piano Repertoire, Book 6 (Belwin-Mills).
MOTCHANE, Marthe M.: An Introduction to Pianistic Styles, Schubert Dances (Peters No.150).
SCHIRMER (Publisher): Schubert Dances (Vol. 1537).
SHEFTEL, Paul: Classics, Romantics, Moderns--Solos for the Intermediate Pianist (C. Fischer, ATF 102).
VOLGER, Heinz: Schubert--Easiest Piano Pieces (Peters No. 5015).

This is an unusual homophonic dance with lush voicing, doubling, and full romantic harmonies. Experimenting with voicing will bring out the inner lines, and careful phrasing and thoughtful rubato will add to the chordal motion. Paired with D. 366, No. 5, this would be an enjoyable recital selection.

Tempo: Glover - Moderato
Banowetz - Moderato
Length: 16 measures
Technique: chords and voicing, sustained and moving notes

No. 4, A Minor <u>Advancing Intermediate</u>

BANOWETZ, Joseph: The Pianist's Book of Classic Treasures (GWM/Kjos).
HALFORD, Margery: Schubert--The First Book (Alfred).
MOTCHANE, Marthe M.: An Introduction to Pianistic Styles, Book 3, Romantic (Bourne).
NIEMANN, Walter: Schubert Dances (Peters No. 150).
SCHIRMER (Publisher): Schubert Dances (Vol. 1537).
SHEFTEL, Paul: Classics, Romantics, Moderns--Solos for the Intermediate Pianist (C. Fischer, ATF 102).

This unusual and creative landler is a study in right hand coordination and control. Sustained and moving notes with opposing touches are frequent. The use of the parallel major in the final measures is a sudden and satisfying surprise, which brings this delightful piece to a convincing end.

Tempo: Glover - Moderato
Banowetz - Moderato
Length: 16 measures
Technique: sustained and moving notes, 2-note phrases

No. 5, A Minor <u>Advancing Intermediate</u>

BANOWETZ, Joseph: The Pianist's Book of Classic Treasures (GWM/Kjos).
NIEMANN, Walter: Schubert Dances (Peters No.150).
SCHIRMER (Publisher): Schubert Dances (Vol. 1537).

SHEFTEL, Paul: Classics, Romantics, Moderns--Solos for the Intermediate Pianist (C. Fischer ATF 102).

The homophonic sound of this landler is contrasted by occasional eighth note melodic lines. It fits quite well with No. 3 of this set, and could be used with it as a B section. The left hand octaves should not become too heavy. Quiet dynamics and a general subdued feeling are quite appropriate.

Tempo: Banowetz - Allegro
Length: 16 measures
Technique: chords and voicing, sustained and moving notes, LH octaves throughout

No. 6, C Major <u>Advancing Intermediate</u>

HALFORD, Margery: Schubert--The First Book (Alfred).
NIEMANN, Walter: Schubert Dances (Peters No.150).
SCHIRMER (Publisher): Schubert Dances (Vol. 1537).

This wonderful landler is rather subtle in its dance-like vibrancy. Its main difficulty is two-note slurs on weak fingers. The second section provides rhythmic interest and contrast through various accents. The ABA form is notated.

Length: 24 measures
Technique: sustained and moving notes, 2-note slurs, waltz bass

No. 7, G Major <u>Advancing Intermediate</u>

While not as interesting as the other landlers in this set, this dance is still enjoyable and satisfying to play. A wide right hand range is covered through leger lines and the use of 8va. Difficult trills on both strong and weak beats may impede the rhythmic flow.

Length: 16 measures
Technique: 8th note scalar patterns and passage work, important accents, jump bass

No. 8, D Major <u>Intermediate</u>

This landler could be useful as an etude for hand coordination, finger facility, tonal balance, and various touches. The right hand is busy and involves some large stretches. Neither line is very tuneful.

Length: 16 measures
Technique: broken chords, large stretches, repeated off beat intervals

No. 9, B Major <u>Advancing Intermediate</u>

The dramatic and powerful opening of this dance consists of stirring minor harmonies which resolve beautifully to the major mode. Within the second phrase there are occasional accidentals for additional harmonic color. The left hand has moving lines which are lovely and should be brought out.

Length: 16 measures
Technique: octaves, octave chords, jump bass

No. 10, B Minor — Advancing Intermediate

This poignant and lovely dance is unusual and innovative, with many textural contrasts and accents on the third beat. There are explicit dynamic directions.

Length: 16 measures
Technique: octave chords, sustained and moving notes, octaves, broken chords, large hand stretches

No. 11, B Major — Advancing Intermediate

The combination of broken chord and double note figurations creates a very Germanic sounding dance. The figurations and harmonies are quite expressive. The right hand has occasional ties over the bar line, while the bass line has an unusual creative pattern.

Length: 25 measures
Technique: broken chords, sustained and moving notes, LH leaps

No. 12, Eb Minor — Intermediate

NIEMANN, Walter: Schubert Dances (Peters No.150).
SCHIRMER (Publisher): Schubert Dances (Vol. 1537).

This is a simple lyrical waltz in a plaintive minor tonality with lovely harmonies and subdued dynamics. This dance is complementary in style and key to No. 13; the two could be combined easily for performance.

Length: 16 measures
Technique: broken 3rds, sustained and moving notes, jump bass

No. 13, Bb Minor — Intermediate

HALFORD, Margery: Schubert--An Introduction to his Piano Works (Alfred).
HALFORD, Margery: Schubert--The First Book (Alfred).

This lovely landler has a plaintive, almost yearning quality. In every respect it fits together with No. 12 of this set, and could be used as a "trio." Accidentals are frequent, and the third beat is often accented.

Length: 16 measures
Technique: broken chords, trills, jump bass

No. 14, Db Major — Advancing Intermediate

The sprightly double dotted rhythms of this landler are made even more lively by interesting accidental alterations and the typically Schubertian waltz bass.

Length: 16 measures

Technique: double dotted rhythms, octaves, jump waltz bass

No. 15, Db Major — Advancing Intermediate

NIEMANN, Walter: Schubert Dances (Peters No.150).
SCHIRMER (Publisher): Schubert Dances (Vol. 1537).

The romantic character of this piece is quite different from the usual waltz-like landler. The tempo can be taken slowly if its expressive qualities are brought out. Full chord grace notes and fp accents add brightness and a touch of surprise to this graceful piece.

Length: 16 measures

Technique: grace notes, broken chords, double notes, sustained and moving notes

No. 16, Ab Major — Advancing Intermediate

This simple graceful dance has a slightly constrained sound and a smooth legato quality. The grace notes accentuate the downbeats. Right hand fingering is important for alternating single and double notes. The offbeat rhythm needs tonal balance to be effective.

Length: 16 measures
Technique: double 3rds, octaves, broken chords, ornaments

No. 17, Eb Major, "Allemande" Advancing Intermediate

Legato thirds are the cohesive factor in this short dance. They appear in various forms, changing the texture, rhythm, and melody. The second eight-measure phrase ends tentatively; it would be quite appropriate to repeat the first section, creating an ABA form and a proper conclusion to the set.

Length: 16 measures
Technique: double 3rds, sustained and moving notes

**EIGHT LANDLER,** D Major, D. 370

MIES, Paul: Schubert--Samtliche Tanze, Band II (G. Henle Verlag 76).

Similarities between these melody-only dances are striking. They all begin and end in D Major, all are in bipartite form and sixteen measures long, and all begin with a third beat pick-up. The differences reveal Schubert's cleverness with melody. Some outline triadic chords, and some move in scalar patterns interspersed with wide intervals. Contrasts in phrasing and articulation that breathe life into seemingly static rows of notes. Within their abbreviated form, these pieces are completely charming.

Length: 128 measures total
Technique: 8th note scalar and arpeggiated patterns, ornamentation, varying articulations

**SIX LANDLER,** Bb Major, D. 374

MIES, Paul: Schubert--Samtliche Tanze, Band II (G. Henle Verlag 76).

These melody-only sketches are graceful and dance-like, but are not as inventive as those of D. 355 or D. 370. They share the common key of Bb Major, the same bipartite form of two eighth-measure sections, and all begin on the third beat. Several have a measured trill effect over the first and second, or second and third beats. They are mostly intervallic in nature, with occasional interlacing scalar patterns.

Length: 96 measures total
Technique: 8th note passagework, ornamentation

## LANDLER, D. 378

Note: All of D. 378 may be found in:

MIES, Paul: Schubert--Samtliche Tanze, Band I (G. Henle Verlag 74).

No. 1, Bb Major — Early Intermediate

AGAY, Denes: Piano Recital (AMSCO).

The minimal handshifts and simple figuration give this landler a pianistic flow. The right hand melody has a meandering, yodelling sound which is typical of many of Schubert's dances. In the first section, omission of the left hand downbeat results in a pleasing off-beat accompaniment. The pedal point in the second section is particularly effective.

Length: 16 measures
Technique: broken chords, LH chords and waltz bass, 8th note scalar patterns and passage work

No. 2, Bb Major — Early Intermediate

SZAVAI/VESZPREMI: Piano Album, Book One (Musica Budapest/Belwin-Mills).

This second landler is very much like the first, melodically, pianistically, and rhythmically. When the left hand downbeat is added, it is sustained through the entire measure, and requires an easy octave span. Added dynamics could enhance the life and spirit of the piece.

Tempo: Szavai/Veszpremi - Allegretto
Length: 16 measures
Technique: scalar and broken chord figurations, 8th note passage work, octave chords and broken chords, waltz bass

No. 3, Bb Major, "Country Dance" <u>Early Intermediate</u>

AGAY, Denes: From Bach to Bartok, Vol. B (Warner).
ANTHONY, George Walter: From Beethoven to Shostakovich (Presser).
HERA and SARMAI: Easy Piano Music from the Period of Romanticism (Musica Budapest/Boosey & Hawkes Z.12.409).
INTERNATIONAL LIBRARY OF PIANO MUSIC, Album Four (University Society).

This light-hearted trifle depends on dynamics and phrasing for its musical expression. Using a variety of articulations to complement the two-note slurs will give the melody vitality.

Tempo: Agay - Con moto
Anthony - Moderato
Length: 16 measures
Technique: broken chords, two-note slurs, jump bass

No. 4, Bb Major — Early Intermediate

AGAY, Denes: Piano Recital (AMSCO).
HERA/SARMAI: Easy Piano Music from the Period of Romanticism (Musica Budapest/Boosey & Hawkes Z.12.409).
INTERNATIONAL LIBRARY OF PIANO MUSIC, Album Four (University Society).

As with Schubert's finest dances, this one is full of exuberant life and spirit. Part of its appeal lies in the fact that it contains more contrast of material and texture than do the first three landler of this set. In the first phrase, light appoggiaturas leap up to high staccato notes with soft dynamics. The second phrase contains a fuller texture with busier rhythms. Although only tonic and dominant seventh harmonies are used, this is an interesting and attractive dance in every way.

Tempo: Agay - Moderately with a lilt
Length: 16 measures
Technique: scalar figures, grace notes, broken interval figuration, LH jump bass

No. 5, Bb Major — Early Intermediate

HERA and SARMAI: Easy Piano Music from the Period of Romanticism (Musica Budapest/Boosey & Hawkes Z.12.409).

This dance groups well with the first two in this set. The continuous eighth note melody flow with accompanying off-beat figures is an important aspect of this landler.

Length: 16 measures
Technique: broken chord and scalar figurations, sustained and moving notes, waltz bass

No. 6, Bb Major <u>Intermediate</u>

HERA and SARMAI: Easy Piano Music from the Period of Romanticism (Musica Budapest/Boosey & Hawkes Z.12.409).

The last three dances of this set fit well together because of their sheer joy and exuberance. In No. 6, right hand doubled intervals comprise the bulk of the motivic material and furnish basis for an attractive opening phrase. The accented rhythmic pulse brings out the lovely quality of this landler.

Length: 16 measures
Technique: grace notes, scalar figures, doubled intervals, waltz bass

No. 7, Bb Major <u>Intermediate</u>

This seventh landler relates to the sixth in the spirited character, and the common use of doubled interval figures. Careful fingering will create the smooth flow suggested by the figuration. These last three landlers would make an enjoyable recital selection.

Length: 16 measures
Technique: doubled intervals, arpeggiated and broken chord figurations, waltz bass

No. 8, Bb Major — Intermediate

This strong and virile dance uses a wide variety of figurations for a comparatively short work. The right hand employs various patterns and chords with occasional appoggiaturas and turns which embellish the melody. Strong octaves, chords, and leaps give the left hand balancing strength.

All eight of these landlers are light, elegant, and of moderate difficulty. They could all be played for an enjoyable performance.

Length: 16 measures
Technique: octaves and octave broken chords, ornaments, chords

**LANDLER,** A and E Major, D. 640, Nos. 1 and 2 — Advancing Intermediate

MIES, Paul: Schubert--Samtliche Tanze, Band II (G. Henle Verlag 76).

Schubert notated these dances in a greatly abbreviated form with only a melody line. Deutsch feels that they were meant for a solo instrument, probably violin. Schubert originally notated some of his piano pieces in this form, revising and/or completing them at a later time.

The melodies given for the two dances of D. 640 are unpianistic, with wide leaps and position changes. They both contain patterns of eighths and sixteenths, but contrast in the arrangement of these within the three-beat measures.

Length: 16 measures each
Technique: upper leger lines, wide interval leaps

## LANDLER, D. 679

Note: All of D. 679 may be found in:

ALFRED (Publisher): Schubert--21 of his Easiest Piano Selections.
MIES, Paul: Schubert--Samtliche Tanze, Band II (G. Henle Verlag 76).

No. 1, Eb Major <u>Intermediate</u>

The two-voice right hand moves in consonant thirds, giving a folkish air of simplicity to this charming dance. The accompaniment is somewhat unusual, employing open intervals of fifths, sixths, and octaves. The Schubertian use of pedal points gives an edge of dissonance to the otherwise bland harmonies. The Landler D. 420, No. 10 in A Major is essentially the same as this one, with a few minor changes in both parts.

Tempo: Alfred - Andante con moto
Length: 16 measures
Technique: waltz bass, 8th note passage work, melody and accompaniment in same hand, double 3rds

No. 2, Eb Major — Intermediate

AGAY, Denes: The Joy of Classics (Yorktown).

The lightly tripping right hand of this landler employs alternate phrasing to that of the left, giving an air of sophistication lacking in D. 679, No. 1. The first section has a waltz bass, but the second employs treble-clef chords and intervals. As a set, these dances exemplify the little dancing dolls on a music box.

Length: 16 measures
Technique: 8th note passage work, jump bass

**ZWEI LANDLER**, D. 680

MIES, Paul: Schubert--Samtliche Tanze, Band II (G. Henle Verlag 76).

The angular dotted rhythms and wide interval leaps used in these dances produce awkward, unmelodious effects. The extremely high register portions are unattractive on the piano. Both landler share characteristics of length, form, key, and rhythmic patterns. The first is a sketch with melody only. The second is a duet on two treble clef staves, with a sustaining third voice in the first section.

Length: 32 measures total

Technique: dotted notes, wide interval leaps, ornamentation

## LANDLER, D. 681

Note: All of D. 681 may be found in:

MIES, Paul: Schubert--Samtliche Tanze, Band II (G. Henle Verlag 76).

No. 1, Eb Major <u>Intermediate</u>

Bright and folk-like, this dance has surprising complexities within its few measures. The right hand is often playing melody and accompaniment concurrently, with an added harmonizing line in the left. Frequent accents on weak beats and changing articulations produce additional flair.

Length: 16 measures

Technique: waltz bass, 8th note passage work, melody and accompaniment in the same hand

No. 2, Bb Major <u>Intermediate</u>

This landler is comprised of parallel intervals in both hands. The right hand outlines the intervals melodically while the left accompanies with the harmonic spelling. The result is a charming, unsophisticated dance with some chromatic interest in the last section.

Length: 16 measures
Technique: sustained and moving notes, 8th note passage work

No. 3, Eb Major — Intermediate

A happy right hand melody is accompanied by chords that avoid the downbeat, producing an asymmetrical feeling within the waltz rhythm of this dance. The melodic treatment is highly sequential, with creative use of the secondary dominant in the second section.

Length: 16 measures
Technique: double 3rds, repeated chords, grace notes

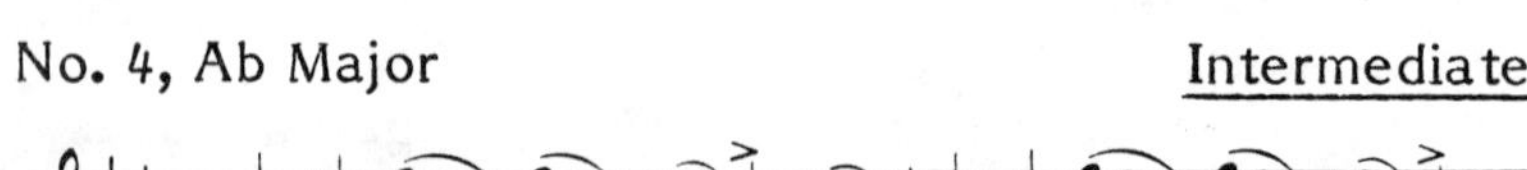

No. 4, Ab Major — Intermediate

The unifying three-note phrase of this landler occurs in varying positions within the measures. The resulting change of accent gives a sense of imbalance that is fascinating. The left hand accompanies with wide interval chords in a pedal point in the opening section, and a waltz bass in the final measures.

Length: 16 measures
Technique: octave chords, waltz bass

No. 5, Ab Major Intermediate

This sentimental dance resembles a folk song, with a simple melody and harmonization in consonant intervals. The right and left hands share a duet, with added chord notes sustaining in the bass. The result is a lovely performance piece.

Length: 16 measures
Technique: sustained and moving notes, ornamentation, "Scoth snap" rhythm

No. 6, Ab Major Intermediate

The folk idea, a common characteristic in D. 681, continues in this graceful dance, with the rhythmic figure seemingly reversed. Both hands double in the opening statement, followed by a typical waltz format. Important rests and articulation details add to the overall charm.

Length: 16 measures
Technique: 2-note phrases, waltz bass, sustained and moving notes

No. 7, Eb Major <u>Intermediate</u>

The right hand carries both melody and accompaniment in this dance, with the left hand harmonizing or providing chordal support. The folk song flavor is present, but the ending of each section on the tonic inversion leaves a feeling of incompletion, creating a "trio" piece that might pair with another of the set.

Length: 16 measures

Technique: melody and accompaniment in same hand, important rests and phrasing, 8th note passage work

No. 8, Bb Major <u>Intermediate</u>

The creative use of intervals and chords in the left hand of this dance produces the waltz feeling in an extraordinary form. With the melody outlined in constantly moving eighth notes, the result is a charming and elegant landler. The landlers of D. 681 are beautiful and would make fine performance choices in groupings or as a whole.

Length: 16 measures

Technique: 8th note passage work, LH intervals and chords, clef changes

## LANDLER, HOMAGE TO THE FAIR LADIES OF VIENNA, D. 734 (Op. 67)

Note: All of D.734 may be found in:

HANSEN (Publisher): Schubert--A Highlight Collection.
MIES, Paul: Schubert--Samtliche Tanze, Band II (G. Henle Verlag 76).
NIEMANN, Walter: Schubert Dances (Peters No.150).
SCHIRMER (Publisher): Schubert Dances (Vol. 1537).
WEINMANN/KANN: Schubert--Landler, Ecossaisen, Menuette (Wiener 50064).

No. 1, G Major — Intermediate

This landler is a fine intermediate piece with solid chords, leaps, and a wide keyboard range. Harmonic movement and voicing is quite pleasing and unusual. The dynamic contrast and tonal changes are a source of musical expression. The ABA form is notated and the B section is in Eb Major with accidentals.

Length: 24 measures
Technique: repeated chords, jump bass, leaps

No. 2, D Major — Intermediate

AGAY, Denes: Easy Classics to Moderns, Vol. 17 (Consolidated).
BRADLEY, Richard: Easy Teaching Pieces for Piano, Vol. 2 (Bradley).

GRANT, Lawrence: Piano Music by the Great Masters (Ashley).

The predominance of thirds and sixths gives this piece a very typical and characteristic Germanic sound. It is simple, charming, and very dance-like. Emphasis on the third beat accentuates the gay mood.

Tempo: Agay - Moderato; ben ritmo
Bradley - Moderato; ben ritmo
Grant - Moderato
Length: 16 measures
Technique: double 3rds, jump bass, octave leaps

No. 3, G Major — Advancing Intermediate

AGAY, Denes: An Anthology, The Romantic Period, Vol. III (Yorktown).

This delightful music box dance uses a light staccato touch throughout. A few grace notes add to the leggiero character. The left hand waltz bass is not as demanding as many examples in this style. The appearance of the melody in the alto voice adds subtlety to the second section.

Tempo: Agay - Scherzando
Length: 24 measures
Technique: grace notes, chords, jump bass, octaves

No. 4, G Major

Advancing Intermediate

AGAY, Denes: An Anthology, The Romantic Period, Vol. III (Yorktown).
AGAY, Denes: Easy Classics to Moderns, Vol. 17 (Consolidated).
GRANT, Lawrence: Piano Music by the Great Masters (Ashley).

The tonic and dominant progressions of this folk-like dance give it an air of simplicity. The broken interval patterns with unusual accents are challenging. The D.C. instruction creates an ABA form (notated in the Mies edition).

Tempo: Grant - Allegretto
Length: 24 measures
Technique: accents, broken intervals, jump bass

No. 5, D Major

Intermediate

AGAY, Denes: Easy Classics to Moderns, Vol. 17 (Consolidated).
GRANT, Lawrence: Piano Music by the Great Masters (Ashley).

The figuration in this simple dance is delightful and Germanic sounding, but there is little or no melody. Therefore, emphasis on the bass line and harmonic movement propels the piece along. Careful and thoughtful phrasing will add to the effectiveness.

Length: 16 measures
Technique: 2 and 4-note slurs, broken intervals

No. 6, A Major — Advancing Intermediate

This light waltz has challenging reading problems which include changing clefs, leger lines, and accidentals. Schubert uses his favorite key scheme of moving a third away from the original tonality, placing the middle section in F Major to create a sudden and satisfying effect. Many different articulations are used, but the character is generally light.

Length: 24 measures
Technique: sustained and moving notes, chords, jump bass, 8th note scalar patterns

No. 7, E Major — Advancing Intermediate

This unique and joyful dance contains a variety of patterns and is coherent and a joy to hear. It is a fine study piece for general right hand facility, involving sustained and moving notes and various articulations. One unusual feature is the asymmetrical twenty measure framework. The ending is light, in keeping with the general context of the piece.

Length: 20 measures
Technique: double 3rds, sustained and moving notes, jump bass

No. 8, C Major

Advancing Intermediate

AGAY, Denes: An Anthology, The Romantic Period, Vol. III (Yorktown).

This simplistic dance is repetitive and child-like. The alternating double and single notes stretch the right hand and employ finger independence. The middle section has interesting harmonic alterations.

Length: 24 measures
Technique: broken chords

No. 9, G Major

Advancing Intermediate

As with many other landlers in this set, the harmonies are repetitious and the melody is predictable. Ties over the bar line add rhythmic interest. This could serve as a facility etude for broken chords, inversions, and hand shifts.

Length: 16 measures
Technique: chord inversions, jump bass

No. 10, C Major

Intermediate

AGAY, Denes: An Anthology, The Romantic Period, Vol. III (Yorktown).

A good sense of rhythm will enhance this lilting dance, with odd rests, accents, and grace notes giving strength to the beat. With its interesting sounds and rhythms, this landler could be paired with a complementary one for performance.

Length: 16 measures

Technique: double 3rds and 6ths, sustained and moving notes, grace notes, jump bass, octaves

No. 11, G Major <u>Advancing Intemediate</u>

Rhythmically, this is an intriguing landler because of its strong third beat emphasis. However, harmonically and melodically it is repetitious, with a redundant "G" pedal point. This dance may be difficult to learn because of excessive leger lines and large leaps.

Length: 24 measures

Technique: sustained and moving notes, broken chords, difficult hand shifts, leger lines, jump bass

No. 12, Bb Major <u>Intermediate</u>

AGAY, Denes: The Joy of Classics (Yorktown).

As do many other waltzes in this set, this simple little dance has repetitious patterns and predictable harmony. However, Schubert manages to interject a good deal of charm into these dances. Accents on the third beats are easy to feel and play. The figuration is slightly demanding but quite pianistic.

Tempo: Agay - Commodo; ben ritmo
Length: 16 measures
Technique: broken chords, ornaments, jump bass

No. 13, G Major <u>Advancing Intermediate</u>

This landler is characterized by expressive harmonies, and could serve as an etude for repeated and changing double notes. Explicitly marked dynamics are important and include sudden changes, which could be exaggerated to help supply the excitement which the piece lacks.

Length: 16 measures
Technique: repeated intervals and chords, jump bass

No. 14, B Major <u>Advancing Intermediate</u>

Although the figuration in this landler is slightly mundane, the harmonies (especially in the second section) are unusual and beautiful, providing this dance with interest and musical expression.

Length: 18 measures
Technique: broken chords, sustained and moving notes

No. 15, G Major — Intermediate

AGAY, Denes: Easy Classics to Moderns, Vol. 17 (Consolidated).
BERINGER, Oscar: Beringer's School of Easy Classics--Schubert (Galaxy).
GRANT, Lawrence: Piano Music by the Great Masters (Ashley).
WELCH, John: Schroeder's First Recital (Studio P/R).

This calm, familiar landler is characterized by elegant charm, style, and grace. The two-measure introduction is an unusual feature and contributes to the sustained mood of the entire dance.

Tempo: Grant - Moderato
Beringer - Allegro moderato
Welch - Moderato
Length: 18 measures
Technique: sustained and moving notes, ornaments, jump bass

No. 16, G Major — Advancing Intermediate

Large chords, alternating with waltz figuration, create unusual contrasts of texture. The two-note slurs, combined with sustained harmony notes, fall on various beats.

Length: 16 measures
Technique: chords with ties, 2-note slurs, jump bass

**LANDLER**, D. 790 (Op. Post. 171)

Note: All of D. 790 may be found in:

HEINRICHSHOFEN/PETERS (Publisher): Schubert Easier Favorites (No. 4051).
MIES, Paul: Schubert--Samtliche Tanze, Band II (G. Henle Verlag 76).
WEINMANN/KANN: Schubert--Landler, Ecossaisen, Menuette (Wiener 50064).

No. 1, D Major — Early Advanced

GEEHL, Henry: Schubert--Compositions of Moderate Difficulty (Ashdown).
NIEMANN, Walter: Schubert Dances (Peters No.150).
SCHIRMER (Publisher): Schubert Dances (Vol. 1537).

This lush and beautiful landler could be thought of in terms of orchestral instruments. It contains smoothly flowing chromatic harmonies and a Romantic sound which is contingent upon expressive dynamics. The sustained and moving notes present a considerable challenge because of the stretches and repetition of held notes. This piece is demanding yet lovely.

Tempo: Deutsches Tempo
Schubert - Alla tedesco
Heinrichshofen - Folk-like

Length: 53 measures
Technique: sustained and moving notes, octaves and octave chords, position changes

No. 2, A Major — Early Advanced

AGAY, Denes: Early Advanced Classics to Moderns, Vol. 47 (Consolidated).
GEEHL, Henry: Schubert--Compositions of Moderate Difficulty (Ashdown).

A simple, yet captivating melody and beautiful expressive harmonies make up this second landler of D. 790. It is a fascinating piece, with the first phrase in eight measures and the second in sixteen. It opens with a fanfare which develops into a difficult second section with many accidentals and demanding figurations.

Tempo: Agay - Vivo e marcato
Length: 24 measures
Technique: leaping octaves, grace notes, sustained and moving notes, chords

No. 3, D Major — Advancing Intermediate

AGAY, Denes: Early Advanced Classics to Moderns, Vol. 47 (Consolidated).
BANOWETZ, Joseph: The Pianist's Book of Classic Treasures (GWM/Kjos).

GEEHL, Henry: Schubert--Compositions of Moderate Difficulty (Ashdown).
NIEMANN, Walter: Schubert Dances (Peters No.150).
SCHIRMER (Publisher): Schubert Dances (Vol. 1537).
SMALL, Allan: Schubert Waltz Sampler (Alfred).
WATERMAN and HARWOOD: The Young Pianist's Repertoire, Book 2 (C. Fischer).

This landler is more like a waltz, with a smooth, lovely wandering melody and a waltz bass replete with interesting harmonic progressions. The melody often outlines diminished seventh chords. An inner melody is a challenge in terms of tonal balance.

Tempo: Banowetz - Allegro
Watermann/Harewood - Allegretto
Length: 16 measures
Technique: broken chords, sustained and moving notes, grace notes, jump bass, melody and accompaniment in the same hand

No. 4, D Major <u>Advancing Intermediate</u>

GEEHL, Henry: Schubert--Compositions of Moderate Difficulty (Ashdown).
NIEMANN, Walter: Schubert Dances (Peters No.150).
SCHIRMER (Publisher): Schubert Dances (Vol. 1537).
SMALL, Allan: Schubert Waltz Sampler (Alfred).

An enchanting waltz with much variety, this landler is very dance-like and full of spirit. The melody involves some sustained and moving notes, legato thirds, and ties across the bar. The chromatic harmonic alterations give a piquant flavor.

Length: 16 measures
Technique: double 3rds, scalar patterns, sustained and moving notes, jump bass

No. 5, B Minor — Advancing Intermediate

NIEMANN, Walter: Schubert Dances (Peters No.150).
SCHIRMER (Publisher): Schubert Dances (Vol. 1537).

This strange and quiet landler is characterized by beautiful, plaintive, and adventurous harmonies and a subdued, almost wistful nature. Expressive possibilities are numerous and should be explored. Initial reading may be tricky because of abundant ties and accidentals. The dynamic level of "ppp" to "f" is unusual.

Length: 24 measures
Technique: chords, sustained and moving notes, tonal balance, important ties, accidentals

No. 6, G# Minor — Early Advanced

NIEMANN, Walter: Schubert Dances (Peters No.150).
SCHIRMER (Publisher): Schubert Dances (Vol. 1537).

This landler, as with many in this set, embodies Schubert at his best and most mature. Although there is none of the fun and frivolity of many of his other dances, there is an intense and very poignant beauty.

The dissonances and unusual chord progressions add to the somber mood, which needs sensitivity to the rhythmic tension. The full chords and spans of a ninth may be challenging to some performers.

Length: 24 measures

Technique: 2-note slurs, sustained and moving notes, thick chords, octaves

No. 7, Ab Major — Advancing Intermediate

KALMUS (Publisher): Schubert--An Easy Album for Piano Solo (Belwin-Mills #3876).

NIEMANN, Walter: Schubert Dances (Peters No.150).

ROWLEY, Alec: The Easiest Original Schumann (Hinrichsen No. 6/Peters).

SCHIRMER (Publisher): Schubert Dances (Vol. 1537).

Right hand triplets and detached left hand figures give this dance a delightful character. The serene mood comes from the sustained and moving notes, smooth melody, and echo effects. The many ties over the bar line in both sixteen-measure sections produce endings with an unfinished sound. If this dance is paired with one of complementary style and key, it would be a fine performance choice.

Tempo: Rowley - Allegretto
Kalmus - Allegretto

Length: 32 measures

Technique: sustained and moving notes, leaps, chords, tonal balance, many ties

No. 8, Ab Minor, or "Country Dance" Early Advanced

KALMUS (Publisher): Schubert--An Easy Album for Piano Solo (Belwin-Mills #3876).
NIEMANN, Walter: Schubert Dances (Peters No.150).
ROWLEY, Alec: The Easiest Original Schumann (Hinrichsen No. 6/Peters).
SCHIRMER (Publisher): Schubert Dances (Vol. 1537).
ZEITLIN, Poldi: Schubert Dances for Piano (Presser).

As with many in this set, this dance has beautiful harmonies and a plaintive melody. The key signature, clef changes, and accidentals cause reading problems, but once learned it is quite pianistic.

Tempo: Rowley - Listesso tempo
Kalmus - L'istesso tempo
Zeitlin - Tempo rubato
Length: 32 measures
Technique: ornaments, octaves, jump bass, clef changes

No. 9, B Major Early Advanced

ZEITLIN, Poldi: Schubert Dances for Piano (Presser).

This beautiful and effective landler, typical of others in this set, uses a waltz bass and running eighth notes. The second section in B Major modulates through A Major to B Minor, and back to B Major.

Tempo: Zeitlin - Lesto
Length: 17 measures
Technique: jump bass, 8th note passage work, accidentals

No. 10, B Major — Early Advanced

This landler is a delicate, romantic waltz with an easy flow. Careful observation of the dynamics and phrasing will enhance the lilting charm. The chromatic harmonic alterations are fascinating.

Length: 16 measures
Technique: ornaments, 8th note passage work, jump bass, accidentals

No. 11, Ab Major — Early Advanced

SCHIRMER (Publisher): Schubert Dances for the Piano (Vol. 1537).

This landler is characterized by a mature romantic style, replete with lovely flowing melodic lines and stirring harmonies. The harmonic movement seems almost too dramatic and full of motion to warrant the soft dynamics. The second beat is often emphasized by a rest and the grace note preceding it lends an off-balance feeling.

Length: 16 measures
Technique: ornaments, sustained and moving notes, jump bass

No. 12, E Major <u>Advancing Intermediate</u>

This entire set of landler is one of Schubert's more beautiful and creative works and would be a delightful performance choice. Consistant with the rest, this dance is lovely and mature, containing quiet dynamics for sensitive expression. There is not much contrast within the figuration, but the effect is elegant.

Length: 22 measures
Technique: broken intervals, sustained and moving notes, waltz bass, ties across the bar

## LANDLER, D. 814

These four landler are an arrangement by Schubert of four duets D. 814 that may be found in "Selected Piano Works for Four Hands--Franz Schubert," edited by Anton Door (Dover).

Note: All of D. 814 may be found in:

WEINMANN/KANN: Schubert--Landler, Ecossaisen, Menuette (Wiener 50064).

No. 1, Eb Major <u>Advancing Intermediate</u>

This landler is based on clever and interesting textural contrasts, its chief characteristic being an alternating second figure found throughout in a variety of forms (double thirds, octaves, and octave chords).

Equally exuberant and exciting as many of the others, it will nevertheless suffer without scrupulous attention to dynamic nuancing.

Length: 16 measures

Technique: double 3rds and octaves, sustained and moving notes, octave chords

No. 2, Ab Major — Advancing Intermediate

This lovely selection begins like a lullaby, with smooth legato figures in both hands. The second phrase employs especially beautiful and unexpected harmonies centering around the minor ii. Staccato left hand figures are juxtaposed against a legato right hand, necessitating much coordination and sensitivity.

Length: 16 measures

Technique: sustained and moving notes, melody and accompaniment in the same hand

No. 3, C Minor — Early Advanced

This landler is a difficult and demanding octave study, full of beautiful harmonies. At the quick tempo the left hand jumps and leaps are very challenging. Both hands use detached octave figures. The dynamics and accents add additional dramatic emphasis.

Length: 17 measures

Technique: octaves, octave chords, 3rd beat accents

No. 4, C Major

Advancing Intermediate

A lovely and mature work, this landler is characterized by its interesting dynamic contrast. It begins with the marking "con sordini" (muted) and ends forte. The second section is unusual in that it is extended beyond the usual 8 to 12 measures. This entire set would make a concise, challenging, and enjoyable performance selection for the advancing intermediate or early advanced pianist. In the duet arrangement the problems are minimal.

Length: 20 measures

Technique: broken chords, sustained and moving notes, double 3rds, octaves

## MINUETS AND TRIOS, D. 41

Note: All of D. 41 may be found in:

MIES, Paul: Schubert--Samtliche Tanze, Band I (G. Henle Verlag 74).
WEINMANN/KANN: Schubert--Walzer und Deutsche Tanze (Wiener 50063).

No. 1, F Major <u>Intermediate</u>

ALFRED (Publisher): Schubert--17 of his Most Popular Piano Selections.
DEXTER, Harry: Selected Piano Works--Schubert (Hansen).
HANSEN (Publisher): Schubert--A Highlight Collection.
HERMANN, Kurt: Schubert, Schumann, and Weber (Kalmus 9541/Belwin-Mills).
KALMUS PIANO SERIES: Schubert--An Easy Album for Piano Solos (Belwin-Mills).
NIEMANN, Walter: Schubert Dances (Peters No.150).
ROWLEY, Alec: The Easiest Original Schubert (Hinrichsen No. 6/Peters).
SCHIRMER (Publisher): Schubert Dances (Vol. 1537).
SHEALY, Alexander: Schubert--his greatest Piano Solos (Ashley).
VOLGER, Heinz: Schubert--Easiest Piano Pieces (Peters No. 5015).

Sounding remarkably like "Oh, Clementine," this accessible minuet has a fanfare beginning and a tonic and dominant orientation. The sharp dotted rhythm gives it an aggressive, bold quality. The contrasting trio utilizes moving eighths and sixteenths at a softer dynamic level.

Tempo: Alfred - Allegretto
Herrmann - Allegretto
Rowley - Allegretto
Kalmus - Allegretto
Length: 38 measures
Technique: sustained and moving notes, octaves, harmonic and broken intervals

No. 2, C Major — Intermediate

DEXTER, Harry: Selected Piano Works--Schubert (Hansen).
HANSEN (Publisher): Schubert--A Highlight Collection.
HERA/ SARMAI: Easy Piano Music from the Period of Romanticism (Musica Budapest/Boosey & Hawkes).
NIEMANN, Walter: Schubert Dances (Peters No.150).
SCHIRMER (Publisher): Schubert Dances (Vol. 1537).
SHEALY, Alexander: Schubert--his greatest Piano Solos (Ashley).
SMALL, Alan: Schubert Waltz Sampler (Alfred).

The harmonies and rhythmic permutations are interesting features of this otherwise mundane waltz. Aside from these it is repetitious, with easily learned patterns. The accompaniment in the trio evolves from repeated triads to broken eighth note triads, then to Alberti sixteenth notes.

Length: 36 measures
Technique: octave chords, octaves, repeated chords, Alberti patterns, 8th and 16th note passage work

No. 3, F Major Intermediate

ALFRED (Publisher): Schubert--21 of his Easiest Piano Selections.
DEXTER, Harry: Selected Piano Works--Schubert (Hansen).
HANSEN (Publisher): Schubert--A Highlight Collection.
SCHIRMER (Publisher): Schubert Dances (Vol. 1537).
SHEALY, Alexander: Schubert--his greatest Piano Solos (Ashley).

This minuet is more interesting than the others, although it retains the same dotted note fanfare. Melodically, it is still unsophisticated but the harmonies are more attractive. Precision with rhythm and dynamics will add to its character.

Tempo: Alfred - Allegro Maestoso
Length: 32 measures
Technique: octaves, sustained and moving notes, ornaments, double 3rds

No. 4, A Minor Advancing Intermediate

DEXTER, Harry: Selected Piano Works--Schubert (Hansen).
HANSEN (Publisher): Schubert--A Highlight Collection.
SCHIRMER (Publisher): Schubert Dances (Vol. 1537).
SHEALY, Alexander: Schubert--his greatest Piano Solos (Ashley).

The dramatic minuet portion of this piece is the highlight of the work, with the short trio in A Major offering contrast in dynamics and form. The difficulties include leaping octaves in dotted rhythms, left hand repeated chords, and embellishments.

Length: 36 measures
Technique: octaves, repeated chords, ornaments

No. 5, Bb Major <u>Intermediate</u>

DEXTER, Harry: Selected Piano Works--Schubert (Hansen).
HALFORD, Margery: Schubert--The First Book for Yound Pianists (Alfred).
HANSEN (Publisher): Schubert--A Highlight Collection.
SCHIRMER (Publisher): Schubert Dances (Vol. 1537).

Reminiscent of Haydn, this minuet and trio evoke charm and elegance through classical simplicity and drama. Echo dynamics and dotted note patterns enhance this effect. This would be a pleasant performance selection.

Length: 32 measures
Technique: octaves, ornaments, sustained and moving notes, 8th and 16th note passage work

No. 6, Bb Major <u>Advancing Intermediate</u>

DEXTER, Harry: Selected Piano Works--Schubert (Hansen).
HANSEN (Publisher): Schubert--A Highlight Collection.
SCHIRMER (Publisher): Schubert Dances (Vol. 1537).

In Schubert's more mature works innovative harmonies often add a very beautiful quality. However, in this minuet and trio, they simply sound strange. This particular work is characterized by a classical style. Schubert attempts to contrast a dramatic minuet with a calm and smooth trio, but the technical demands are difficult, making this contrast hard to achieve.

Length: 32 measures
Technique: octaves, octave chords, repeated chords, awkward hand position changes, ornaments

No. 7, F Major — Advancing Intermediate

DEXTER, Harry: Selected Piano Works--Schubert (Hansen).
HANSEN (Publisher): Schubert--A Highlight Collection.
NIEMANN, Walter: Schubert Dances (Peters No.150).
SCHIRMER (Publisher): Schubert Dances (Vol. 1537).
SHEALY, Alexander: Schubert--his greatest Piano Solos (Ashley).

This powerfully dramatic minuet, of performance calibre, is extremely pianistic and enjoyable to play. Solid and broken chords make up most of the material. The entire piece works best when played by a sensitive pianist who can make the most of the contrast between the minuet and delicate trio. The challenges in the trio are the ornamentation and tonal balance.

Length: 44 measures
Technique: octaves, octave chords, sustained and moving notes, broken chord and interval patterns, ornaments

No. 8, C Major <u>Intermediate</u>

ALFRED (Publisher): Schubert--21 of his Easiest Piano Selections.
HALFORD, Margery: Schubert--The First Book for Yound Pianists (Alfred).
HERA/SARMAI: Easy Piano Music from the Period of Romanticism (Musica Budapest/Boosey & Hawkes).
SHEALY, Alexander: Schubert--his greatest Piano Solos (Ashley).

This minuet produces a profound sense of monotony; it would probably sound prosaic even if played extremely well. The trio is pleasant when a light legato tone is used in the upper register and if the repeated chord accompaniment is quite subdued.

Tempo: Alfred - Allegro Moderato
Length: 32 measures
Technique: repeated and broken chords, 16th note patterns

No. 9, F Major <u>Advancing Intermediate</u>

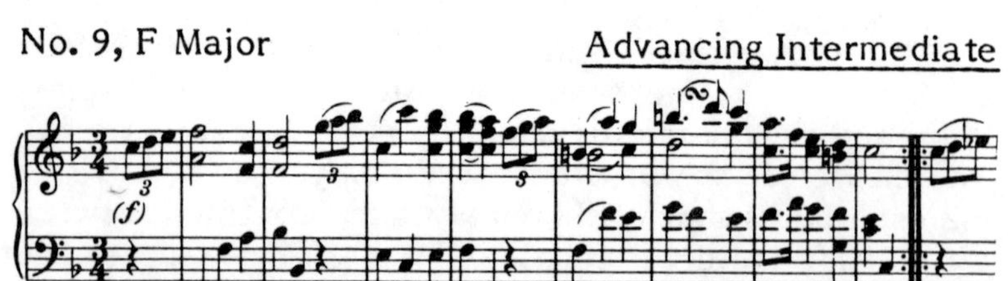

AGAY, Denes: Easy Classics to Moderns, Vol. 17 (Consolidated) trio only.
ACKERMAN, Gloria: Piano Guide for the Second Year Student (Belwin-Mills) trio only.
DEXTER, Harry: Selected Piano Works--Schubert (Hansen).
GRANT, Lawrence: Piano Music by the Great Masters (Ashley) trio only.
HANSEN (Publisher): Schubert--A Highlight Collection.
NIEMANN, Walter: Schubert Dances (Peters No.150).
SCHIRMER (Publisher): Schubert Dances (Vol. 1537).
SHEALY, Alexander: Schubert--his greatest Piano Solos (Ashley).

This minuet is accessible even though it contains many triplet figures and upbeat trills. The trio offers a chance to work on a light detached tone. Important rests should be carefully observed. The constant repeated chord accompaniment in the trio will be a problem for any but the most sensitive performer.

Tempo: trio - Allegro Scherzando
Length: 52 measures
Technique: ornaments, octaves, repeated chords, scalar patterns, sustained and moving notes

No. 10, Bb Major — Advancing Intermediate

DEXTER, Harry: Selected Piano Works--Schubert (Hansen).
HANSEN (Publisher): Schubert--A Highlight Collection.
NIEMANN, Walter: Schubert Dances (Peters No.150).
SCHIRMER (Publisher): Schubert Dances (Vol. 1537).

The unifying motive of this piece is the prevailing ornamental figure. The extreme echo dynamics provide flair and spice. The left hand has melodic material as well as accompanimental patterns. The harmonic progressions are engrossing.

Length: 41 measures

Technique: ornaments, double 3rds, octaves, scalar patterns, sustained and moving notes

No. 11, D Major — Intermediate

DEXTER, Harry: Selected Piano Works--Schubert (Hansen).
HANSEN (Publisher): Schubert--A Highlight Collection.
SCHIRMER (Publisher): Schubert Dances (Vol. 1537).
SHEALY, Alexander: Schubert--his greatest Piano Solos (Ashley).

This martial sounding minuet employs dotted rhythms to achieve its effect, contrasting sharply with the plodding, even eighth notes in the trio. Dynamic nuance will liven up this dance.

Length: 36 measures

Technique: dotted rhythms, various articulations, octaves

No. 12, D Major — Advancing Intermediate

DEXTER, Harry: Selected Piano Works--Schubert (Hansen).
HANSEN (Publisher): Schubert--A Highlight Collection.
NIEMANN, Walter: Schubert Dances (Peters No.150).
SCHIRMER (Publisher): Schubert Dances (Vol. 1537).
SHEALY, Alexander: Schubert--his greatest Piano Solos (Ashley).

Changing rhythms are the most challenging aspect of this orchestral sounding minuet and trio, which contrast in mood and dynamics. Coordination between the hands and varying articulations are noteworthy.

Length: 36 measures
Technique: 16th note passage work, ornaments, sustained and moving notes, octave chords, repeated chords and intervals

No. 13, D Major <u>Intermediate</u>

SHEALY, Alexander: Schubert--his greatest Piano Solos (Ashley).

This march-like minuet and trio will be enhanced by playing with as much zeal, fire, and spirit as possible. Although the trio has notated contrasts, the vibrant nature of this piece is carried through its entirety. Precise dotted rhythms are incorporated throughout. Observing the dynamic differences provides sparkle.

Length: 33 measures
Technique: various dotted rhythms, octaves, octave chords, sustained and moving notes, scalar figures, broken interval figures

No. 14, D Major Advancing Intermediate

SHEALY, Alexander: Schubert--his greatest Piano Solos (Ashley).

This etude-like piece begins with expansive octaves that give way to quick scalar figures which determine the tempo. This dance is built of scales and broken intervals and will be technically challenging to perform.

Length: 32 measures
Technique: octaves, scales, broken interval figurations, ornaments

No. 15, D Major Advancing Intermediate

SHEALY, Alexander: Schubert--his greatest Piano Solos (Ashley).

This excellent minuet and trio is reminiscent of Haydn because of its fun and good-natured exuberance. Harmonically, this is one of the more interesting and daring of this set. The contrasts between the minuet and the trio are highly successful. This would be a fine performance choice, and a rewarding study for the advancing intermediate pianist.

Length: 32 measures
Technique: octaves, broken chords, scalar figures, broken interval figurations

No. 16, G Major Advancing Intermediate

HERA/SARMAI: Easy Piano Music from the Period of Romanticism (Musica Budapest/Boosey & Hawkes).
SHEALY, Alexander: Schubert--his greatest Piano Solos (Ashley).

The trio of No. 16 provides a lovely and subtle contrast to the more vigorous minuet. The repeated notes against the left hand double thirds are enchanting. Musically played, this would work well as a performance selection.

Length: 32 measures
Technique: repeated notes and octaves, LH double 3rds, scalar passages

No. 17, C Major Advancing Intermediate

HERA/SARMAI: Easy Piano Music from the Period of Romanticism (Musica Budapest/Boosey & Hawkes).
SHEALY, Alexander: Schubert--his greatest Piano Solos (Ashley).

This dance pairs an intermediate level minuet with a musically more challenging trio. The minuet is a strong march-like piece, as are many others in this set, while the trio is delicate and pianistic. Broken interval figurations call for a variety of touches. Tonal balance and dynamics are important.

Length: 32 measures
Technique: legato vs. staccato, octave chords, sustained and moving notes, broken interval figurations

No. 18, F Major | Intermediate

ANTHONY, George Walter: Beethoven to Shostakovich, Easy, Vol. 2 (Presser).
DEXTER, Harry: Selected Piano Works--Schubert (Hansen).
GLOVER and HINSON: Piano Literature, Volume One - Intermediate A (Belwin-Mills FDL878).
HALFORD, Margery: Schubert--The First Book for Yound Pianists (Alfred).
HANSEN (Publisher): Schubert--A Highlight Collection.
HERRMANN, Kurt: Schubert, Schumann, and Weber (Kalmus 9541/Belwin-Mills).
NIEMANN, Walter: Schubert Dances (Peters No.150).
PALMER, Willard: Seven Centuries of Keyboard Music (Alfred).
SCHIRMER (Publisher): Schubert Dances (Vol. 1537).
SHEALY, Alexander: Schubert--his greatest Piano Solos (Ashley).
VOLGER, Heinz: Schubert--Easiest Piano Pieces (Peters No. 5015).

Unlike most of the other minuets in this set, this one has a subdued quality throughout. It is reminiscent of Beethoven's well-known Minuet in G. A sensitive and expressive performance will enhance its beauty. Bare textures and important rests are pronounced and should not be blurred by the damper pedal.

Length: 31 measures
Technique: 2-note slurs, double 3rds, sustained and moving notes, scalar figures, trill-like figurations

No. 19, Bb Major — Advancing Intermediate

In this dance the left hand gains added importance, with many chromatic alterations which are pleasing complements to the right hand legato thirds. The classical sounding trio has a repetitive double note accompaniment, with grace notes that embellish the leaping single note melody.

Length: 32 measures
Technique: double 3rds, ornaments, repeated intervals, sustained and moving notes

No. 20, G Major — Intermediate

ALFRED (Publisher): Schubert--21 of his Easiest Piano Selections.
HERA/SARMAI: Easy Piano Music from the Period of Romanticism (Musica Budapest/Boosey & Hawkes).
SHEALY, Alexander: Schubert--his Greatest Piano Solos (Ashley).

This minuet is very full-sounding, while the trio is lighter with repeated notes and scalar figures. Played sensitively, this piece would be suitable for a performance.

The minuets in this set were written when Schubert was just sixteen, and contain many inconsistencies of a young composer. They also reveal many unrestrained feelings of youthful exuberance.

Length: 32 measures

Technique: chords, octaves, scales, repeated intervals, broken chords

## MINUETS, D. 91

Note: All of D. 91 may be found in:

MIES, Paul: Schubert--Samtliche Tanze, Band I (G. Henle Verlag 74).

No. 1, D Major <u>Advancing Intermediate</u>

This minuet has a classical construction and sound. The first section has a dignified martial quality to its homophonic character; the second section becomes more florid, with flurries of sixteenth note scales in the right hand.

Both trios, separated by a repetition of the minuet, have a more romantic flavor, with cantabile melodies and quiet dynamics. The first, in A Major, has a slow tune accompanied by left hand broken chords. The second, in D Major, is similar in construction but has added complexity in both melody and accompaniment.

This is a lovely minuet, with delightful contrasts that offer a wide opportunity for sensitive playing.

Length: 48 measures
Technique: octaves, scalar patterns, sustained and moving notes, ornamentation

No. 2, A Major — Advancing Intermediate

As in No. 1, this minuet has a sturdy, march-like air that contrasts dynamically with the quiet, subdued trios. The abrupt change from major to tonic minor adds a welcome subtlety to the harmonic structure in the minuet and second trio. Both trios illustrate Schubert's love for melody. The first is awkwardly accompanied by repeated intervals over a sustained bass note. The second is creatively supported by a treatment of broken chords, and its beauty totally overshadows the other portions, making them relatively unsatisfying.

Length: 48 measures
Technique: octaves, chords, ornamentation, broken chords, repeated intervals, sustained and moving notes

**MINUET**, D. 334, A Major, or "Allegretto" — Advancing Intermediate

MIES, Paul: Schubert--Samtliche Tanze, Band I (G. Henle Verlag 74).
SHEALY, Alexander: Schubert--his greatest Piano Solos (Ashley).

The lovely melodies in both minuet and trio of D. 334 are such that the rhythmic qualities of the dance give way to the cantabile characteristics of the song. The minuet is serene and unhurried, with sustaining chords under a melody that delights with frequent tied suspensions. The chromatic passing tones in all voices produce poignant, romantic coloring in the harmonic progressions. The trio becomes more rhythmic, with left hand treble clef triads underpinning a melody of more complexity. This is a beautiful piece that gives wide oportunity for sensitive playing, and would be a wonderful performance choice.

Length: 86 measures
Technique: sustained and moving notes, ties, important phrasing and accents, both hands in treble clef, dynamic range

**MINUET**, D. 335, E Major — Advancing Intermediate

MIES, Paul: Schubert--Samtliche Tanze, Band I (G. Henle Verlag 74).
SHEALY, Alexander: Schubert--his greatest Piano Solos (Ashley).

This bright rondo-like minuet begins with classical simplicity in the first section, but has some surprises in its continuation. The long second section opens by developing the triplet thematic phrase, halting at a fermata, and recapping in sonata-like form. The two trios, divided by a repetition of the minuet, contrast in dynamics. They both have a song-like treatment of the right hand, accompanied by broken chords and sustaining pedal points. Each trio shares the formal ABA treatment of the minuet. In its entirety, this is a cleverly written piece with a sparkling good humor that could brighten any program.

Length: 75 measures
Technique: 8th note passage work, triplet scalar patterns, sustained and moving notes, melody and accompaniment in the same hand

**MINUET**, D. 336, D Major Intermediate

MIES, Paul: Schubert--Samtliche Tanze, Band I (G. Henle Verlag 74).
VOLGER, Heinz: Schubert--Easiest Piano Pieces (Peters No. 5015).

Simple harmonies and straightforward ABA construction give a folk character to this minuet. The A sections are single-line melodies with chordal accompaniments. The B section contrasts with unison scalar patterns. The trio also follows an ABA pattern, with material that shows little relationship to the minuet. The A sections are "music box" tunes with left hand accompaniments in the treble clef. The B section utilizes fanfare octaves, giving an abrupt change of mood.

Length: 56 measures
Technique: octaves, scalar patterns, ornamentation, sustained and moving notes

**MINUETS**, D. 380

Note: All of D. 380 may be found in:

MIES, Paul: Schubert--Samtliche Tanze, Band I (G. Henle Verlag 74).

No. 1, E Major <u>Intermediate</u>

A stately classical sound characterizes this minuet, which contrasts full, evenly moving chords with occasional sixteenth note scalar patterns. Trio I relates to the minuet in its melodic motives, but has a more romantic flavor due to the broken chords with pedal points that outline the theme. Trio II returns to the classical sound, although the pedal point is retained in some measures. The elegant contrasts enhance this performance choice.

Length: 51 measures
Technique: sustained and moving notes, broken chords, 16th note scalar patterns, chords

No. 2, A Major <u>Intermediate</u>

A processional flavor pervades this minuet and both trios, with dotted rhythm and full repeated chords unifying all three. Contrasts are present also, with the trio sections receiving new and creative accompanying patterns; the second trio moves into D Major. This is a delightful, vigorous dance that is tactilely enjoyable to perform.

Length: 48 measures
Technique: octaves and octave chords, sustained and moving notes, 16th note scalar and broken chord patterns

No. 3, C Major <u>Intermediate</u>

The processional-like quality of D. 380, No 2 is retained in this minuet, with melodic and rhythmic similarities that are unmistakable. This set of minuets has a martial quality that unifies them into an intriguing performance choice.

Length: 17 measures
Technique: octave chords, 16th note scalar patterns, broken chords, sustained and moving notes

**MINUET,** C# Minor, D. 600 <u>Early Advanced</u>

MIES, Paul: Schubert--Samtliche Tanze, Band II (G. Henle Verlag 74).

The yearning poignancy and strong scope of expression in this regal minuet suggest instruments, with the left hand line reminiscent of pizzicati basses. The harmonic language and beauty compare to a baroque movement from a French overture. The highly dramatic language is not typical of Schubert's smaller pieces and dances. This is a beautiful work with very musical, expressive, and sensitive dynamics and articulations. It is speculated that D. 610, in the relative E Major, is the companion trio. These would be a beautiful pair for performance.

Length: 30 measures
Technique: octaves, sustained and moving notes, scalar passages in both hands, accidentals

**TRIO,** E Major, D. 610 Early Advanced

MIES, Paul: Samtliche Tanze, Band II (G. Henle Verlag 76).

This trio was probably written to pair with the Minuet in C# Minor, D.600. It has a delicate charm embodied in the high register scoring of both hands. The unifying motive of a dotted eighth/sixteenth pick-up followed by even eighth notes is subjected to frequent position changes. It is often accompanied by thirds that parallel the harmonies inherent in the melodic outlining. In the last section the left hand takes over the melody with an added duet line, while the right hand adds a static pedal point.

Paired with the minuet, this would make a delightful performance choice.

Length: 32 measures
Technique: sustained and moving notes, eighth note passage work, changing clefs, ornamentation, octaves, double 3rds

TWO MINUETS, D. 995, C Major and F Major <u>Intermediate</u>

MIES, Paul: Schubert--Samtliche Tanze, Band II (G. Henle Verlag 76).
SHEALY, Alexander: Schubert--his Greatest Piano Solos (Ashley).

Closely related in mood and key, these two minuets share a martial air of exuberance, with trios of somewhat lighter character. Written in C Major, the first dance opens with vigorous fanfare octaves, initiating the dotted eighth/sixteenth pick-up motive developed throughout. This motive is voiced heavily in the two section minuet, interspersed with brilliant scalar passages. Its scoring in the two-section trio is more gentle and song-like, displaying a classic treatment in the second half which moves through creative harmonic transitions to prepare for the D.C. minuet.

The second minuet and trio, found only in the Mies edition, is written in F Major, and utilizes even eighth and sixteenth notes to impart its militant forcefulness (very reminiscent of the well-known March Militaire). The delicate contrasting trio is of special interest, with its ABA structure a sonatina in miniature, complete with thematic development and recapitulation. The charm of the filigreed melody, with a murmuring inner voice and pedal point bass, reveals Schubert in his most winsome mood. A particularly delightful performance choice, this dance will captivate both player and listener.

These dances have come down to us in a complete pianoforte version but were probably scored for a chamber ensemble. According to Mies, they were written in 1813 and are some of the earliest of this form to have survived.

I. Length: 45 measures
Technique: octaves and octave chords, 16th note scalar patterns, sustained and moving notes, clef changes, dynamics

II. Length: 48 measures
Technique: repeated notes, octaves and octave chords, sustained and moving notes, ornamentation

**WALTZ,** C# Major, D. 139 <u>Advancing Intermediate</u>

MIES, Paul: Samtliche Tanze, Band I
(G. Henle Verlag 74).

This waltz, composed early in Schubert's career, is brisk and militant, with "ff" dynamics throughout. The right hand octaves move in varying patterns of steps and skips, accompanied by heavy octave and seventh chords in the left hand. The awkward key is aggravated by many accidentals in the middle section. Written in A Major, the trio provides a welcome contrast, with agile arpeggiated patterns moving in a wide keyboard range over thick bass chords on beats one and three.

Length: 73 measures
Technique: octaves, thick chords, eighth note arpeggios

**WALTZES,** D. 145 (Opus 18)
"Atzenbrugger Deutsche"

Note: All of D. 145 may be found in:

MIES, Paul: Schubert--Samtliche Tanze, Band I
(G. Henle Verlag 74).
WEINMANN/KANN: Schubert--Walzer und Deutsche Tanze (Wiener 50063).

No. 1, E Major <u>Advancing Intermediate</u>

NIEMANN, Walter: Schubert Dances (Peters No.150).
SCHIRMER (Publisher): Schubert Dances (Vol. 1537).
SHEALY, Alexander: Schubert--his greatest Piano Solos (Ashley).
SHEFTEL, Paul: Classics, Romantics, Moderns--Solos for the Intermediate Pianist (C. Fischer ATF 102).

This martial sounding waltz has many difficulties, including thick uncomfortable chords, wide leaps, accidentals, and leger lines. Schubert's dynamics (ff-p) add to the vivid character. Each of the two sections are made up of a vigorous opening and a softer syncopated ending. There are also ties across the barline which add to its vibrancy.

Length: 32 measures
Technique: thick chords, octaves, wide leaps, syncopation, accidentals, ties and accents

No. 2, B Major — Advancing Intermediate

AGAY, Denes: Dances--Baroque to Jazz, Vol. C (Warner).
NIEMANN, Walter: Schubert Dances (Peters No.150).
SCHIRMER (Publisher): Schubert Dances (Vol. 1537).
SHEALY, Alexander: Schubert--his greatest Piano Solos (Ashley).

This lovely legato work is reminiscent of a lullaby, with the pedal point adding to the calming effect. The consistent left hand accompaniment challenges in the sustained and moving notes that encompass more than an octave. Phrasing and accents add to the character.

Length: 24 measures
Technique: octave chords, sustained and moving notes, large stretches, ornaments

No. 3, A Minor Advancing Intermediate

SHEALY, Alexander: Schubert--his greatest Piano Solos (Ashley).

One can almost picture people dancing to this lively waltz. It is made up of two distinct themes. The first is in fortissimo unison octaves. The second theme (at a softer level) retains the octaves in the right hand, but has a typical waltz accompaniment in the left hand. Articulations and accents add animation to this waltz.

Length: 48 measures
Technique: various articulations, octaves, large reaches, leaps

No. 4, C# Minor Early Advanced

NIEMANN, Walter: Schubert Dances (Peters No.150).
SCHIRMER (Publisher): Schubert Dances (Vol. 1537).
SHEALY, Alexander: Schubert--his greatest Piano Solos (Ashley).

As with many of Schubert's waltzes, this dance exemplifies a certain joyous exuberance found in much Viennese music. The large chords in the right hand and the wide leaps in the left hand are challenging. The chromatic treatment of the sequences in the second section add harmonic zest to this otherwise straightforward dance (The Niemann and Schirmer editions omit No. 3; henceforth their numbers are one behind the Mies, which is our definitive source--Ed.).

Length: 16 measures
Technique: scalar and broken chord figures, LH jump bass

No. 5, G Major — Intermediate

NIEMANN, Walter: Schubert Dances (Peters No.150).
SCHIRMER (Publisher): Schubert Dances (Vol. 1537).
SHEALY, Alexander: Schubert--his greatest Piano Solos (Ashley).
SHEFTEL, Paul: Classics, Romantics, Moderns--Solos for the Intermediate Pianist (C. Fischer ATF 102).

The lovely melody of this dance has filigreed scales and broken chords covering a wide keyboard range. The major/minor relationship is presented in two separate eight-measure phrases. The first is in E Minor using forte dynamics, while the second is in G Major with pianissimo markings. The smooth and elegant sound of this accessible waltz contrasts well with the rest of the set.

Length: 16 measures
Technique: scalar and broken chord figures, LH jump bass

No. 6, B Minor — Intermediate

AGAY, Denes: Easy Classics to Moderns, Vol. 17 (Consolidated).

ALFRED (Publisher): Schubert--21 of his Easiest Piano Selections.
BANOWETZ, Joseph: The Pianist's Book of Classic Treasures (GWM/Kjos).
CLARK and GOSS: Piano Literature, Books 3-4a-4b (Summy-Birchard).
HERRMANN, Kurt: Easy Schubert, Schumann, and Weber (Kalmus 9541/Belwin-Mills).
HUGHES, Edwin: Master Series--Schubert (G. Schirmer).
McGRAW, Cameron: Four Centuries of Keyboard Music, Vol. 3 (Boston).
NEVIN, Mark: 50 Best Loved Piano Solos--Bach to Bartok (Boston 14062).
NEVIN, Mark: Piano Masterpieces for the Young, Vol. 2 (Willis).
NIEMANN, Walter: Schubert Dances (Peters No.150).
OLSON, BIANCHI, BLICKENSTAFF: Repertoire 5b (C. Fischer).
SCHIRMER (Publisher): Schubert Dances (Vol. 1537).
SHEALY, Alexander: Schubert--his greatest Piano Solos (Ashley).
SHEFTEL, Paul: Classics, Romantics, Moderns--Solos for the Intermediate Pianist (C. Fischer ATF 102).
SMALL, Allan: Schubert Waltz Sampler (Alfred).
VOLGER, Heinz: Schubert--Easiest Piano Pieces (Peters No. 5015).
WILLS, Vera: The Purple Book #2 (G. Schirmer 3450).

The dissonances, pedal points, and occasional wide intervals create a very plaintive and yearning sound in this piece. Employing subdued dynamics and using a light touch will enhance the character. Feeling one pulse per measure while still observing the mazurka-like accents will also aid in the performance of this waltz.

Tempo: (vary among editions)
Length: 33 measures
Technique: dotted rhythms, jump bass, important phrasing and accents

No. 7, Eb Major — Advancing Intermediate

NIEMANN, Walter: Schubert Dances (Peters No.150).
SCHIRMER (Publisher): Schubert Dances (Vol. 1537).

This waltz has a light and fleeting quality that can be enhanced by mature playing. The form is ABA, with the A section varied upon its repetition. The stronger B section has fz accents and a definitive left hand pedal point, changing character more than overall dynamics.

Length: 24 measures
Technique: jump bass, octaves, octave chords

No. 8, Gb Major — Advancing Intermediate

NIEMANN, Walter: Schubert Dances (Peters No.150).
SCHIRMER (Publisher): Schubert Dances (Vol. 1537).
ZEITLIN, Poldi: Schubert Dances for Piano (Presser).

Long melodic lines characterize this lyrical waltz, which centers in Eb Minor for the first six measures. The right hand has the difficult task of having to bring out and shape the melody while also subduing broken interval accompaniment figures. Although a fairly pianistic key to play, Gb Major can be a rather difficult key to read.

Length: 16 measures
Technique: sustained and moving notes, melody and accompaniment in the same hand, jump bass

No. 9, F# Minor  Advancing Intermediate

NIEMANN, Walter: Schubert Dances (Peters No.150).
SCHIRMER (Publisher): Schubert Dances (Vol. 1537).
ZEITLIN, Poldi: Schubert Dances for Piano (Presser).
ZEITLIN and GOLDBERGER: The Solo Book IV (Consolidated).

The beautifully poignant melody running throughout this waltz provides excellent right hand scale practice. The left hand plays a simple chordal accompaniment, with the right hand scalar melody crossing under or over.

Tempo: Zeitlin - Ugualmente
Zeitlin and Goldberger - Allegretto
Length: 24 measures
Technique: scales, ornaments, awkward hand-crosses, clef changes

No. 10, B Minor  Advancing Intermediate

NIEMANN, Walter: Schubert Dances (Peters No.150).
SCHIRMER (Publisher): Schubert Dances for the Piano (Vol. 1537).

This quiet homophonic waltz is almost like a lullaby because of its pianissimo dynamics and rhythmic rocking patterns. A sophisticated use of the pedal will maintain the character. The subtle harmonic changes enhance the beauty of the piece.

Length: 16 measures
Technique: octave chords, important phrasing and pedal

No. 11, B Major — Advancing Intermediate

NIEMANN, Walter: Schubert Dances (Peters No.150).
SCHIRMER (Publisher): Schubert Dances (Vol. 1537).
SHEALY, Alexander: Schubert--his greatest Piano Solos (Ashley).

This jovial dance is light-hearted and cheerful. Employing fortissimo dynamics, the middle section is harmonically transitory and leads to the repetition of the theme in intervals rather than octaves.

Length: 24 measures
Technique: octaves, jump bass, accidentals

No. 12, E Major — Advancing Intermediate

NIEMANN, Walter: Schubert Dances (Peters No.150).
SCHIRMER (Publisher): Schubert Dances (Vol. 1537).
SHEALY, Alexander: Schubert--his greatest Piano Solos (Ashley).

This waltz opens with a rousing chordal triplet fanfare. It is later altered to a single note melody employing the same rhythms. Both sections use sudden and dramatic dynamic changes, adding to the lively nature of this otherwise tedious piece.

Length: 32 measures
Technique: repeated chords, octaves, leger lines, leaps

With the exception of Nos. 3 and 12, D. 145 would make an excellent performance choice.

**WALTZES**, D. 146 (Op. 127)
("Last Waltzes," "Farewell Waltzes," or "Letzte Walzer")

Note: All of D. 146 may be found in:

MIES, Paul: Schubert--Samtliche Tanze, Band I (G. Henle Verlag 74).
WEINMANN/KANN: Schubert--Walzer und Deutsche Tanze (Wiener 50063).

No. 1, D Major <u>Intermediate</u>

NIEMANN, Walter: Schubert Dances (Peters No.150).
SCHIRMER (Publisher): Schubert Dances (Vol. 1537).

Repeated chords, octaves, and pedal points create a fanfare-like sound. This waltz, which is much easier than it sounds, would be enhanced by a quick tempo to achieve a lively exuberance. The harmonies vacillate between major and minor modes to create an attractive effect. The dolce trio, while employing material which is consistent with the waltz, provides a lovely contrast.

Length: 48 measures
Technique: repeated chords and octaves, scales, sustained and moving notes

No. 2, A Major — Advancing Intermediate

NIEMANN, Walter: Schubert Dances (Peters No.150).
SCHIRMER (Publisher): Schubert Dances (Vol. 1537).

The folk-like exuberance of the first waltz in this set is continued here in a slightly different texture. The chief tonality is A Major, but it has a tentative modulation that makes it harmonically enjoyable. Accents on the third beat and the two-note slurs give a light airy quality.

Length: 16 measures
Technique: double notes, sustained and moving notes, octaves

No. 3, E Major — Advancing Intermediate

NIEMANN, Walter: Schubert Dances (Peters No.150).
SCHIRMER (Publisher): Schubert Dances (Vol. 1537).

Although not particularly captivating, this piece might provide enjoyment. Schubert wrote two trios for this waltz. The first trio is in A Major and is 26 measures long. The second, a short trio in E Major, is listed in Grove's as D. 135. It offers some contrast of dynamics and figurations. Its material is very similar to that of the waltz except that the dotted rhythms are moved from the upbeat to the second beat.

Length: 77 measures
Technique: clef changes, scalar figures, octave chords, sustained and moving notes

No. 4, A Major — Advancing Intermediate

NIEMANN, Walter: Schubert Dances (Peters No.150).
SCHIRMER (Publisher): Schubert Dances (Vol. 1537).

This heavy and ponderous waltz retains the character of the other waltzes of this set. The difficulties include octaves and large chords in both hands. The trio provides contrast in its extremely elegant character. The dynamic changes add spice to this dramatic piece.

Length: 64 measures
Technique: octaves and octave chords, scalar figures, repeated chords

No. 5, F Major — Advancing Intermediate

BERINGER, Oscar: Beringer' School of Easy Classics--Schubert (Galaxy).
NIEMANN, Walter: Schubert Dances (Peters No.150).
SCHIRMER (Publisher): Schubert Dances (Vol. 1537).
SCHWERDTNER, Hans-Georg: Sonatinas, Sonatas, Pieces (Schott 6695AP).

Large arpeggios, chords, and octaves in both hands contribute to the forceful and propelling sound of this waltz. The trio is quiet and lovely and provides a delightful contrast. In Schubert's original autograph the trio was written in Ab Major. The Mies and Weinmann/Kann editions adhere to this key. The others use the key of Bb Major.

Tempo: Beringer - Tempo di valse
Length: 87 measures
Technique: arpeggios, chords, sustained and moving notes, octaves, scalar patterns

No. 6, D Major — Advancing Intermediate

SHEALY, Alexander: Schubert--his greatest Piano Solos (Ashley).

The trio of this waltz is infinitely more interesting than the first section which is characterized by monotonous scales and harmonies. The lightly animated trio uses detached chordal figures with accented downbeats. The sudden dynamic contrasts in this section could be exaggerated to make the piece more attractive.

Length: 56 measures
Technique: scales, chords, octaves, sustained and moving notes, varying articulation

No. 7, B Minor — Advancing Intermediate

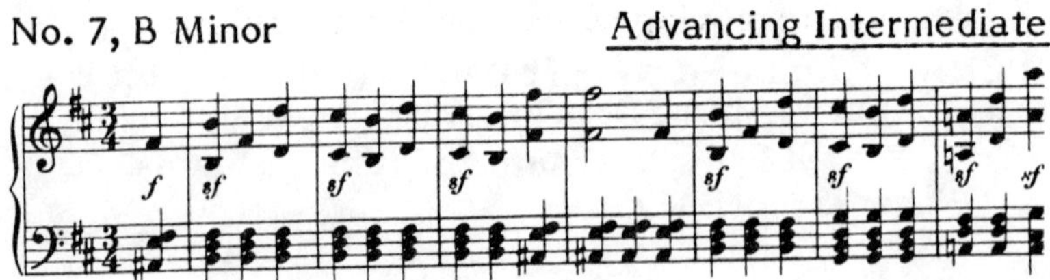

The most attractive aspect of this dance is the extreme contrast in character between the waltz and the trio. The melodramatic waltz uses a sinister sounding B Minor tonality while the trio employs a light-hearted G Major. Similarities between the two sections include ponderous repeated accompanimental chords and melodic chord outlining.

Length: 48 measures

Technique: repeated chords, octaves, scalar patterns, sustained and moving notes

No. 8, G Major — Advancing Intermediate

NIEMANN, Walter: Schubert Dances (Peters No.150).
SCHIRMER (Publisher): Schubert Dances (Vol. 1537).
SHEALY, Alexander: Schubert--his greatest Piano Solos (Ashley).

Two sections of equal attractiveness combine to create this pleasant dance. The waltz, appearing in G Major and B Minor, is in a crisp folk style with snapped, dotted rhythms and accents on the third beats. The legato trio creates a very smooth contrast with right hand intervals accompanied by broken chords. Sensitive dynamics and careful finger control will enhance this "Last Waltz" for performance.

Length: 45 measures

Technique: large chords, octaves, sustained and moving notes, varying articulation

No. 9, C Major — Advancing Intermediate

AGAY, Denes: Easy Classics to Moderns, Vol. 17 (Consolidated) trio only.
GRANT, Lawrence: Piano Music by the Great Masters (Ashley) trio only.
NIEMANN, Walter: Schubert Dances (Peters No.150).
SCHIRMER (Publisher): Schubert Dances (Vol. 1537).

A calm, tranquil mood is projected throughout this waltz. Dynamics play an extremely important role, especially with balancing the sprightly right hand octaves and the subdued left hand accompaniment. The homophonic trio provides a pleasing contrast at an easier level.

No. 10, F Major — Early Advanced

This waltz is one of Schubert's most technically demanding. The first section contains scalar octaves while the trio is made up of eighth note broken chord figures. This piece is harmonically innovative; once mastered it is attractive and could make an excellent right hand etude.

Length: 62 measures
Technique: octave scales, scalar figures, chords, sustained and moving notes, 8th note passage work

No. 11, Bb Major — Advancing Intermediate

Careful tonal balance and meticulous articulations will enhance the flowing effect suggested by this piece. The sustained, directionless character of the trio provides a drastic contrast to the waltz. Accentuating the nuances of the left hand will lend an air of cohesiveness.

Length: 52 measures
Technique: hand-crosses, sustained and moving notes, scales, octave chords, octaves

No. 12, G Minor — Advancing Intermediate

NIEMANN, Walter: Schubert Dances (Peters No.150).
SCHIRMER (Publisher): Schubert Dances (Vol. 1537).

This unusual and unique waltz is reminiscent of a German peasant dance. Its minor mode creates almost a plaintive, yearning effect. The abrupt change to G Major in the last line is very effective. Various syncopations across the bar lines result in beautiful suspensions. Although Schubert abandons the trio, he often retains the basic rounded binary form in waltzes 12 through 19.

Length: 24 measures
Technique: octaves and octave chords, ties across the bar lines, waltz bass

No. 13, C Major — Advancing Intermediate

This jubilant waltz with its boisterous gaiety has an infectious quality. Large leaps and double thirds provide technical challenges. To enhance its character, one pulse per measure and attention to accents are appropriate.

Length: 16 measures
Technique: large chords, octaves, double 3rds, large leaps

No. 14, G Major — Advancing Intermediate

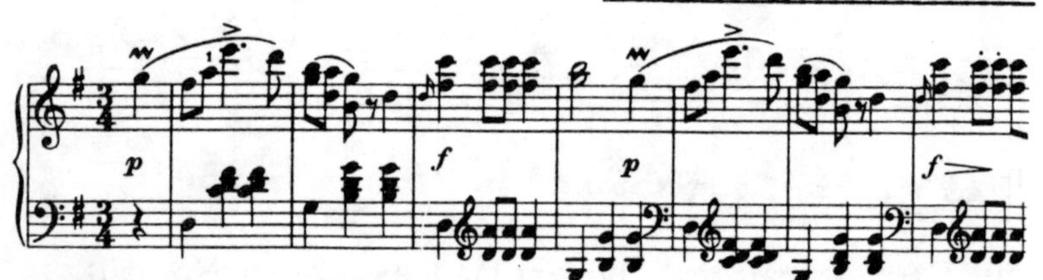


NIEMANN, Walter: Schubert Dances (Peters No.150).
SCHIRMER (Publisher): Schubert Dances (Vol. 1537).
SMALL, Allan: Schubert Waltz Sampler (Alfred).

This particular waltz could not have been written by any other than Schubert. Its lighthearted figuration and surprising dynamics give it its thoroughly engaging and delightful sound. The soaring melody has a beautiful and unexpected dissonance. Combined with waltz No. 13 (or any of Nos. 12 through 19), this would be excellent for a performance.

Length: 24 measures
Technique: ornaments, jump bass, repeated 5ths

No. 15, Bb Major Intermediate

HALFORD, Margery: Schubert--An Introduction to his Piano Works (Alfred).
HALFORD, Margery: Schubert--The First Book (Alfred).
NIEMANN, Walter: Schubert Dances (Peters No.150).
SCHIRMER (Publisher): Schubert Dances (Vol. 1537).
SMALL, Allan: Schubert Waltz Sampler (Alfred).

The most arresting feature of this simple, quiet waltz is the startling non-harmonic tone found in measures one and three. The unstable harmonic sense is further shaken by a G Minor opening and subsequent modluation to Bb Major. Challenges include right hand melody and accompaniment in the same hand.

Length: 17 measures
Technique: 2-note slurs, melody and accompaniment in the same hand, jump bass

No. 16, F Major Advancing Intermediate

NIEMANN, Walter: Schubert Dances (Peters No.150).
SCHIRMER (Publisher): Schubert Dances (Vol. 1537).

Two similar eight-measure phrases are used to create entirely different characters in this lovely and delightful waltz. The first mood is jubilant, yet strong and forceful. The second is lighter, more elegant, and dolce. The whole waltz is harmonically innovative and appealing. The first phrase vacillates between F Major and G and D Minor. Combined with Nos. 15 and 16, this waltz would be a satisfying performance selection.

Length: 16 measures

Technique: chords, sustained and moving notes, octaves, large reaches, varying articulations

No. 17, Bb Major — Advancing Intermediate

NIEMANN, Walter: Schubert Dances (Peters No.150).
SCHIRMER (Publisher): Schubert Dances (Vol. 1537).

Both Bb Major and G Minor are used equally in this short waltz. The right hand has a lovely legato melody with a pedal point accompaniment in the inner voice. The left hand supports with a simple waltz bass. Dynamics are pianissimo with light and attractive third beat accents. Phrasing and melodic shape are probably the most important aspects to be considered.

Length: 16 measures

Technique: melody and accompaniment in the same hand, jump bass

No. 18, Bb Major — Advancing Intermediate

NIEMANN, Walter: Schubert Dances (Peters No.150).
SCHIRMER (Publisher): Schubert Dances (Vol. 1537).

This waltz is similar in construction to No. 17. The lovely sustained quality of the melody is supported by the inner pedal points. Dominant harmonies are prominent throughout, even in the short G Minor section. Careful phrasing and lovely tone are essential.

Length: 16 measures
Technique: melody and accompaniment in the same hand, jump bass

No. 19, F Major <u>Advancing Intermediate</u>

Dotted rhythms, crisp articulations, and delicate octaves give this attractive waltz a lighter, appealing character. Although a trio is not indicated, the middle section serves that function, providing much drama and contrast.

Length: 24 measures
Technique: octaves, sustained and moving notes, various articulations, jump bass

No. 20, D Major <u>Advancing Intermediate</u>

In this final waltz of D. 146, Schubert returns to the ABA form of waltz-trio-waltz. In the initial waltz, the left hand accompaniment uses a detached first beat, with an ensuing emphasis on the second beat in the manner of a Viennese Waltz. The lengthy G Major trio requires right hand coordination for double notes, sustained and moving notes, and a variety of touches. The left hand employs a simple waltz bass, but clef changes make reading awkward. Detached notes indicated in the Urtext are sparing yet vital to the overall character of the piece.

Length: 40 measures
Technique: octaves, sustained and moving notes, important phrasing, double 3rds, varying articulation

The eight waltzes without trios (Nos. 12 through 19) could be combined for a lovely performance choice. In the longer dances the trios are more attractive than the waltz sections, and could perhaps be combined for a studio recital.

## **WALTZES**, D. 365 (Op. 9)

Note: All of D. 365 may be found in:

MIES, Paul: Schubert--Samtliche Tanze, Band I (G. Henle Verlag 74).
NIEMANN, Walter: Schubert Dances (Peters No.150).
SCHIRMER (Publisher): Schubert Dances (Vol. 1537).
WEINMANN/KANN: Schubert--Walzer und Deutsche Tanze (Wiener 50063).

No. 1, Ab Major, "Country Waltz" <u>Intermediate</u>

CLARK and GOSS: Piano Literature, Book 5b (Summy-Birchard).
DEXTER, Harry: Selected Piano Works--Schubert (Hansen).

FROST, Bernice: First Classic Collection (J. Fischer/Belwin-Mills 8754).
HANSEN (Publisher): Schubert-A Highlight Collection.
HERRMANN, Kurt: Easy Schubert, Schumann, and Weber (Kalmus 9541/Belwin-Mills).
HUGHES, Edwin: Master Series--Schubert (G. Schirmer).
KALMUS (Publisher): Schubert--An Easy Album for Piano Solo (Belwin-Mills).
KING-ORDEN, Esther: 100 Classics for Young Pianists (Shattinger-Hansen 0111).
McGRAW, Cameron: Four Centuries of Keyboard Music, Book 4 (Boston).
ROWLEY, Alec: The Easiest Original Schubert (Hinrichsen No. 6/Peters).
SHEALY, Alexander: Schubert--his greatest Piano Solos (Ashley).
SMALL, Alan: Schubert Waltz Sampler (Alfred).
VOLGER, Heinz: Schubert--Easiest Piano Pieces (Peters No. 5015).
WEYBRIGHT, June: Course for Pianists, Book 5 (American Academy).
WILLS, Vera: The Purple Book #1 (G. Schirmer 3449).

This familiar waltz has an Eb pedal point throughout the first section which cleverly obscures a definite sense of an Ab tonic. The harmonies and the style are basically classical. It is not difficult and is a pretty piece for study and performance.

Tempo: vary among editions
Length: 16 measures
Technique: sustained and moving notes, jump bass, pedal point

No. 2, Ab Major, "Trauerwalzer" — Advancing Intermediate

BANOWETZ, Joseph: The Pianist's Book of Classic Treasures (GWM/Kjos).
CLARK and GOSS: Piano Literature, Book 5b (Summy-Birchard).
DEXTER, Harry: Selected Piano Works--Schubert (Hansen).
GEEHL, Henry: Schubert--Compositions of Moderate Difficulty (Ashdown).
HANSEN (Publisher): Schubert-A Highlight Collection.
HUGHES, Edwin: Master Series--Schubert (G. Schirmer).
KALMUS (Publisher): Schubert--An Easy Album for Piano Solo (Belwin-Mills).
KING-ORDEN, Esther: 100 Classics for Young Pianists (Shattinger-Hansen 0111).
McGRAW, Cameron: Four Centuries of Keyboard Music, Book 4 (Boston).
ROWLEY, Alec: The Easiest Original Schubert (Hinrichsen No. 6/Peters).
SHEALY, Alexander: Schubert--his greatest Piano Solos (Ashley).
SMALL, Alan: Schubert Waltz Sampler (Alfred).
VOLGER, Heinz: Schubert--Easiest Piano Pieces (Peters No. 5015).

This beautiful "trauerwalser" deserves its popularity. Legato techniques are combined with lovely harmonies which stray far from the tonic. The many voices provide ample opportunity for sensitive tonal balance.

Tempo: Banowetz - Allegretto
Length: 16 measures
Technique: sustained and moving notes, melody and accompaniment in same hand, waltz bass, accidentals

No. 3, Ab Major | Advancing Intermediate

AGAY, Denes: Classics to Moderns, Intermediate, Vol. 37 (Consolidated).
BRADLEY, Richard: Bradley's Level Six Classics (Bradley).
CLARK and GOSS: Piano Literature, Book 5b (Summy-Birchard).
DEXTER, Harry: Selected Piano Works--Schubert (Hansen).
GRANT, Lawrence: More Classics to Contemporary Piano Music (Ashley).
HANSEN (Publisher): Schubert-A Highlight Collection.
HUGHES, Edwin: Master Series--Schubert (G. Schirmer).
KALMUS (Publisher): Schubert--An Easy Album for Piano Solo (Belwin-Mills).
KING-ORDEN, Esther: 100 Classics for Young Pianists (Shattinger-Hansen 0111).
McGRAW, Cameron: Four Centuries of Keyboard Music, Book 4 (Boston).
ROWLEY, Alec: The Easiest Original Schubert (Hinrichsen No. 6/Peters).
SHEALY, Alexander: Schubert--his greatest Piano Solos (Ashley).
SMALL, Alan: Schubert Waltz Sampler (Alfred).
VOLGER, Heinz: Schubert--Easiest Piano Pieces (Peters No. 5015).
WILLS, Vera: The Purple Book #1 (G. Schirmer 3449).

Technically this charming waltz is relatively easy, but it requires a slightly more advanced level of musicianship to take advantage of the breathtaking dynamic effects. A good sense of rhythm is also needed.

Tempo: varies among editions
Length: 16 measures
Technique: double 3rds, broken chords, sustained and moving notes, jump bass

No. 4, Ab Major — Intermediate

DEXTER, Harry: Selected Piano Works--Schubert (Hansen).
HALFORD: Margery: Schubert--The First Book (Alfred).
HALFORD, Margery: Schubert--An Introduction to his Piano Works (Alfred).
HANSEN (Publisher): Schubert-A Highlight Collection.
VOLGER, Heinz: Schubert--Easiest Piano Pieces (Peters No. 5015).

This calm and serene waltz begins quietly and is fortified in the second half by stronger harmonies and a melody in legato thirds. The expansion of movement and dynamics is best kept within a small range. An Eb pedal point similar to that in No. 1 of this set is found throughout 10 of the 16 measures.

Length: 16 measures
Technique: sustained and moving notes, double 3rds, scalar patterns

No. 5, Ab Major — Advancing Intermediate

DEXTER, Harry: Selected Piano Works--Schubert (Hansen).
HANSEN (Publisher): Schubert--A Highlight Collection.

A music box-like delicacy and a light leggiero touch will enhance the character of this waltz. Containing many instances of sustained and moving notes, double notes, amd melodic voicing, this makes an excellent study for finger independence in both hands.

Length: 16 measures
Technique: double 3rds and 6ths, sustained and moving notes, jump bass, important rests

No. 6, Ab Major Intermediate

AGAY, Denes: Classics to Moderns, Intermediate Vol. 37 (Consolidated).
BRADLEY, Richard: Bradley's Level Six Classics (Bradley).
DEXTER, Harry: Selected Piano Works--Schubert (Hansen).
GRANT, Lawrence: More Classic to Contemporary Piano Music (Ashley).
HANSEN (Publisher): Schubert--A Highlight Collection.

Featuring octaves, double thirds, and various articulations in the right hand, this predictable waltz is an excellent study for general facility.

Tempo: Grant - Moderato
Length: 16 measures
Technique: octaves, double 3rds, jump bass

No. 7, Ab Major — Advancing Intermediate

DEXTER, Harry: Selected Piano Works--Schubert (Hansen).
HANSEN (Publisher): Schubert--A Highlight Collection.

Two widely contrasting sections characterize this waltz. In the first, the left hand has a lovely sustained and moving note pattern, while in the second, it has a basic waltz bass. The melody in both sections is beautiful and thoughtfully shaped.

Length: 16 measures
Technique: octaves, sustained and moving notes, scalar patterns

No. 8, Ab Major — Intermediate

DEXTER, Harry: Selected Piano Works--Schubert (Hansen).
HANSEN (Publisher): Schubert--A Highlight Collection.
HERRMANN, Kurt: Easy Schubert, Schumann, and Weber (Kalmus 9541/Belwin-Mills).

This waltz is refreshingly simple; it consists solely of a single note melody accompanied by Alberti-like figures. There are many large stretches in the left hand, but these can be facilitated by a slower tempo. The lower notes of the left hand often form a countermelody to the right hand, giving it a duet quality.

Tempo: Herrmann - Allegro Commodo
Length: 16 measures
Technique: Alberti-like figures, broken intervals, large stretches

No. 9, Ab Major Intermediate

DEXTER, Harry: Selected Piano Works--Schubert (Hansen).
HANSEN (Publisher): Schubert--A Highlight Collection.

The difficulties involved in this waltz have to do chiefly with the initial reading. The left hand waltz bass is in the middle keyboard range and generally uses two clef changes per measure. Once the learning process is accomplished, this waltz is rather easy and quite enjoyable to play.

Length: 16 measures
Technique: ornaments, clef changes, jump bass

No. 10, Ab Major Advancing Intermediate

DEXTER, Harry: Selected Piano Works--Schubert (Hansen).
HANSEN (Publisher): Schubert--A Highlight Collection.

Musical sensitivity and good legato technique will aid in a successful performance of this waltz. The wide interval leaps are challenging, but with careful pedalling, a smooth effect can be achieved. There are occasional instances of counterpoint between the lower bass notes and the melody.

Length: 16 measures

Technique: broken intervals, large stretches, inner voice off beat pedal point, sustained and moving notes

No. 11, Ab Major, "Dance" <u>Intermediate</u>

DEXTER, Harry: Selected Piano Works--Schubert (Hansen).

HANSEN (Publisher): Schubert-A Highlight Collection.

SCHWERDTNER, Hans-Georg: Easy Piano Pieces and Sonatinas (Schott 6806AP).

ZEITLIN and GOLDBERGER: The Solo Book III (Consolidated).

This waltz is charming in its simplicity and classical sound. The single line right hand melody involves thoughtful and sensitive shaping. The left hand is a combination of Alberti-like figuration with additional harmonic and sustained notes. The chromatic quasi-melody in the left hand in the second section adds a delightful touch.

Tempo: Zeiltin - Moderato

Length: 16 measures

Technique: Alberti-like figures, sustained and moving notes

No. 12, Ab Major Advancing Intermediate

DEXTER, Harry: Selected Piano Works--Schubert (Hansen).
HALFORD: Margery: Schubert--The First Book (Alfred).
HALFORD, Margery: Schubert--An Introduction to his Piano Works (Alfred).
HANSEN (Publisher): Schubert--A Highlight Collection.

This lighthearted dance sounds best at a quick tempo with one pulse per measure. Important rests at the end of measures enhance the buoyant, lilting rhythm. This is a charming waltz which could pair with another from this set for a delightful performance choice.

Length: 16 measures
Technique: arpeggio, 8th note passage work, sustained and moving notes, waltz bass

No. 13, Ab Major Advancing Intermediate

DEXTER, Harry: Selected Piano Works--Schubert (Hansen).
HANSEN (Publisher): Schubert--A Highlight Collection.

Agility in both hands is called for in the melody, which is mainly in octaves, and the leaping bass, which covers a wide keyboard range. The few well-placed rests add vitality to the second eight measure phrase.

Length: 16 measures
Technique: octaves, jump bass, important ties and accents

No. 14, Db Major — Advancing Intermediate

AGAY, Denes: Classics to Moderns, Intermediate Vol. 37 (Consolidated).
BRADLEY, Richard: Bradley's Level Six Classics (Bradley).
GRANT, Lawrence: More Classic to Contemporary Piano Music (Ashley).
VOLGER, Heinz: Schubert--Easiest Piano Pieces (Peters No. 5015).

This very attractive dance uses a surprising modulation from the tonic key of Db to A Major and back. The sensitive tonal balance between the beautiful melody and accompaniment in the right hand is challenging. This could be a lovely performance choice.

Tempo: Agay - Vivo
Bradley - Vivo
Grant - Vivo
Length: 25 measures
Technique: melody and accompaniment in the same hand, jump bass, sustained and moving notes

No. 15, Db Major — Advancing Intermediate

DEXTER, Harry: Selected Piano Works--Schubert (Hansen).
HANSEN (Publisher): Schubert--A Highlight Collection.

The first eight measures of this delightful and exuberant waltz contain a fine and beneficial exercise in right hand legato thirds. The second section emphasizes the unusual and arresting harmonies. Dynamic and textural contrast in the symmetrical melody provide interest and accessibility for both the pianist and the listener.

Length: 16 measures
Technique: double 3rds, sustained and moving notes, waltz bass

No. 16, A Major — Intermediate

DEXTER, Harry: Selected Piano Works--Schubert (Hansen).
HANSEN (Publisher): Schubert-A Highlight Collection.

The most difficult aspect of this sprightly waltz is deciding on how the ornaments should be executed and keeping them in rhythm with the rest of the piece. The rhythmic and harmonic variances in the second section are extremely refreshing.

Length: 16 measures
Technique: detached ornaments, sustained and moving notes, waltz bass

No. 17, A Major Intermediate

DEXTER, Harry: Selected Piano Works--Schubert (Hansen).
HANSEN (Publisher): Schubert--A Highlight Collection.

This joyful Germanic waltz contains some yodel-like effects in the melody. The dynamic contrasts, accents, and articulation in the second section add to the loveliness of the piece. The accented chords resulting from a contrary motion leap are fun to play (a la Scharwenka's "Polish Dance").

Length: 16 measures
Technique: sustained and moving notes, waltz bass, important accents

No. 18, A Major Intermediate

DEXTER, Harry: Selected Piano Works--Schubert (Hansen).
HANSEN (Publisher): Schubert-A Highlight Collection.

As with many of Schubert's short pieces (the waltzes in particular), this one is filled with German fun and exuberance. A very simple harmonic structure supports a rhythmic melody. The first section is legato and involves much leger line reading. The second is more detached, with important eighth rests and accents ending each measure.

Length: 17 measures
Technique: leger lines, sustained and moving notes, broken chords, important accents and rests

No. 19, G Major Advancing Intermediate

The contrast between the two eight-measure sections in this waltz is striking. The first section involves right hand leaps and hand shifts between beats three and one, with the straightforward melody, harmony, and rhythm. The second legato section has a lovely theme and changing harmonies.

Length: 16 measures
Technique: leaps, broken chords, ornaments, jump bass, clef changes

No. 20, G Major Advancing Intermediate

This powerful and exuberant waltz would make an excellent etude for left hand octaves. These octaves are forceful (almost pesante), making a delightful contrast to the abrupt and quiet ending. A flexible, unhurried tempo will create the proper mood.

Length: 16 measures
Technique: LH octaves, broken chords, jump bass

No. 21, G Major, or "Landler" Intermediate

AGAY, Denes: More Easy Classics to Moderns, Vol. 27 (Consolidated).

BRADLEY, Richard: Bradley's Level Three Classics (Bradley).

BRADLEY, Richard: Easy Teaching Pieces, Vol. 2 (Bradley).

Kept at a constant soft dynamic level, this waltz evokes a charming music box sound. The continuous two-note patterns give a delightful rhythmic impetus. The high range of the melody involves leger line reading. Agay and Bradley alleviate this problem by using an 8va. This is one of Schubert's easier waltzes and is quite enjoyable.

Tempo: Agay - Moderato - ben ritmo
Bradley - Moderato - ben ritmo
Length: 16 measures
Technique: leger lines, 2-note slurs, jump bass, broken chords

No. 22, B Major Advancing Intermediate

Schubert displays his harmonic inventiveness in this pianistic waltz. The B Major key is never firmly established; an unusual and beautiful juxtaposition of B Major and B Minor is used instead. The second section is quite convincingly in G# Minor. Before playing the piece, it would be helpful to go through all the harmonic progressions.

Length: 17 measures
Technique: jump bass, 8th note passage work, accidentals, ornaments

No. 23, B Major — Advancing Intermediate

One can almost picture a goatherd in the Swiss Alps while listening to this yodel-like waltz. Made up of a broken chord melody, it is actually quite simple to play. The second section contains a lovely harmonic sequence. This waltz fits together perfectly with No. 24, the next one in this set.

Length: 16 measures
Technique: broken chords, jump bass, important ties and accents

No. 24, B Major — Advancing Intermediate

Almost like a landler, this waltz pairs well with No. 23, the previous one in this set. Perhaps this one could be played as a trio, repeating the first waltz. Like No. 23, it has a very Swiss-like yodelling sound, characterized by a broken chord melody. The abrupt change to the relative minor and its return within two measures adds a zesty fillip in the second section.

Length: 16 measures
Technique: broken chords, leaps

No. 25, E Major Advancing Intermediate

Right hand agility is a must in this waltz as the third beat trills are often approached and left by a leap. Reading difficulties are encountered because of leger lines and trills. After these obstacles are overcome, the dance is not hard to play, but it is also uninteresting once the initial challenges have worn off.

Length: 16 measures
Technique: chords, broken chords, ornaments, leaps, jump bass

No. 26, E Major Advancing Intermediate

HALFORD: Margery: Schubert--The First Book (Alfred).
HALFORD, Margery: Schubert--An Introduction to his Piano Works (Alfred).

This waltz is a scherzo in most senses of the word, being light, witty, and fast. The interest is found in the right hand which has grace notes, trills, and third beat accents. This is a very pianistic piece which is delightful to hear if it is not played with a heavy hand.

Length: 16 measures
Technique: grace notes, ornaments, broken chords, leaps, jump bass

No. 27, E Major

Intermediate

Leger line reading makes this dance look much harder than it actually is. The right hand melody is consistently in a high register. The first section in C# Minor is expressive and legato, while the second in E Major is buoyant and detached. Emphasizing these character differences will add interest to the piece.

Length: 16 measures

Technique: broken chords, jump bass, leaps

No. 28, A Major

Intermediate

A buoyant, light sound is created by trills and triplets which must be played as stylistically and gracefully as possible. Sudden register changes in the second section create echo effects which can be accentuated by subito dynamics. A fast tempo works the best, and the left hand waltz accompaniment is easier than most because there are no leaps.

Length: 16 measures

Technique: sustained and moving notes, leaps, waltz bass

No. 29, D Major, or "Atzenbrugger Deutche No. 3," "German Dance" — Advancing Intermediate

SMALL, Alan: Schubert Waltz Sampler (Alfred).
VOLGER, Heinz: Schubert--Easiest Piano Pieces (Peters No. 5015).

This romantic waltz is much larger in scope of expression and harmony than many others in this set. Overall it is very pianistic and fairly easy to play, but it can be hard to read because of the leger lines. In the Small and Volger editions, 8va is used instead. Dynamic contrasts will add to the charm of the piece.

Length: 24 measures
Technique: leger lines, leaps, chords, octaves

No. 30, A Major — Advancing Intermediate

This joyful dance is completely waltz-like in idiom. Light and cheerful in character, this would be a good performance choice. The octaves and broken octaves give an added richness to the folk-like melody.

Length: 16 measures
Technique: broken octaves, octaves, jump bass, clef changes

No. 31, C Major, or "Atzenbrugger Deutche No. 6" — Advancing Intermediate

This dramatic waltz opens with a rhythmically ambiguous theme. Because of the many double notes and occasional wide leaps, this fanfare-like dance is rather difficult. However, it is one of Schubert's more exuberant and joyful waltzes and could be worth the effort required.

Length: 19 measures
Technique: sustained and moving notes, double 3rds, large chords, octaves, leaps

No. 32, F Major — Advancing Intermediate

SMALL, Alan: Schubert Waltz Sampler (Alfred).

The jolly gaiety in this subtle and understated waltz will be best enhanced by a light touch and careful regard to dynamic contrasts. The creative harmonic progressions and the key change from F Major to Db Major and back add a colorful flavor. This waltz could be combined with one or two of the next three in the set (which are in the same key) for an enjoyable performance selection.

Length: 24 measures
Technique: scalar patterns, sustained and moving notes, octaves, jump bass

No. 33, F Major Advancing Intermediate

SMALL, Alan: Schubert Waltz Sampler (Alfred).

As with many of Schubert's waltzes, this one is filled with polka-like Germanic gusto. Phrasing is crucial, as is close observation of the dynamics and accents. The pianissimo dynamic level notated seems inappropriate for this exuberant piece. This would make a satisfying performance selection if paired with another of the last waltzes in this set.

Length: 32 measures
Technique: repeated chords, jump bass

No. 34, F Major Advancing Intermediate

An unusual feature of this waltz is its two measure introduction in which the pianissimo accompaniment pattern is presented with "fp" accents on beat three. This third beat accent is a unifying motive to No. 33. The harmonic modulation from F to Db and back is similar to that of No. 32. These last six waltzes would make a successful performance selection.

Length: 18 measures
Technique: double 6ths, sustained and moving notes, jump bass, clef changes

No. 35, F Major — Advancing Intermediate

SMALL, Alan: Schubert Waltz Sampler (Alfred).

This is another of Schubert's Germanic melodies which is reminiscent of yodelling, accompanied by I-V7 harmonies which fit the jocular mood. An attractive harmonic modulating sequence in the second section offers a delightful contrast.

Length: 16 measures
Technique: stretches, double 3rds, 8th note passage work, jump bass

No. 36, F Major — Intermediate

SMALL, Alan: Schubert Waltz Sampler (Alfred).

This beautiful homophonic piece has hymn-like form, voicing, and cadences. A large hand is helpful as there are many wide interval chords. The beautiful harmonic progressions in the second section are Schubert at his best.

Length: 16 measures
Technique: large stretches, chords

This is an exceptional group of 36 waltzes. A judicious grouping, particularly of the last six, would provide pleasurable performance possibilities.

## **WALTZES**, D. 779 (Op. 50)
### "Valses Sentimentales"

Note: All of D. 779 may be found in:

MIES, Paul: Schubert--Samtliche Tanze, Band II (G. Henle Verlag 76).

No. 1, C Major — Advancing Intermediate

HANSEN (Publisher): Schubert-A Highlight Collection.
NIEMANN, Walter: Schubert Dances (Peters No.150).
SCHIRMER (Publisher): Schubert Dances (Vol. 1537).
VOLGER, Heinz: Schubert--Easiest Piano Pieces (Peters No. 5015).

This first charming waltz exemplifies Schubert's melodic prowess. The right hand carries two lines throughout. The lower is often the melody and uses hand and finger control to delineate it. A regular pulse, one per measure, is an important feature of this and all waltzes of the set. The character may be enhanced by changes in articulation.

Length: 16 measures
Technique: double 3rds, jump bass, sustained and moving notes, important rests and accents

No. 2, C Major — Advancing Intermediate

HANSEN (Publisher): Schubert-A Highlight Collection.
NIEMANN, Walter: Schubert Dances (Peters No.150).
SCHIRMER (Publisher): Schubert Dances (Vol. 1537).

The sixteenth/two eighth note pickup figure which characterized the first waltz of the set is thoroughly integrated into the thematic material of this lovely dance. The precise dotted rhythms have some unexpected alterations. Abrupt modulations with little or no preparation create a surprising effect.

Length: 24 measures
Technique: repeated chords, sustained and moving notes, double 3rds, scales, jump bass, changing clefs

No. 3, G Major — Advancing Intermediate

HANSEN (Publisher): Schubert-A Highlight Collection.
HERRMANN, Kurt: Easy Schubert, Schumann, and Weber (Kalmus 9541/Belwin-Mills).
NIEMANN, Walter: Schubert Dances (Peters No.150).
SCHIRMER (Publisher): Schubert Dances (Vol. 1537).

Cross-phrasing between the melody and the accompaniment is the most arresting feature of this smooth waltz. The continuous eighth note melody needs shape and phrasing. The middle section involves some tricky leger line reading.

Length: 24 measures
Technique: jump bass, 8th note passage work, clef changes

No. 4, G Major — Advancing Intermediate

ZEITLIN, Poldi: Schubert Dances for Piano (Presser).

This ballroom-like waltz uses a lilting combination of elegant themes. The first section combines chordal patterns with leaping eighth notes which are marked as two-note phrases. Dynamics are "mf" to "ff", and although accents are often found on the second and third beats, the main pulse should never be obscured. This is the last of the waltzes in this set using the sixteenth dotted note motive. Nos. 1, 2, and 4 are recommended as a performance group.

Tempo: Zeitlin - L'istesso
Length: 16 measures
Technique: chords, clef changes, jump bass, 8th note passage work, 2-note phrases

No. 5, Bb Major — Advancing Intermediate

AGAY, Denes: Dances--Baroque to Jazz, Vol. C (Warner).

As with many of Schubert's dances, this is a joyful German waltz. A lilting feel and leggiero touch will help maintain the mood and character of the piece. Right hand leaps and quick double thirds require care to create the light assured sound they need. This simple sounding waltz is a rewarding study.

Tempo: Agay - Moderato
Length: 24 measures
Technique: broken chords, double 3rds, jump bass, RH jumps

No. 6, Bb Major <u>Intermediate</u>

ZEITLIN, Poldi: Schubert Dances for Piano (Presser).

The prevalent three-chord eighth note figure and the accented third beats give this waltz its happy character. Technical difficulties include full right hand chords and leaping octaves. Harmonically, this waltz is much more interesting than others in this set, using seventh and diminished seventh chords, and chromatic leading tones. Dynamic contrasts add much to the character of the piece and gives zest to groupings within the set.

Tempo: Zeitlin - Brioso
Length: 16 measures
Technique: repeated chords, full chords, octaves, jump bass

No. 7, Bb Major <u>Advancing Intermediate</u>

Continuous melodic eighth notes, a common feature of these Valses Sentimentales, create a highly gratifying sound in this waltz. The eighth notes outline melodic and broken chord figures and cover a wide keyboard range. Ornaments on the downbeats add to the character of this piece.

Length: 16 measures

Technique: ornaments, broken chords, jump bass, 8th note passage work, leger lines

No. 8, D Major <u>Advancing Intermediate</u>

This outstanding, vibrant waltz is very enjoyable to play, and sounds much harder than it actually is. Subtle and creative articulations will add greatly to the overall musical expression. This dance contrasts effectively with neighboring waltzes.

Length: 16 measures

Technique: sustained and moving notes, octaves, 2-note phrases

No. 9, D Major <u>Advancing Intermediate</u>

Unusual and innovative hemiola effects between the two hands combine with light and airy ascending lines, producing a quaint and amiable piece. The second section contains a lovely sequence resulting in contrasting minor harmonies.

Length: 16 measures

Technique: broken chords, 8th note passage work, jump bass, leger lines

No. 10, G Major, or "German Dance" Intermediate

NEVIN, Mark: 50 Best Loved Piano Solos--Bach to Bartok (Boston 14062).

This simple waltz is one of the most appealing and accessible of the set. In the first section the single line melody with a I, IV, V waltz bass is uncomplicated. The second section has a more complex finale, utilizing double thirds in a lovely harmonic pattern. The opening dotted rhythm serves only as an upbeat to measures one and nine, with two-note phrases being the prominent motive.

Tempo: Nevin - Moderato
Length: 16 measures
Technique: 2-note phrases, jump bass, double 3rds

No. 11, G Major Advancing Intermediate

Schubert's genius at bringing out various waltz qualities is epitomized by No. 11. Dynamic contrast and a light touch will portray the dance-like character. The use of upper register evokes a music box sound, while the broken chords give a yodelling effect. The circular and ascending melodic patterns bring to mind a series of light pirouettes.

Length: 16 measures
Technique: 8th note passage work, jump bass, leger lines

No. 12, D Major Intermediate

AGAY, Denes: An Anthology of Piano Music, The Romantic Period, Vol. III (Yorktown).
BERINGER, Oscar: Beringer's School of Easy Classics--Schubert (Galaxy).
HANSEN (Publisher): Schubert-A Highlight Collection.
NIEMANN, Walter: Schubert Dances (Peters No.150).
SCHIRMER (Publisher): Schubert Dances (Vol. 1537).
VOLGER, Heinz: Schubert--Easiest Piano Pieces (Peters No. 5015).
ZEITLIN, Poldi: Schubert Dances for Piano (Presser).

This sprightly waltz has distinct hemiola phrasing which gives it style and verve. Sustained and moving notes in the right hand provide the principal challenge.

Length: 24 measures
Technique: sustained and moving notes, jump bass, stretches

No. 13, A Major Advancing Intermediate

AGAY, Denes: An Anthology of Piano Music, The Romantic Period, Vol. III (Yorktown).
BISHOP, Stephen: Oxford Keyboard Classics--Schubert (Oxford).
HANSEN (Publisher): Schubert--A Highlight Collection.
HUGHES, Edwin: Master Series--Schubert (G. Schirmer).
LANNING, Russell: Music by the Masters (Musicord/Belwin-Mills).

NIEMANN, Walter: Schubert Dances (Peters No.150).
ROYAL CONSERVATORY OF MUSIC: Piano Examination Repertoire 6 (Frederick Harris 8304).
SCHIRMER (Publisher): Schubert Dances (Vol. 1537).
SHEALY, Alexander: Schubert--his greatest Piano Solos (Ashley).
SHEFTEL, Paul: Classics, Romantics, Moderns--Solos for the Intermediate Pianist (C. Fischer, ATF 102).
SMALL, Alan: Schubert Waltz Sampler (Alfred).
VOLGER, Heinz: Schubert--Easiest Piano Pieces (Peters No. 5015).
WILLS, Vera: The Purple Book #2 (G. Schirmer 3450).
ZEITLIN, Poldi: Schubert Dances for Piano (Presser).

This popular waltz has a smooth and pretty, almost dainty sound and is quite pianistic. There is wide opportunity for sensitive playing and experimentation with different balance of voices. Schubert uses many hemiolas and suspensions which add to the attractiveness of the waltz.

Length: 40 measures
Technique: sustained and moving notes, jump bass, hemiolas, important ties

No. 14, D Major — Advancing Intermediate

Schubert's jolly musical sense of humor is well exemplified in this piece. Sudden fortissimo chords interrupt the quiet, sedate, and dolce melody. In addition, chromatic harmonic movement in the second half adds a certain element of surprise. Double thirds are the main technical difficulty.

Length: 16 measures
Technique: double 3rds, octave chords, jump bass, important accents and rests

No. 15, F Major — Advancing Intermediate

This simplistic waltz depends on dynamic and articulation contrast for its appeal and interest. Light accents and marcato touch should be taken in the context of the quiet dynamics. Harmonies include chromatic movement with a shift to D Minor in the second section.

Length: 24 measures
Technique: scalar patterns, jump bass

No. 16, C Major — Advancing Intermediate

As in No. 11, Schubert uses the element of surprise quite deftly. The opening bars, with their garulous boldness, suggest quite a different nature from the light, tinkly sounds which follow. In addition, the harmonic elements are not always clear, lending another aspect of surprise. Dynamic contrast should be sharply executed.

Length: 17 measures
Technique: large chords, octaves, scalar patterns and 8th note passage work, jump bass

No. 17, C Major <u>Intermediate</u>

RICHTER, Ada: Great Piano Music, Vol. Three (Presser).

This light-hearted dance is quite pianistic and appealing in a buoyant and exuberant way. Bouncy broken chord figures give a jovial sound. The two sections contrast in dominant and tonic tonal areas. To maintain the character of this waltz, the rests at phrase endings should be observed carefully.

Length: 26 measures
Technique: scales, broken and solid chords, jump bass

No. 18, Ab Major <u>Intermediate</u>

HANSEN (Publisher): Schubert-A Highlight Collection.
NIEMANN, Walter: Schubert Dances (Peters No.150).
SCHIRMER (Publisher): Schubert Dances (Vol. 1537).

This simple waltz contains similar figuration throughout, which facilitates learning, but is rather repetitious. Melodic patterns are quite pianistic but require some hand stretching. The extremely high register at the end may cause reading difficulty.

Length: 17 measures
Technique: broken chords, jump bass

No. 19, Ab Major

Advancing Intermediate

HANSEN (Publisher): Schubert-A Highlight Collection.
HERRMANN, Kurt: Easy Schubert, Schumann, and Weber (Kalmus 9541/Belwin-Mills).
NIEMANN, Walter: Schubert Dances (Peters No.150).
SCHIRMER (Publisher): Schubert Dances (Vol. 1537).
ZEITLIN, Poldi: Schubert Dances for Piano (Presser).

This unusual dance involves unique melody, accompaniment, haronies, and pedal points. The right hand carries two voices, consisting of a melody beneath a higher off-beat pedal point. Both of these voices need thoughtful shaping and beautiful tone. The accompaniment provides passing tones which create a counter melody using both parallel and contrary motion. These passing harmonies and the use of the ii chord and its secondary dominant create lovely surprises. Musical demands are much more than the technical requirements.

Length: 16 measures
Technique: broken intervals, jump bass, melody and accompaniment in the same hand

No. 20, Ab Major

Advancing Intermediate

HANSEN (Publisher): Schubert-A Highlight Collection.
NIEMANN, Walter: Schubert Dances (Peters No.150).
SCHIRMER (Publisher): Schubert Dances (Vol. 1537).

The predominant octave melody gives this waltz a lively Viennese character which is typical of Schubert's best waltzes. An interesting chromatic movement in measures five through seven is the only exception to fairly prosaic harmonies. Dynamic contrasts are rich and should be brought out as much as possible. Paired with the next waltz in this set (No. 21), this would be an excellent performance selection.

Length: 16 measures

Technique: octaves, chords (solid and broken), jump bass

No. 21, Eb Major — Advancing Intermediate

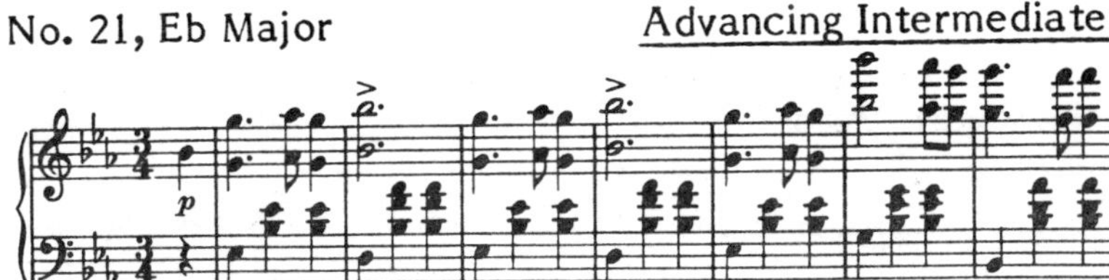


HANSEN (Publisher): Schubert-A Highlight Collection.
NIEMANN, Walter: Schubert Dances (Peters No.150).
SCHIRMER (Publisher): Schubert Dances (Vol. 1537).

Because of its harmonies, rhythms, figurations, and phrase structure, this waltz seems to be an extension of the previous waltz (No. 20). The octaves in a high register give it a crystalline music box quality which is appealing. This waltz could serve as a B or trio section, followed by a repeat of No. 20.

Length: 16 measures

Technique: octaves, jump bass

No. 22, Eb Major — Advancing Intermediate

HANSEN (Publisher): Schubert--A Highlight Collection.
NIEMANN, Walter: Schubert Dances (Peters No.150).
SCHIRMER (Publisher): Schubert Dances (Vol. 1537).

Prevalent broken chord figuration creates the same Swiss-like yodelling effect that is found in many of these waltzes. The largest technical problem involves right hand shifts and hand stretches. The charming ending has harmonic changes which are both surprising and delightful.

Length: 24 measures
Technique: broken chords, large stretches, jump bass, dynamic range (ff-pp)

No. 23, Eb Major — Intermediate

The opening diminished seventh and abrupt movement of tonal centers is unsettling and very effective. The first four bars are dark and somber, contrasting with the remainder of the piece which is very light-hearted. Lilting eighth notes with unusual second beat accents are particularly attractive in the second section.

Length: 16 measures
Technique: scalar double 3rds, jump bass, 8th note passage work

No. 24, Bb Major — Intermediate

The first section of this subtle, constrained waltz is in a poignant G Minor, at a piano dynamic level. The melody is in single notes and can be shaped thoughtfully. The second section, however, is in the buoyant key of Bb Major at a forte dynamic level, replete with double notes and soaring phrases. These contrasts are the essence of this inviting piece.

Length: 16 measures

Technique: sustained and moving notes, broken chords, ornamentation, waltz bass and jump bass

No. 25, G Major — Advancing Intermediate

This waltz opens with a typical I-V relationship which sets up the bold and surprising harmonies in the next section. Its uneven phrase patterns are unusual and appealing. In the second section, constantly changing articulations and fz accents add to the dance's vitality.

Length: 24 measures

Technique: double 3rds, repeated chords, sustained and moving notes, jump bass

No. 26, C Major — Intermediate

This waltz has a quaint, naive quality which gives it a simple folk-like sound. Schubert's use of nonharmonic tones on strong beats creates an extremely beautiful element of the unexpected. The harmonies and dynamics in the last four measures give an elegant flavor to the waltz. Dynamic contrasts should be exaggerated for the most effective expression.

Length: 16 measures
Technique: broken chords, large stretches, jump bass

No. 27, Eb Major — Advancing Intermediate

HANSEN (Publisher): Schubert-A Highlight Collection.
HERRMANN, Kurt: Easy Schubert, Schumann, and Weber (Kalmus 9541/Belwin-Mills).
NIEMANN, Walter: Schubert Dances (Peters No.150).
SCHIRMER (Publisher): Schubert Dances (Vol. 1537).
VOLGER, Heinz: Schubert--Easiest Piano Pieces (Peters No. 5015).
ZEITLIN, Poldi: Schubert Dances for Piano (Presser).

A wide range of changing articulations and the contrast of major and minor modes give this simplistic, mundane waltz some variety. The staid melody reflects a solid peasant dance, although it is quiet and light. The two sections juxtapose piano and forte dynamics and Eb and C Major tonalities. Double grace notes accentuate the accented third beats.

Length: 24 measures
Technique: broken chords, ornamentation, jump bass

No. 28, Eb Major — Advancing Intermediate

The first section is gay and cheerful with subdued dynamics. The second section begins in the parallel minor and contains many melodic and harmonic surprises. The doubling of the melody in the left hand voice is an engaging touch.

Length: 16 measures
Technique: octaves, jump bass

No. 29, Eb Major — Advancing Intermediate

At first glance, the right hand texture, with its combination of broken chords and double notes, appears to be quite dense and thick. However, after some scrutiny and practice, a certain heirarchy of moving notes will become clear. Both hands have contrapuntal lines. The sixteenth note pickup to the phrase adds zest.

Length: 24 measures
Technique: broken chords, sustained and moving notes, waltz bass

No. 30, C Major — Advancing Intermediate

The lively Germanic character of this waltz is typical of Schubert, but the surprising hemiola effect in the second section is totally unexpected and rewarding.

Length: 16 measures

Technique: broken chords, double 3rds, scalar patterns, jump bass, unusual phrases and accents

No. 31, A Minor/C Major — Advancing Intermediate

AGAY, Denes: The Joy of Romantic Piano, Book I (Yorktown).

In a sound reminiscent of a concertina, the melodic right hand is challenging with leaps and quick hand shifts. Downbeat emphasis through trills and third beat accents are frequent.

Length: 16 measures

Technique: scalar patterns, ornamentation, double 3rds, jump bass, RH leaps

No. 32, C Major — Intermediate

ZEITLIN, Poldi: Schubert Dances for Piano (Presser).

This lilting waltz is quite simple and pianistic but repetitious in melodic patterns and harmonies. Creative use of dynamics and articulations will add charm and animation.

Tempo: Zeitlin - Affabile
Length: 24 measures
Technique: broken chords, octave chords, jump bass

No. 33, Ab Major <u>Advancing Intermediate</u>

This sprightly waltz, with its contrast of eighth notes and detached quarters, gives opportunity for sensitive phrasing. The third beat accents provide added vitality.

Length: 16 measures
Technique: broken chords, double 3rds, jump bass with wide leaps, changing clefs

No. 34, Ab Major <u>Advancing Intermediate</u>

HANSEN (Publisher): Schubert--A Highlight Collection.
NIEMANN, Walter: Schubert Dances (Peters No.150).
SCHIRMER (Publisher): Schubert Dances (Vol. 1537).

The homophonic sound of this waltz contrasts with the melody and accompaniment style found in others of this set. The beautiful texture is comprised of left hand octaves and harmonic intervals and right hand notes in two and three voices. Dynamic differences can add appeal.

Length: 16 measures
Technique: octaves, repeated chords, double 3rds, important accents and rests

Although performance of D. 779 in its entirety is impractical due to its length, selective groupings would provide entertaining performance choices. To make these choices, the purchase of the two Mies volumes is recommended, as they are the only available source that contains all of D. 779 (as well as many other unavailable Schubert dances).

**WALZER GENNANT**, G Major, D. 844, "Albumblatt" Advancing Intermediate

MIES, Paul: Schubert--Samtliche Tanze, Band II (G. Henle Verlag 76).
WEINMANN/KANN: Schubert--Walzer und Deutsche Tanze (Wiener 50063).

This unusual, quiet, and hymn-like waltz has a beautiful "religioso" feeling. One of Schubert's later waltzes, it contains many syncopations which add to the harmonic variety by creating lovely suspensions. The homophonic structure would indicate bringing out the melody but there are interesting inner voices that could also be stressed.

Length: 16 measures
Technique: chords and voicing, sustained and moving notes, important ties and accents

# WALTZES, D. 924 (Op. 91a)
## "Grazer Walzer"

Note: All of D. 924 may be found in:

MIES, Paul: Schubert--Samtliche Tanze, Band II
(G. Henle Verlag 76).
NIEMANN, Walter: Schubert Dances (Peters No.150).
SCHIRMER (Publisher): Schubert Dances (Vol. 1537).

No. 1, E Major — Advancing Intermediate

This charming waltz is characterized by a delicate music box sound. Reading the leger lines is the most difficult aspect. The second section contains some large reaches which will need flexibility and a light touch. Dynamic contrast and clarity of ornaments will add to the buoyant nature of this piece.

Length: 25 measures
Technique: broken chords, ornamentation, octaves, jump bass, leger lines

No. 2, E Major — Advancing Intermediate

This awkward waltz is rather dull, with unvaried melody and predictable harmonies. However, it still contains Schubert's occasional crystalline elegance, characterized by the high register found in many of his other waltzes. Dynamic contrast will bring out the latent charm and help obviate the hiccuping effect caused by the syncopation.

Length: 16 measures
Technique: ornamentation, octaves, jump bass, syncopation

No.3, E Major — Advancing Intermediate

At first appearance, this waltz seems unappealing. However, a deeper look reveals a musical expression in the form of dynamic contrasts and the often hidden pedal points. A quick waltz tempo and careful, sensitive shaping of the melodic lines will enliven this rather bland waltz.

Length: 16 measures
Technique: broken chords, sustained and moving notes, jump bass, leger lines

No. 4, A Major — Advancing Intermediate

Obviously composed with dancing as its intent, this piece is very exuberant and waltz-like. However, the charm of the waltzes in D. 779 is not evident in this piece or the set as a whole. Harmonies are quite prosaic and the motivic figuration is very Germanic sounding, yet redundant.

Length: 24 measures
Technique: high leger lines, broken chords, jump bass

No. 5, A Major <u>Advancing Intermediate</u>

The abundance of octaves gives this piece the Viennese sound which is characteristic of so many Schubert waltzes. Although melodically mundane, it is harmonically surprising. Style and energy in performance will enliven this waltz.

Length: 16 measures
Technique: octaves, jump bass, clef changes

No. 6, A Major <u>Advancing Intermediate</u>

The yodelling-like broken chord melody in this waltz remains rather innocuous throughout, displaying the generally uninspired quality found in this set of dances. However, there are occasional moments of harmonic interest.

Length: 16 measures
Technique: ornamentation, leger lines, clef changes, waltz bass, 8th note passage work

No. 7, A Minor <u>Advancing Intermediate</u>

This waltz is stylistically more exciting than the other Grazer Walzer. The initial A Minor section is very powerful and heavy, contrasting well with the lighter C Major section. Both sections are characterized by music box sounds. The second ending with an abrupt key change from C to A Minor leaves an unfinished feeling.

Length: 18 measures
Technique: broken octaves, chords, jump bass

No. 8, A Major — Advancing Intermediate

This piece is characterized by a high register theme which seems tedious. It is rather difficult to play because of continuous position changes.

Length: 24 measures
Technique: broken chords, broken octaves, 2-note phrases, leger lines, jump bass

No. 9, C Major — Advancing Intermediate

AGAY, Denes: More Easy Classics to Moderns, Vol. 27 (Consolidated).

BRADLEY, Richard: Bradley's Classics for Piano, The Second Level (Bradley B12M42/Columbia).

BRADLEY, Richard: Bradley's Level Four Classics (Bradley).

BRADLEY, Richard: Easy Teaching Pieces, Vol. 2 (Bradley).

GRANT, Lawrence: More Classic to Contemporary Piano Music (Ashley).
HERRMANN, Kurt: Easy Schubert, Schumann, and Weber (Kalmus 9541/Belwin-Mills).
RICHTER, Ada: Great Piano Music, Vol. 3 (Presser).
SHEFTEL, Paul: Classics, Romantics, Moderns--Solos for the Intermediate Pianist (C. Fischer ATF 102).
VOLGER, Heinz: Schubert--Easiest Piano Pieces (Peters No. 5015).
WATERMANN/HAREWOOD: The Young Pianist's Repertoire, Book Two (Faber).

Offering more harmonic interest than many of these Grazer Walzer, this dance is considerably more enjoyable. Shaping the right hand inner voice melody is a challenge. A quick and lively tempo is suitable for this waltz. The Richter and Waterman/Harewood volumes are the only multi-period collections that correctly notate the second four measures in the high register.

Tempo: varies among editions
Length: 16 measures
Technique: jump bass, RH harmonic intervals

No. 10, A Major <u>Advancing Intermediate</u>

As with many other waltzes in this set, No. 10 is characterized by a sprightly melody that suffers from too much repetition. The dynamic contrasts will add interest.

Length: 44 measures
Technique: broken chords, stretches, ornamentation, leger lines, arpeggiated patterns, jump bass

No. 11, G Major <u>Advancing Intermediate</u>

This waltz has more innate charm than many of the others in this set. The initial reading is difficult because of the inner voice inverted mordents, the wide position changes, the accidentals, and the left hand clef changes. Once learned, this music box waltz will be enjoyable.

Length: 24 measures
Technique: sustained and moving notes, broken chords, ornamentation, leaps, stretches, repeated intervals, jump bass

No. 12, E Major <u>Advancing Intermediate</u>

This charming, pleasant, and accessible waltz could provide a dramatic ending to the set. Harmonically it is interesting and creative with diminished seventh chords. Although fun to play, the initial reading may be difficult. The arpeggiated figures are challenging.

Length: 48 measures
Technique: full chords, arpeggiated figures, leaps, jump bass, octaves

WALTZES, D. 969 (Op. 77)
"Valses Nobles"

Note: All of D. 969 may be found in:

HANSEN (Publisher): Schubert--A Highlight Collection.
INTERNATIONAL LIBRARY OF PIANO MUSIC, Vol. IV (University Society).
MIES, Paul: Schubert--Samtliche Tanze, Band II (G. Henle Verlag 76).
NIEMANN, Walter: Schubert Dances (Peters No.150).
SCHIRMER (Publisher): Schubert Dances (Vol. 1537).

No. 1, C Major — Advancing Intermediate

BASTIEN, James: Piano Literature, Vol. 4 (GWM/Kjos).
CLARK and GOSS: Piano Literature, Book 6b (Summy-Birchard).
GLOVER, David Carr: Piano Repertoire, Level Six (Belwin-Mills).
LANNING, Russell: Music by the Masters (Musicord/Belwin-Mills).
SHEFTEL, Paul: Classics, Romantics, Moderns--Solos for the Intermediate Pianist (C. Fischer ATF 102).
SMALL, Alan: Schubert Waltz Sampler (Alfred).

A boisterous German exuberance, typical of Schubert's compositions, is found in this dance. Its predominant motivic figures are octaves and large chords, giving it an introductory fanfare-like quality. The movement within the inner voices adds a creative and challenging touch.

Tempo: Lanning - Vivace
Glover - Vivace
Bastien - Allegro
Length: 16 measures
Technique: octaves, octave chords, LH leaps

No. 2, A Major Advancing Intermediate

SMALL, Alan: Schubert Waltz Sampler (Alfred).

As with the first waltz in this set, this dance is full of Viennese sound and spirit. Although predominantly in octaves, "p" is used equally as often as "f," providing an elegant contrast. The second beat accents are zestful.

Length: 18 measures
Technique: octaves, jump bass, important accents

No. 3, C Major Advancing Intermediate

By far one of Schubert's most creative and exciting waltzes, this epitomizes his apparent sense of fun and exuberance. While technically demanding due to the constant figuration of octaves with thirds enclosed, it is quite rewarding and well worth the effort. Exaggerating the dynamic contrasts will add spice to this wonderful piece. The innovative harmonic writing in the second section is particularly delightful. The climactic effect of the extended octave scales is stunning.

Length: 58 measures
Technique: octaves, octave chords

No. 4, G Major <u>Advancing Intermediate</u>

CLARK and GOSS: Piano Literature, Book 6b (Summy-Birchard).
SMALL, Alan: Schubert Waltz Sampler (Alfred).

Octaves in the upper register of the keyboard create the Viennese music box sound which is very characteristic of many of Schubert's waltzes. Aside from the octaves the only difficulty in this piece is position changes. The octaves are a characteristic of the first five waltzes in this set, but this dance utilizes dotted rhythms.

Length: 25 measures
Technique: octaves, jump bass

No. 5, C Major <u>Advancing Intermediate</u>

SMALL, Alan: Schubert Waltz Sampler (Alfred).

As with the other waltzes in this set, this one is filled with sparkling vigor. Harmonically, it is quite creative, with the C Major key center not firmly established until the last few measures of the first section. This, and the sequential patterns, create a wonderful and intriguing waltz.

Length: 32 measures
Technique: octaves, octave chords, jump bass

No. 6, C Major <u>Intermediate</u>

SZAVAI/VESZPREMI: Piano Album, Book 1 (Belwin-Mills).

The mood of this sixth waltz is in sharp contast to the first five, eliminating the octaves and substituting an unsophisticated folk sound melody in the manner of D. 365. The short two and three-note phrases give a light tripping effect and their sequential treatment is charming.

Length: 16 measures
Technique: sustained and moving notes, waltz bass, 2-note phrases

No. 7, E Major <u>Advancing Intermediate</u>

CLARK and GOSS: Piano Literature, Book 6b (Summy-Birchard).
ZEITLIN, Poldi: Schubert Dances for Piano (Presser).

This waltz is quite refreshing in its unique use of thematic material. The sixteenth note figures which act as grace notes give this dance a certain vigorous snap and bounce which makes it delightful to play and hear. There are a few large leaps and stretches but basically this is not a difficult selection.

Length: 24 measures

Technique: octaves, repeated chords, large leaps and stretches

No. 8, A Major | Advancing Intermediate

This unusual dance is more like a march than a waltz. The dynamic contrasts are the source of musical expression and could be exaggerated. The full rolled chords are not consistent in their appearance and dissonant harmony in the last line is surprising, as though Schubert did not do a final editing of this piece.

Length: 24 measures

Technique: rolled chords, full chords, octaves, repeated notes

No. 9, A Minor | Intermediate

BASTIEN, James: Piano Literature, Vol. 4 (GWM/Kjos).
LANNING, Russell: Music by the Masters (Musicord/Belwin-Mills).

SHEFTEL, Paul: Classics, Romantics, Moderns--Solos for the Intermediate Pianist (C. Fischer ATF 102).

This familiar fiery and colorful waltz is a welcome and refreshing addition to the others in this set. Although in the key of A Minor, the waltz occasionally ventures through other tonalities which adds spice. Observing and exaggerating the dynamic contrasts, and feeling one pulse per measure, will propel the piece forward. The re-emergence of the sixteenth note grace-note-like pattern of No. 7 results in an innovative ending touch.

Tempo: Bastien - Maestoso
Lanning - Allegro non troppo
Length: 36 measures
Technique: octaves, octave chords, repeated octaves, LH leaps

No. 10, F Major — Early Intermediate

SMALL, Alan: Schubert Waltz Sampler (Alfred).
VOLGER, Heinz: Schubert--Easiest Piano Pieces (Peters No. 5015).
ZEITLIN, Poldi: Schubert Dances for Piano (Presser).

The sweet Viennese melody which characterizes this lovely waltz is like a happy folk song. It is short and simple, yet amiable and demure. With sensitive expression and careful observance of the various dynamic and articulation markings, this can be enjoyable to play and hear.

Tempo: Zeitlin - Cantando
Length: 16 measures
Technique: sustained and moving notes, jump bass, 8th note passage work

No. 11, C Major Intermediate

SMALL, Alan: Schubert Waltz Sampler (Alfred).
ZEITLIN, Poldi: Schubert Dances for Piano (Presser).

Just as Schubert is explicit in his dynamic preferences, the performer must be explicit in following them. This piece is in the good-natured bold style of many of the Valses Nobles. The repeated chords provide the challenge.

Tempo: Zeitlin - Impetuoso
Length: 16 measures
Technique: repeated chords, octave chords, jump bass

No. 12, C Major Advancing Intermediate

SHEALY, Alexander: Schubert--his Greatest Piano Solos (Ashley).
SMALL, Alan: Schubert Waltz Sampler (Alfred).

This exciting and energetic waltz closes this set of twelve, which could be performed in total by even the advanced pianist. As with the others, the octaves in upper registers create a Viennese-like sound which exudes a certain liveliness and charm.

Length: 36 measures
Technique: octaves, scalar octaves, jump bass, LH repeated chords

**WALTZ,** Ab Major, D. 978 <u>Intermediate</u>

MIES, Paul: Samtliche Tanze, Band II
(G. Henle Verlag 76).

Graceful broken chords and octaves are used as motivic patterns in this waltz. Ties over the first beat of many measures add impetus to the rhythmic flow. The first section moves in consonant harmonies, but the second section receives heightened harmonic tension from an octave pedal point in the waltz bass line.

Length: 28 measures
Technique: broken octaves, waltz bass, ties over the bar line, sustained and moving notes

**WALTZ,** G Major, D. 979 <u>Early Advanced</u>

MIES, Paul: Samtliche Tanze, Band II
(G. Henle Verlag 76)

This short waltz is surprisingly difficult. The right hand octaves move in widening intervals, ending in ungainly leaps as each section ends. The left hand waltz bass has its share of wide leaps also, but moves more gracefully.

Length: 16 measures
Technique: octaves, wide interval leaps, waltz bass

**TWO WALTZES,** G Major and B Minor, D. 980 — Early Advanced

MIES, Paul: Samtliche Tanze, Band II (G. Henle Verlag 76).

The two waltzes of this set complement each other well, but seem unfinished without a D.C. that repeats the first in G Major.

The first waltz begins each section with hemiolas that totally obscure the triple rhythm. There is a fascination in this structure, but dancers would face certain confusion in the ambiguities to the ear.

The second waltz is a straightforward, sturdy combination of right hand chords and left hand octaves, offering a decided contrast to the vagaries of its companion.

Length: 40 measures
Technique: dotted patterns, waltz bass, octaves, repeated chords

## II. IMPROMPTUS

The designation "impromptu" was an invention of the Bohemian pianist and composer Jan Worzischek (1791-1825), with antecedents in short piano works called Ecologues, Rhapsodies, and Dithyrambs, by a fellow countryman, Jan Tomachek (1774-1850). The works of these composers are unknown beyond their own locale, but Schubert adopted their concept of short piano works into his own personal and far-reaching statement of musical form. These epigrammatic character pieces are improvisatory, expressing a feeling of intimate, spontaneous revelation.

There are two sets of Impromptus, both written in 1827, and each containing four pieces that are musically complete, with clear ideas and textures. Each has its own distinctive character and formal structure, melding together as a set with, as Kathleen Dale describes it, a quality of "unified diversity."

Of the first set, D. 899 (Op. 90), Nos. 1 and 2 were published during Schubert's lifetime; numbers three and four were published in 1857. The second set, Op. 142 (D. 935) was published in 1838 by Diabelli. Robert Schumann, and later Albert Einstein regarded this set of four pieces as a sonata, broken up to be more sellable, but the Schubert autographs show the specific title of "Impromptus" on the manuscript.

## **FOUR IMPROMPTUS,** D. 899 (Op. 90)

Note: All of D. 899 may be found in:

DEXTER, Harry: Selected Piano Works--Schubert (Hansen).
EPSTEIN, Julius: Schubert--Shorter Works (Dover).
HANSEN (Publisher): Schubert-A Highlight Collection.
KALMUS (Publisher): Schubert--Impromptus, Moments Musicaux for Piano Solo (Belwin-Mills No. 3886).
SHEALY, Alexander: Schubert--his greatest Piano Solos (Ashley).

No. 1, C Minor — Advanced

This dramatically beautiful impromptu opens with an ambiguous and startling unison octave "G." This is followed by a lovely and simplistic melody which is the substance and cohesive factor of the entire piece. Schubert varies this main theme in many ingenious ways, from harmonic enrichment to diminution and augmentation of various aspects. Broken chords and repeated note triplets often accompany the theme, producing many tricky occurences of 2 vs. 3. Schubert points out many mood changes through various dynamic and textural contrasts. Harmonically, this is an extremely creative work. At measure 152, a refreshing shift of key to G Major (with a C Major key signature) eventually moves to C Major, alternating with flirtatious sallies back to C Minor, right up to the final four measures in C Major. Extensive use of repeated notes and chords requires an awareness of pulse and tonal balance to avoid fatigue.

Tempo: Allegro Molto Moderato
Length: 204 measures
Technique: 2 vs. 3, 4 vs. 3, various dotted rhythms, double notes, chords, repeated notes and chords, Alberti bass figures, sustained and moving notes, wide dynamic range (ppp-ff), octaves, triplet and 16th note broken chords

No. 2, Eb Major — Early Advanced

AGAY, Denes: An Anthology, The Romantic Period, Vol. III (Yorktown).
BRIMHALL, John: Original Piano Masterworks, Levels 3 and 4 (Hansen).

This lovely impromptu is characterized by a floating, sweeping main theme which is comprised of various diatonic and chromatic scalar passages. Played with a very light touch, the waterfall-like shape will enhance the musical ideas. The contrasting B section is quite dark and dramatic, containing many arresting harmonic progressions. An excellent piece for harmonic study and overall structure, this would also be a welcome performance choice.

Tempo: Allegro
Length: 283 measures
Technique: 3/4 hemiolas, alternating triplets and duplets, diatonic scales, chromatic passage work, arpeggios, wide stretches, chords, sustained and moving notes, accidentals, dynamic range, broken octaves

No. 3, Gb Major

Early Advanced

This impromptu reveals Schubert at his most pensive and introspective. Four of these editions follow the original key of Gb Major. The Kalmus edition transposes the key to G Major. Schubert originally wrote it in Gb Major but altered it to G Major at his publisher's insistence. The beautiful cantabile melody is accompanied by murmuring broken chords. This accompaniment must be used to bring out unusual and emotional harmonic changes, which are the essence of musical expression in this work. Although technically accessible, this piece requires intense concentration to perform it musically. The Kalmus version is 172 measures in length, eliminating the cut time notation.

Tempo: Andante
Length: 87 measures
Technique: 4 vs. 3, sustained and moving notes, broken chords, LH trills, wide stretches, accidentals

No. 4, Ab Major

Advanced

BRADLEY, Richard: Bradley's Level Seven Classics (Bradley).
BRADLEY, Richard: Bradley's Classics for Piano--The Fourth Level (Bradley/Columbia B14M21).
HEINRICHSHOFEN/PETERS (Publisher): Schubert--Easier Favorites (No.4051).
WILLIS (Publisher): Famous Piano Solos (106627).

Although in Ab Major, this impromptu begins pianissimo in Ab Minor, which in retrospect creates a satisfying sense of tonal and emotional ambiguity. Broken chord figures create the unifying features which produce a delicate rippling effect. Dynamic contrast and tonal balance are of utmost importance. The C# Minor trio contrasts with repeated instead of broken chords. This impromptu is long, but relatively easy to learn due to the clarity of structure and repetition of ideas. Lilt and sense of long line keeps it from being monotonous.

Tempo: Allegretto
Length: 276 measures
Technique: 16th note broken chord passage work, sustained and moving notes, accidentals, repeated chords, endurance problems

**FOUR IMPROMPTUS,** D. 935 (Op. 142)

Note: All of D. 935 may be found in:

EPSTEIN, Julius: Schubert--Shorter Works (Dover).
HANSEN (Publisher): Schubert-A Highlight Collection.
KALMUS (Publisher): Schubert--Impromptus, Moments Musicaux for Piano Solo (Belwin-Mills No. 3886).

No. 1, F Minor — Advanced

In a quasi-rondo form (almost like a sonata movement), this overly long impromptu suffers from redundancy. Its themes have none of the profile and beauty of many of the other impromptus, in particular those of Op. 90. The opening theme is a declamatory statement that grows into an appoggiatura-dominated idea which Schubert fortunately develops quite well. A variety of key changes and dynamic contrasts aid the musical treatment. In addition, many of the harmonic progressions are very beautiful. In one section the music poises on the tip of its toes, as it were, on a high Eb half note before rippling into a downward cascade of broken chord notes. An appassionato melody dialoguing between treble and bass, crosses back and forth over the right hand accompanying figure. A recapitulation of both sections, with a final return of the opening theme, ends this Impromptu.

Tempo: Allegro moderato
Length: 235 measures
Technique: wide stretches, ornamentation, broken chord and interval figurations, arpeggios, full chords, octaves, sustained and moving notes, hand-crosses, 16th note passage work

No. 2, Ab Major — Early Advanced

AGAY, Denes: Early Advanced Classics to Moderns, Vol. 47 (Consolidated).

ALFRED (Publisher): Schubert--17 of his Most Popular Selections.

BRIMAHLL, John: Original Piano Masterworks, Levels 3 and 4 (Hansen).

DEXTER, Harry: Selected Piano Works--Schubert (Hansen).

GEEHL, Henry: Schubert--Compositions of Moderate Difficulty (Ashdown).

INTERNATIONAL LIBRARY OF PIANO MUSIC, Vol. IV (University Society).

HALFORD, Margery: Schubert--An Introduction to his Piano works (Alfred).
HUGHES, Edwin: Master Series--Schubert (G. Schirmer).
MEDLEY, Bill and Pat: Standard Literature, Volume 3 (Hal Leonard HL00240903).
SHEALY, Alexander: Schubert--his greatest Piano Solos (Ashley).

This lovely and serene impromptu opens with a beautiful, homophonic, almost hymn-like sound. A striking harmonic movement within the inner voices offers a wide opportunity for sensitive tonal balance. The B section, or trio, is characterized by flowing triplets with several recognizable melodic lines. A simple restatement of the original 46-measure main section follows, with a four-measure coda. This shorter and more concise impromptu will be a tremendously satisfying performance choice.

Tempo: Allegretto
Length: 148 measures
Technique: voicing, broken chords, full chords, sustained and moving notes

No. 3, Bb Major — Advanced

AGAY, Denes: Classics to Moderns, Theme and Variations, Vol. 77 (Consolidated).
DEXTER, Harry: Selected Piano Works--Schubert (Hansen).
HEINRICHSHOFEN/PETERS (Publisher): Schubert--Easier Favorites (No. 4051).

The very familiar theme of this effective work is taken from Schubert's stage play, "Rosamunde." The five variations retain the theme's basic harmonic movement and contour, and much of the same underlying rhythmic motion. The harmonic progressions are basically simple. Variation I has melody and accompaniment in the same hand, with a four-voice division. Variation II is a light, tripping filigree of sixteenth notes outlining the melody. Variation III is in the key of Bb Minor. Variation IV is in the key of Gb Major and is structured in broken chords. Variation V, again in Bb Major, features fleeting triplet figures in scalar patterns and arpeggio passages. A nine-measure chordal coda restates the theme, ending the piece quietly.

Tempo: Andante
Length: 132 measures
Technique: octaves, broken chords with melody intertwined, sustained and moving notes, ornamentation, arpeggios, broken octaves, Alberti-like figures, 16th note passage work

No. 4, F Minor <u>Advanced</u>

This wonderful impromptu is both brilliant and frenetic. The initial capricious idea becomes more and more exuberant, whipping itself into quite a frenzy even when pianissimo. The quick tempo, which is appropriate to the piece, also causes technical difficulties in the cadenza-like scalar passages. Hemiolas are creatively and effectively used. The left hand accompaniment has the seeds of a tremolo effect, developed with split chords and octaves. The rhythm is driving and should maintain momentum. Although technically difficult, this piece lies well under the hands. This audience pleaser would be an excellent performance selection.

Tempo: Allegro scherzando
Length: 525 measures
Technique: cadenza-like passages, scales, double 3rds, arpeggios, broken chords, octave chords, trills, parallel diatonic and chromatic scales

## MOMENTS MUSICAL

Kathleen Dale aptly describes this set of six pieces as "poems in sound." They are short works in song form, revealing great diversity in form, content, and spirit, and expressing Schubert's tremendous individuality as a composer for the piano. They were published as a set in July of 1828 as D. 780 (Op. 94). Two of the six were published at earlier dates. Number three was originally titled "Air Russe" and included in a volume called Album Musicale, printed in 1823. Number six appeared in a second 1824 edition of Album Musicale under the title "Plaintes d'un Troubadour."

## MOMENT MUSICAL, D. 780 (Op. 94)

Note: All of D. 780 may be found in:

DEXTER, Harry: Selected Piano Works--Schubert (Hansen).
EPSTEIN, Julius: Schubert--Shorter Works (Dover).
HANSEN (Publisher): Schubert--A Highlight Collection.
KALMUS PIANO SERIES: Schubert Impromputs, Moments Musicaux, Phantasies, and Allegretto, Andante, March, Scherzos (Belwin-Mills 3886).
SHEALY, Alexander: Schubert--his greatest Piano Solos (Ashley).

No. 1, C Major — Advancing Intermediate

HEINRICHSOFEN/PETERS (Publisher): Schubert Easier Favorites (Urtext N.4051).
KALMUS PIANO SERIES: Schubert--An Easy Album for Piano Solos (Belwin-Mills).

ROWLEY, Alec: The Easiest Original Schubert (Hinrichsen No. 6/Peters).

The subtleties of this lovely short work are musically challenging, and are tremendously satisfying in the learning and performing process. There are complex rhythms, involving duple and triple subdivisions, and two against three patterns. The phrases are of varying lengths, with innovative use of extension and diminution throughout. The harmonic progressions are a source of delightful surprise, revealing Schubert at his creative best. The ABA form is extremely accessible. The A sections have a fanfare opening, surprising in the delicate dynamic levels that predominate. The B section contrasts in key and in rhythmic and melodic scoring, but retains the quiet, hushed dynamics. This "musical moment" is extremely pianistic and would be a joy in performance.

Tempo: Moderato
Length: 95 measures
Technique: octaves, full chords, sustained and moving notes, broken chords

No. 2, Ab Major — Advancing Intermediate

AGAY, Denes: An Anthology, The Romantic Period, Vol. III (Yorktown).

The rondo form of this lilting piece utilizes two contrasting ideas. The first builds in fascinating irregular phrases of full chords in a recurring dotted note motive. The second contrasts with a single note cantabile melody over a broken chord accompaniment. Subtle changes of patterns and harmony within the Ab

Major and F# Minor sections call for a thoughtful and sensitive approach that will reveal the beauty of this piece to the listener. This would be a wonderful performance choice.

Tempo: Andantino
Length: 93 measures
Technique: octave chords, ornamentation, wide broken chords, sustained and moving notes

No. 3, F Minor — Advancing Intermediate

AGAY, Denes: An Anthology, The Romantic Period, Vol. III (Torktown).
ALFRED (Publisher): Schubert--17 of his Most Popular Selections.
ALFRED (Publisher): Schubert--21 of his Easiest Piano Selections.
BRIMHALL, John: My Favorite Classics, Level Two (Hansen).
BRIMHALL, John: Original Piano Masterworks, Levels 3 and 4 (Hansen).
CURTIS, Helen: Fundamental Piano Series, Book Four (Lyon & Healy).
CHRISTOPHER, John: Two Hundred Years of Piano Music, 112 Pieces (McAfee/Belwin-Mills DM245).
DANA, Walter: My Favorite Classics, Level Four (Hansen).
GEEHL, Henry: Schubert--Compositions of Moderate Difficulty (Ashdown).
HALFORD, Margery: Schubert--The First Book (Alfred).
HEINRICHSHOFEN/PETERS (Publisher): Schubert Easier Favorites (Urtext N.4051).
HUGHES, Edwin: Master Series--Schubert (G. Schirmer).

INTERNATIONAL LIBRARY OF PIANO MUSIC: Vol. IV (University Society).
KING-ORDEN, Esther: 100 Classics for Young Pianists (Shattinger-Hansen 0111).
NAHUM, WOLFE, KOSAKOFF: Piano Classic (J. Fischer/Belwin-Mills).
ROYAL CONSERVATORY OF MUSIC: Piano Examination Repertoire 8 (Frederick Harris 8078).
SCHIRMER (Publisher): 59 Solos You Like to Play.
VOLGER, Heinz: Schubert--Easiest Piano Pieces (Peters No. 5015).
WARNER (Publisher): Super Classics for Piano.
WILLS, Vera: The Yellow Book #2 (G. Schirmer 3446).

The delicate lilting spirit of this delightful piece has made it probably the most famous of this set. It is short and utilizes a single thematic idea throughout. The minor tonality and the rather hollow divided chord accompaniment produce a plaintive effect, but a change to parallel major in the ending bars provides a bright alteration of mood within the clearly defined character of the piece. This could be an excellent introductory etude for double thirds and sixths, and grace notes played on the beat. It could also be useful for study of structural logic and harmonic analysis of movement from minor to parallel major. Beyond being an excellent teaching piece, it would be an asset in any performance situation.

Tempo: Allegro Moderato
Length: 78 measures
Technique: ornamentation, divided chords, double 3rds and 6ths, jump bass

No. 4, C# Minor — Advancing Intermediate

AGAY, Denes: Easy Classics to Moderns, Vol. 17 (Consolidated).
ALFRED (Publisher): Schubert--21 of his Easiest Piano Selections.
ALFRED (Publisher): Schubert--17 of his Most Popular Selections.
GEEHL, Henry: Schubert--Compositions of Moderate Difficulty (Ashdown).

This fleeting, toccata-like piece is in ABA form, with the A sections featuring a perpetual motion effect in right hand sixteenth notes over left hand detached eighth notes. These sections are challenging, with patterns that alter slightly and melodic ideas dependent on sensitive control in tonal balance. The B section is a delightful contrast in mood, moving abruptly into Db Major, and building on a homophonic theme of sparkling vivacity. Schubert's markings accentuate the syncopated rhythm, and his soft dynamics produce a breathless quality of tremendous intensity. This could be a stunning piece for a performer with clean, crisp, technique.

Tempo: Moderato
Length: 179 measures
Technique: 16th note passage work, octaves, broken intervals and chords, staccato, vs. legato

No. 5, F Minor — Advancing Intermediate

AGAY, Denes: Early Advanced Classics to Moderns, Vol. 47 (Consolidated).
HALFORD, Margery: Schubert--The First Book (Alfred).

High spirited and tactilely exhilarating, this piece is a delight on its own merit and provides dramatic contrast within the set. It is rather short, with an attractive repetitive rhythmic motive that gives way to a light filigree theme of divided chords and intervals. There is wide dynamic range and varying articulations and accents, producing a performance vehicle for exaggerated, stylish playing.

Tempo: Allegro vivace
Length: 111 measures
Technique: quick repeated chords, octaves and octave chords, 8th note passage work

No. 6, Ab Major — Advancing Intermediate

ALFRED (Publisher): Schubert--17 of his Most Popular Selections.
SCHIRMER (Publisher): Schubert Dances for the Piano (Vol. 1537).

Ending the set quietly, this piece is a beautifully poetic study in tonal balance that will benefit from a sensitive performance. The homophonic structure, with exquisite subtleties of tied-over harmonic changes, allows shaping of the melodic phrase within the larger context of the piece itself. The trio contrasts in key by way of some interesting enharmonic movement, but retains the quiet, almost somber mood of the A sections. Schubert's gift for melody and creative sense of harmony are admirably demonstrated in this lovely piece.

Tempo: Allegretto
Length: 119 measures
Technique: sustained and moving notes, full chords

## SHORTER WORKS

Included in this section are the short pieces of Schubert that have either no ties with other forms (such as the Drei Klavierstucke) or whose groupings are small (such as the Scherzi). These pieces come from different periods of the composer's life, and share no particular commonalities in form, texture, or intent. The shorter forms seem especially well-suited to Schubert's quasi-improvisatory and intimate expressiveness.

Recent scholarship has resulted in changes of category for some pieces originally considered "shorter works" in the Brietkopf and Hartel scores. The "Five Pieces for Pianoforte," or "Funf Klavierstucke," are now designated as the Sonata in E Major, D. 459. The "Adagio" and "Rondo," Op. 145 (D. 505 and 506) are considered to be movements of sonatas D. 625 and D. 566 respectively. A work called "Piece for Pianoforte" in A Major (D. 604) is now placed as the third movement of the Sonata in F# Minor (D. 571). The Adagio in E Major (D. 612) is the second movement of the Sonata in E Major (D. 613). Reviews of these works will be found in the sonata or sonata fragment sections of this book.

**ALLEGRETTO,** C Minor, D. 915 Advancing Intermediate

AGAY, Denes: An Anthology, The Romantic Period, Vol. III (Yorktown).
ANTHONY, George Walter: Schubert to Shostakovich, Vol. 2 (Presser).
BANOWETZ, Joseph: The Pianist's Book of Classic Treasures (GWM/Kjos).
BISHOP, Stephen: Oxford Keyboard Classics--Schubert (Oxford).
EPSTEIN, Julius: Schubert--Shorter Works (Dover).
FERGUSON, Howard: A Keyboard Anthology, Second Series, Book IV (Belwin-Mills).
HALFORD, Margery: Schubert--An Introduction to his Piano Works (Alfred).
HUGHES, Edwin: Master Series--Schubert (G. Schirmer).
KALMUS (Publisher): Schubert--An Easy Album for Piano Solo (Belwin-Mills).
KALMUS (Publisher): Schubert--Impromptus, Moments Musicaux for Piano Solo (Belwin-Mills No. 3886).
KRAUSE, Annamaria: German Piano Music (Musica Budapest/Boosey & Hawkes Z12137).
ROWLEY, Alec: The Easiest Original Schubert (Hinrichsen No. 6/Peters).
SZAVAI and VESZPREME: Album for Piano, #2 (Belwin-Mills).

According to Kathleen Dale, this short work seems to be a "Moment Musical in everything but its title," and forms a charming link to those works of that name written in the same year, 1827. It is poetic in character and reflects the Schubertian idiom quite clearly. As with many of Schubert's significant ideas, the opening melody is presented in quiet unison between hands, outlining the tonic C Minor triad. The material within this 6/8 ABA form offers abrupt changes from minor to its relative or tonic major, unexpected interruptions by pungently discordant groups of notes, canonic imitations of thematic fragments, and wide variations in dynamic levels. The Ab Major B section is calm and "religioso," written in full chords that are slow-moving and harmonically exquisite. This composition represents a microcosm of what is most endearing in the works of this composer, and would be a beautiful performance choice.

Tempo: Allegretto
Length: 160 measures
Technique: 8th note passage work, double 3rds, sustained and moving notes, important rests and accents, octave chords, pp-ff

ANDANTE, D. 29, C Major — Early Intermediate

EPSTEIN, Julius: Schubert--Shorter Works (Dover).
FERGUSON, Howard: A Keyboard Anthology, First Series, Book IV (Belwin-Mills).
HALFORD, Margery: Schubert--The First Book (Alfred).
HUGHES, Edwin: Master Series--Schubert (G. Schirmer).
KALMUS PIANO SERIES: Schubert--An Easy Album for Piano Solos (Belwin-Mills).

This lovely, unassuming piece, written in 1812, uses the same thematic material as the first movement of a string quartet listed by Deutsch as D. 3; the quartet has been lost, but the four voice structure of the piano version would tend to support the composer's original intentions.

Structured in a loosely-organized ABA form, this piece offers a tantalizing glimpse into Schubert's developing style of composition. The main thematic idea is presented briefly in an opening statement, treated in wildly diverse position changes in the closing measures of the B section, and developed to the greatest degree in the extended recapitulation. The composer's attention is drawn to other thematic fragments within this short composition, and he deals with them at will, in an almost intuitive fashion, defying the logic of his classical predecessors. The performer is drawn to these arresting tidbits through their compositional accentuation, as if Schubert were pointing out minute details that might otherwise be ignored.

In describing this work, the noted Schubert authority Kathleen Dale says, "there may be seen an already remarkable power of moulding the formal structure of a short piece to enhance the unity of style in the pianoforte writing."

Tempo: Andante
Length: 63 measures
Technique: octaves and octave chords, broken chords, dotted rhythms, sustained and moving notes

**FANTASY,** C Minor, D. 993 <u>Advanced</u>
(Largo for Harpsichord)

DEMUS, Jorg: Franz Schubert--Fantasy (Largo) D. 993 (Presser).

Published for the first time in 1980 by Theodore Presser, this early work by Schubert was found as a manuscript in the private collection of Consul Otto Tausig of Malmo, Sweden. The visiting pianist, Jorg Demus, recognized its value and was instrumental in bringing it to the public; other pianists had played it and considered it insignificant. It was introduced prior to publication, with an accompanying article, by the <u>Piano Quarterly</u>, Winter 1978-79/Number 4.

The manuscript bears the title "Largo for Clavicembalo"; the title "Fantasy" has been supplied by the editor, recognizing the influence of Mozart's Fantasy, K. 475. The works share the Largo, Andantino Largo form (although Schubert inserts a brief Allegro), the common key of C Minor, and stylistic similarities that are undeniable. Schubert expresses his own individuality in the use of uneven phrase lengths, asymmetric blocks of rhythmic subdivision, and the romantically inclined third-relationships in tonal alteration.

Length: 92 measures
Technique: complex rhythmic subdivision, tremolandos, ornamentation, 16th and 32nd scalar and arpeggiated patterns, broken chords, sustained and moving notes

**MARCH,** E Major, D. 606 Advancing Intermediate

EPSTEIN, Julius: Schubert--Shorter Works (Dover).
KALMUS PIANO SERIES: Schubert (Belwin-Mills 3886).

This sturdy, vigorous march suffers from a paucity of thematic material, making it unsatisfying despite Schubert's daring harmonic alterations in sequential treatment. The trio is lighter and more frivolous in character, with a clever inter-voice tune built in trill-like half steps. As in the march, the first section presents the melodic statement and the second section develops it through sequential manipulation.

Tempo: Allegro con brio
Length: 84 measures
Technique: octaves and octave chords, melody and accompaniment in same hand, clef changes, widely contrasting dynamics, sustained and moving notes

## **SCHERZOS**, D. 593, Op. Post.

Note: All of D. 593 can be found in:

EPSTEIN, Julius: Schubert--Shorter Works (Dover).
HALFORD, Margery: Schubert--An Introduction to his Piano Works (Alfred).
HEINRICHSHOFEN/PETERS (Publisher): Schubert--Easier Favorites (Urtext No. 4051).
KALMUS (Publisher): Schubert--Impromptus, Moments Musicaux for Piano Solo (Belwin-Mills No. 3886).

No. 1, Bb Major — <u>Early Advanced</u>

AGAY, Denes: Easy Classics to Moderns, Vol. 17 (Consolidated).
ALFRED (Publisher): Schubert--17 of his Most Popular Piano Selections.
BASTIEN, James: Piano Literature, Book 4 (GWM/Kjos).
BERINGER, Oscar: Beringer's School of Easy Classics--Schubert (Galaxy).
CURTIS, Helen: Fundamental Piano Series, Book 5 (Lyon-Healy).
ECKSTEIN, Maxwell: Sonatina Album (C. Fischer L509).
FERGUSON, Howard: A Keyboard Anthology, Second Series, Book III (Belwin-Mills).

GEEHL, Henry: Schubert--Compositions of Moderate Difficulty (Ashdown).
GEORGII, Walter: Leichte Klaviermusik, Band I (G. Henle).
HUGHES, Edwin: Master Series--Schubert (G. Schirmer).
INTERNATIONAL LIBRARY OF PIANO MUSIC, Vol. IV (University Society).
KALMUS (Publisher): Schubert--An Easy Album for Piano Solo (Belwin-Mills).
PETERS (Publisher): Sonatinen Album (#1233A).
ROWLEY, Alec: The Easiest Original Schubert (Hinrichsen No. 6/Peters).
SCHIRMER (Publisher): Schubert Dances (Vol. 1537).
SHEALY, Alexander: Schubert--his greatest Piano Solos (Ashley).
THOMPSON, John: Modern Course for Piano, Book 6 (Willis).
WEYBRIGHT, June: Course for Pianists, Book 6 (American Academy).

This well-known scherzo is delightful in a kind of "tongue-in-cheek" manner. It embodies the grace and elegance of the dance within classical formal parameters. Though the repetition is endless, it is advantageous for learning purposes. The rhythmic divisions of beat might prove hazardous to the uninitiated. The student quickly learns the first lilting triplet figure and has difficulty from then on keeping an even pulse. Tasteful use of rubato and dynamic contrast will add to the charm of this harmonically creative scherzo. The trio provides a complete contrast in its quiet sustained and moving notes and running left hand eighth note passages.

Tempo: Allegretto
Length: 130 measures
Technique: ornamentation, scalar patterns, arpeggios, sustained and moving notes, jump bass, 8th note passage work, full chords

No. 2, Db Major — Early Advanced

Beautiful and occasionally surprising harmonies are the most arresting feature of this work. The tempo should be chosen with measure 51 as the criteria or disaster will ensue. The key changes (from Db Major to E Major and Ab) in the trio render the reading process challenging, but they are logical. The trio is characterized by a lovely melody in a persistent dotted figure. The entire work is simplistic in style yet quite elegant. Frequent repetitions help in the learning. In contrast to the excessively familiar Scherzo No. 1, this piece is relatively unknown and would provide a welcome addition to performance literature.

Tempo: Allegro moderato
Length: 146 measures
Technique: arpeggios, staccato and parallel scales, ornamentation, sustained and moving notes, 8th note passage work

These two scherzi are amusing excursions for the performer. The second is the more difficult, with fleeting passage work in each hand. Both have delightful contrasts in thematic material, and will be effective for public performance.

**THREE PIANO PIECES,** D. 946, "Drei Klavierstucke" — Early Advanced

All of D. 946 may be found in:

EPSTEIN, Julius: Schubert--Shorter Works (Dover).

No. 1, Eb Minor

Labelling the form of this piece is difficult. Dale describes it as "either a scherzo with two trios, or a rondo in which the episodes are more independent than usual in the older rondo form." It seems most logical to consider it a broad tripartite composition, with the last section an exact duplicate of the opening portion.

The primary theme is a single line melody, often doubled at the octave. Triplet broken chords accompany, but gain importance as the music develops, becoming the dominant feature as the secondary theme appears. A third idea is interspersed, juxtaposing the triple against duple rhythms, producing a taut building of tension to the dramatic climax. The section ends with an abrupt series of soft detached chords that serve as a bridge to the new key and mood of the Andante. The contrasts are marked by the tonality change to B Major, the richer voicing in both melody and accompaniment, and the improvisational nature of the haunting song-like theme. An enharmonic modulation of octave chords leads back to the repeat of the A section.

Tempo: Allegro Assai
Length: 278 measures
Technique: octaves and octave chords, broken chords, 2 vs. 3, scalar patterns, ornamentation, important rests and accents

No. 2, Eb Major

Although similar in structure to the first piece, this movement reverses the dramatic content with pensive, thoughtful material interrupted by an energetic section altered in both key and meter. It opens with a pastoral folk song in 6/8, harmonized in thirds, with an eighth note accompaniment. The secondary idea provides new intensity, with murmuring thirds and tremolo effects that ebb and flow in widely contrasting dynamic levels, like a violent thunderstorm that tortures the countryside and then rumbles away in the distance. The sunshine returns with the folk song, ending in quiet chords that bridge to the Listesso section, written in Ab Minor with a 2/2 time signature. This portion of the work is inordinately long, with awkward broken chords that contain a melody within the repetitious wanderings of altering modality and tonality. A reprise of the Eb Major folk song provides a happy ending to the drama.

Tempo: Allegretto
Length: 236 measures
Technique: octaves and octave chords, 3rds, tremolo intervals, scalar and chromatic patterns, changing clefs, sustained and moving notes

No. 3, C Major

Somewhat less complex than the two preceding pieces, this cheerful work retains the same tripartite form, with beginning and ending sections exactly alike. An ending coda provides a dramatic finish to the set as a whole. Piquant syncopations within the opening octave melody set a robust mood that develops in intensity to a brilliant chordal cadence. A whisper soft Neopolitan modulation to the key of Db Major introduces the B section which is typically Schubertian. The infectious dance gambols through innovative modulations in a tip-toeing manner, with occasional bursts of forte chords. The reprise of the A section is approached through a chromatic shift to the original key of C Major. The coda dazzles with bravura technical effects, ending with the syncopated chords of the A section cadence.

Tempo: Allegro
Length: 251 measures
Technique: octaves and octave chords, ties over bar lines, important rests and accents, changing clefs, scalar patterns

The "Drei Klavierstucke" were composed in 1828, but appeared in print for the first time in 1868, anonymously edited by Brahms. These compositions, like the Impromptus, are lyrical works, displaying moods that may change abruptly from thoughtful pensiveness to dramatic bombast. The Schubertian authority Kathleen Dale proposes that these pieces may have been the nucleus of a third set of Impromptus, being similar in style and nature, with "distinct originality of formal structure making them historically valuable." According to a Schubert biographer M.J.E. Brown, they represent the "first departure by a major composer from the dominance of the sonata over piano forms."

**TEN VARIATIONS ON AN ORIGINAL THEME,** F Major, D. 156 Advanced

EPSTEIN, Julius: Schubert--Shorter Works (Dover).

The theme for this enticing set of variations reveals Schubert's penchant for creating exquisite melody. His thematic idea is presented quietly, with delicate dynamic nuances that call for careful tonal balance and expressive phrasing between the song-like tune and its simple three-voice accompaniment.

Variations 1 through 7 are typical fare, reminiscent of Mozart or Beethoven in basic idea, but bearing the mark of Schubert's personal style of composition. The first retains the mood of the theme, with the subdued melody spinning out over murmuring triplets within the inner voices. Ensuing variations offer wide contrasts in mood. Numbers two, three, and six are technically demanding, while one, four, and five call for expressive sensitivity. The delicate scherzando of the seventh variation is a delight.

The vigorous dotted rhythms of number eight lead into structural alterations that characterize the final variations, which are freer, more daring, and connected together in a climactic sweep to the end. Cadenza-like bars of unmeasured filigree patterns bridge variations eight to nine, and ten to the ending coda. Variation nine is a lovely improvisation with sensual romantic effects. The lilting dance quality of number ten, composed in 3/8, offers immediate contrast in tempo and mood. It builds in intensity to a final fermata, giving way to a quiet whirlwind of freely interpreted passage work. The coda is a brilliantly conceived microcosm of the entire set of variations, moving through a short presto, adagio, and tempo 1 to the final virtuosic presto ending.

Tempo: (Thema) Andante
Length: 365 measures
Technique: sustained and moving notes, broken chords, arpeggios and scales, ornamentation

**VARIATIONS ON A THEME BY ANSELM HUTTENBRENNER,** A Minor, D. 576 Early Advanced

EPSTEIN, Julius: Schubert--Shorter Works (Dover).
HALFORD, Margery: Schubert--An Introduction to his Piano Works (Alfred).

A thoughtful economy of material and restraint in development characterizes this theme and thirteen variations. The initial sixteen measure statement is a quiet and introspective trio, with every voice gaining importance in the variations to come. Each part seems to capture Schubert's imagination and he deals with them in a curiously inconsistent fashion, juxtaposing and intertwining, but always pointing out their beauty through innovative treatment.

The composition of the variations is unsurprising, most often structured in a homophonic thematic treatment which retains the rhythmic simplicity of the initial statement, while pairing it with rippling patterns of sixteenth notes. Variations five, six, nine, and thirteen appear in the tonic major, through key signature alteration. Dramatic intensity is apparently not the composer's intent, as he breaks the building momemtum of effect in variations six and eleven with a return to the serenity of the original theme. These brief gems reveal Schubert's genius in melodic and harmonic manipulation within the basic rhythmic framework. Variation thirteen is a fitting finale to the set, being graceful and good-humored rather than dazzling in brilliance. It is a quick, dance-like movement in 3/8 time, characterized by abrupt changes in modality and dynamic levels.

This set of variations is sadly neglected, probably because of exclusion from collections of piano literature. Its relatively short length, its moderate technical demands, and above all, its sheer loveliness should make it a composition heard more often.

Tempo: Andantino
Length: 305 measures
Technique: octaves and octave chords, 16th and 32nd note passage work, changing clefs, sustained and moving notes, melody and accompaniment in same hand

**VARIATIONS ON A WALTZ BY DIABELLI,** C Minor, D. 718 — Advancing Intermediate

BISHOP, Stephen: Oxford Keyboard Classics--Schubert (Oxford).
EPSTEIN, Julius: Schubert--Shorter Works (Dover).
ZEITLIN and GOLDBERGER: The Solo Book IV (Consolidated).

This short work owes its existence to a contest sponsored by Anton Diabelli, publisher and minor composer, who drafted the initial theme. According to Kathleen Dale, Schubert "changes its strident major into a wistful minor, and by endowing it with a graceful melodic curve and a number of iridescent harmonies, transforms it into a waltz so tenderly ethereal that even an angel might dance to it." Other contributors to the contest were Czerny, Moscheles, Weber, Hummel, and the ten-year-old Liszt. Beethoven received the contest piece, and although he considered it a "cobblers patch," he used it for an incomparable set of 35 variations, finished two years after the competition deadline.

The phrasing and the tied suspensions in this piece allow for sensitive interpretation. A few peculiar measures feature reaches of a tenth in the right hand which must retain the tied inner voices. This challenge might be solved by a rolled left hand chord which includes the lower right hand note. Performance of these variations would be worthwhile.

Tempo: Zeitlin and Goldberger - Moderato
Length: 64 measures
Technique: waltz bass, sustained and moving notes, ties over bar lines

## SONATAS

Most published volumes of the Schubert sonatas contain the eleven works based on the Brietkopf and Hartel editions of 1897. The G. Henle edition, used as the source for this book, contains newly edited printings of the eleven sonatas in the first two volumes, with the unfinished or altered works in volume three. In the third volume there are two complete sonatas, D. 459 and D. 566, which we have chosen to review in this chapter, with explanations included.

The sonatas of Schubert provide an insightful record of his musical growth from the early days of his career to its very end. Only three were published in his lifetime. None of the sonatas received their deserved attention until nearly one hundred years after his death. Franz Liszt admired them but never included any in his concert repertoire. They were similarly neglected by Anton Rubenstein, d'Albert, Busoni, Padarewski, Sauer, and Godowsky; these famous pianists apparently did not trust the effectiveness of these works with the public.

The Schubert Sonatas lack the motivic construction of the Beethoven works of this genre. Instead, they reflect his sensitive nature in lyrical, personal terms. Melody furnished the initial impulse; development is often achieved by making subordinate material important through tonally adventurous modulations. The early sonatas reflect a certain immaturity, but they become increasingly more unified in thought and more profound in intensity, culminating in their highest point of perfection in D. 958, D. 959, and D. 960, composed in his last year.

The Schubertian authority, Kathleen Dale, has listed some innovations within the sonata style that reflect Schubert's originality. They are:

1. Varied treatment of the rondo form.
2. Invention of a new type of movement for a finale.
3. Transformation of the slow movement into a poem of sound.

4. Approach to the recapitulation through subtle and unexpected means.
5. Restatement of the opening phrase of the movement during its very last bars.
6. Unusual but logical choice of keys for various sonata movements.
7. Contrast between styles of sonata movements or even successive sonatas.[1]

**SONATA,** E Major, D. 459 <u>Advanced</u>

BADURA-SKODA, Paul: Schubert Klaviersonaten Band III (G. Henle Verlag 150).

**Allegro moderato**

Classical in form and conception, this allegro reveals its romantic tendencies only in its adventurous harmonic modulations. The themes are simple, textures are open, and thematic development is predictable. The single line melodies are accompanied by chords that evolve into inner voice moving lines or Alberti patterns.

The development section is brief and builds upon the movement's principal theme, accompanied by repeated pedal points in various voices within the chordal construction. The recapitulation has a thematic restatment of the first subject in A Major and the second in the tonic E Major.

Length: 124 measures
Technique: 16th note scalar patterns, sustained and moving notes, ornamentation, Alberti patterns, octaves and octave chords

## Scherzo

The subdued theme of this sonata/allegro scherzo opens with a unison melody that broadens into four voice counterpoint. The uneven phrase lengths produce a delightful tension within the melodic idea. This melody is repeated in octaves, paired with a murmuring broken chord inner voice over sustained bass pedal points. A secondary theme sings out in the bass register, with the pedal points providing the same sustaining support. The right hand has challenging broken octaves, phrased in opposing patterns.

A brief development follows, based on a new phrase motif characterized by syncopated movement within the four voices. Innovative pairings of voices are joined in delightful interwoven patterns. A straightforward recapitulation ends the movement.

Tempo: Allegro
Length: 237 measures
Technique: sustained and moving notes, octaves and octave chords, 8th note scalar patterns and passage work, broken chords and octaves

## Adagio (C Major)

This adagio in 3/8 time is built on a lovely wistful song in C Major. The simplicity of its opening statement quickly gives way to ornamented embellishment within the melodic line that becomes more complex as the movement develops. A secondary idea of a more florid nature receives similar developmental treatment. Rhythmic patterns create some confusion in this movement, with triplets and patterns of three sixteenth notes confusingly interspersed.

Length: 114 measures

Technique: complex rhythmic subdivision, broken chords and octaves, sustained and moving notes, ornamentation, chromatic and arpeggiated patterns

**Scherzo con trio** (A Major/D Major)

This is the second scherzo within this sonata, but this A Major effort is in the expected form, complete with trio. The sprightly theme in 3/4 takes an arpeggiated figure, often in unison, as its unifying motive. Hemiola effects, achieved by phrasing, produce a lilting, off-beat result that is attractive, with harmonic suspensions and uneven phrases adding additional elan. The D Major trio builds around a contracted broken chord, with the unison treatment evolving into a conversational sparring between the hands. Its subdued dynamics and sustained quality contrast effectively with the more vigorous scherzo.

Tempo: Allegro

Length: 83 measures

Technique: arpeggiated patterns, octave chords, changing clefs, sustained and moving notes

**Allegro patetico**

This finale will challenge with its variety of technical effects, giving the performer a chance to dazzle with whirlwind flurries of sound. It is musically shallow and will cloy quickly.

Length: 105 measures

Technique: complex rhythmic subdivision, broken chords, 2-note phrases, double 6ths, octaves, chromatic figures, arpeggios, hand-crosses

Known in earlier Schubert editions as "Funf Klavierstucke" or "Five Piano Pieces," recent scholarship has titled this group as a sonata. The unusual inclusion of two scherzo movements is puzzling; whether Schubert intended to retain both in the finished score may never be known, since there are incomplete autographs. The complete work comes from a first edition published by C.A. Klemm in 1843. There is conflicting information about this sonata, so the confusion as to its background remains.

**SONATA,** A Minor, D. 537 (Op. Post. 164) — Early Advanced

BUONAMICI, G: Schubert--Ten Sonatas for Piano (G. Schirmer).

KALMUS PIANO SERIES: Franz Schubert--Sonatas for Piano, Part II.

MIES, Paul: Schubert--Klaviersonaten, Band I (G. Henle Verlag 146).

PETERS (Publisher): Schubert Sonaten, Band II (No. 488).

**Allegro, ma non troppo**

This movement clearly reveals Schubert's struggle to make the sonata/allegro form a vehicle of personal expression. A major difference in his approach is recognized by Kathleen Dale, who says "Schubert makes so much of both subjects in the exposition that they are almost disqualified from appearing in the necessarily shortened development and are consequently replaced by an episode in the remote key of Ab." This "Neopolitan" key alteration, appearing with total abruptness, is a favorite device in Schubert's harmonic bag of tricks. Another is his penchant for beginning the recapitulation in the sub-dominant. This tonality change is the only alteration in an otherwise exact repetition of the exposition. The addition of a coda-like restatement of the opening theme brings the movement to a close.

There are thematic motives that serve to unify the loosely organized material of this 6/8 movement. The quarter/eighth rhythm introduced in the principal theme appears throughout, with brief reversals of the pattern in both the exposition and the recapitulation. The broken triad in unison between the hands is periodically expanded and altered rhythmically. The somber eighth note pedal points return again and again. With these threads interwoven into the varying thematic ideas, the performer may sense the overall design of the movement and meld each lovely section into an integrated whole.

Length: 199 measures
Technique: octaves and octave chords,
sustained and moving notes, changing clefs,
repeated notes, 16th note passage work

**Allegretto quasi Andantino** (E Major)

The rondo form of this slow movement offers an excellent medium for Schubert's melodic genius. Each section displays a transparent beauty. As a whole, it is a composition of unsophisticated but enchanting loveliness. The initial idea opens in E Major. Ensuing harmonic changes offer tonal relationships that seem far-fetched, but gain their own logic under the composer's skilled hands.

The simplicity in thematic presentation masks some unexpected difficulties for the performer. The song-like melodies of the A and C sections are voiced in octaves, calling for smooth legato playing and dynamic shaping of phrases. The accompanying patterns offer the most hazards, especially in the A section broken chords, where wide leaps test the pianist's accuracy and dynamic control. The filigreed sixteenth notes of the B section offer welcome relief, although they present additional challenges in tonal balance. Expressive ability will be necessary in this movement, but the satisfaction of achievement will be enormous.

Length: 146 measures
Technique: octaves, jump bass, broken chords and arpeggios, 2-note slurs, sustained and moving notes, changing clefs

**Allegro vivace**

In describing this movement, Kathleen Dale observes that it is "designed in a dual form altogether new to the sonatas." The first half starts in the tonic minor and closes in the tonic major. The coda simulates a recapitulation but reverses the key pattern.

The music is quick and vivacious, with mercurial mood changes of child-like intensity. A feeling of imbalance is produced by uneven phrase lengths, abrupt dynamic changes, dramatic measure rests, and a constant shift of modality and tonality. The opening scalar statement with rhythmic variation in every measure sets the pace for the entire movement. The good humor and "joie de vivre" apparent in every new idea are irresistible.

Length: 367 measures

Technique: 16th note scalar patterns and passage work, sustained and moving notes, abrupt dynamic changes (ppp-ff), key signature changes, clef changes, repeated chords, 2-note phrases

This sonata was written in 1817 and published posthumously about 1852. Statements from three authoritative writers on Schubert give some insight into the work. M.J.E. Brown calls it "timid in development and ornamentation." Ferguson states that "by the time he was twenty, Schubert had found has own way of dealing with larger instrumental forms and ,with this sonata. his individual genius has already appeared." Dale concurs, saying that "each of the three movements is different in construction from any of his previous works." She describes it as "restrained and beautiful," and shows the composer's "striving to overcome the restrictions of traditional form."

Beyond the formal understanding of this work, the performer will find music of delightful accessibility, with its own inner logic in intensity and development. The sonata is neither inordinately long nor difficult. The twists and turns of thematic presentation provide appealing discoveries on every page.

**SONATA**, E Minor, D. 566 <u>Advanced</u>

BADURA-SKODA, Paul: Schubert Klaviersonaten, Band III (G. Henle Verlag 150).

**Moderato**

This sonata/allegro movement has appealing themes and moments of real beauty, but is marred by ineffective development and unwieldy repetitions. It reveals much of what Schubert was to become, but the immaturity is apparent and is of questionable musical value.

Length: 97 measures
Technique: octaves and octave chords, sustained and moving notes, broken chords and intervals, scalar and arpeggiated patterns, ornamentation

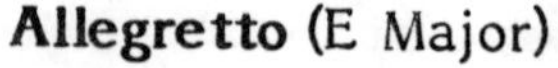

**Allegretto** (E Major)

The classical orientation of this slow movement is attractive, but it shares the uneven inspiration of the first movement. Its moments of beauty are not frequent enough to sustain interest throughout the repetitious material.

Length: 227 measures
Technique: melody and accompaniment in the same hand, 16th note passage work, broken chords and octaves, 2 vs. 3, ornamentation

**Scherzo** (Ab Major)

This Ab Major scherzo and trio is the most appealing of the movements in the sonata. Its playful ebullience is heightened by abrupt contrasts between the sharp, percussive chords and lilting conversational phrases. The Db Major trio opens with a simple tune accompanied by murmuring eighth notes. The second section has short, conversational moments before returning to the original material.

Tempo: Allegro vivace
Length: 153 measures
Technique: octaves and octave chords, sustained and moving notes, arpeggiated patterns, changing clefs, 8th notes passagework

**Rondo,** E Major, D. 605 (Op. 145, No. 2)

This challenging rondo shares the uneven quality of preceding movements, with moments of fun followed by long periods of redundancy. There are some innovative modulations, enhanced by wide dynamic contrasts, driving rhythms, and irregular phrase lengths.

Tempo: Allegretto
Length: 290 measures
Technique: sustained and moving notes, ornamentation, arpeggios, octaves, large chords, wide leaps

This sonata has an extraordinary history of publication. Each movement was published separately at widely divergent times; they were not combined into one work until 1948, in an edition prepared by Kathleen Dale. Autographs exist only of the first movement and trio; the second movement and scherzo come to us only in copy form. The Rondo finale was originally published as Op. 145, No. 2 (D. 506). It was paired with a greatly abbreviated version of the Adagio from the incomplete Sonata in F Minor, D. 625.

**SONATA,** Eb Major, D. 568 (Op. 122) <u>Early Advanced</u>

BUONAMICI, G: Schubert--Ten Sonatas for Piano (G. Schirmer).
KALMUS PIANO SERIES: Franz Schubert--Sonatas for Piano, Part II.
MIES, Paul: Schubert--Klaviersonaten, Band I (G. Henle Verlag 146).
PETERS (Publisher): Schubert Sonaten, Band II (No. 488).

**Allegro moderato**

Although the composer follows traditional sonata/allegro form in the key choices of the thematic subjects, he yields to a developing idiosyncrasy in the elongation of the secondary theme in the exposition. The ensuing development section is shortened, perhaps to balance the length of the movement.

The primary theme opens with a unison second inversion triad, followed by a chordal section. The triad motif appears later over an Alberti-like broken chord accompaniment. The secondary theme is a graceful dance tune accompanied by light, detached chords. The lengthy treatment of this idea includes its statement in both hands, with differing accompanying figures including the Alberti pattern introduced earlier. The exposition ends in flurries of quiet notes, with restatements of the triad motif in each hand.

The brief development consists of a sixteenth note arpeggiated figure opposed by repeated chords. Its sequential treatment involves numerous position changes and shifts between hands. The transition into the recapitulation is startling, with a thematic restatement of fascinating variation. The primary theme is somewhat shortened, but the secondary theme spins out to the same whispering, understated conclusion.

Length: 259 measures
Technique: 16th note scalar and arpeggiated patterns, broken chords, ornamentation, sustained and moving notes, hand-crosses, changing clefs, octaves

**Andante molto** (G Minor)

The theme of this slow movement could belong to Haydn or Mozart, but its ensuing treatment reveals the maturing genius of Schubert. The simplicity of the thematic ideas, paired with rather thick harmonic underpinnings, offers opportunity for thoughtful, expressive interpretation. The straightforward eighth and sixteenth note treatment of the initial material is altered dramatically by the introduction of a sharply dotted note melody, accompanied by repeated chords, scored in six subdivisions per beat. The juxtaposition of rhythmic values is an intriguing study for the performer. The return of the primary theme, contrasted with the sextuplet rhythm in the inner voices, heightens the complexity of development. A restatement of the secondary idea leads into a brief coda-like return to the transparent classical quality of the beginning.

Length: 122 measures

Technique: complex rhythmic subdivision, octaves and octave chords, sustained and moving notes, important rests and accents, changing clefs

**Menuetto** (C Minor)

BERINGER, Oscar: Beringer's School of Easy Classics--Schubert (Galaxy).

Graceful elegance characterizes this minuet and trio, recalling the classical roots of the form, but with the longer phrases of developing romanticism. The homophonic writing is crystalline in its simplicity, allowing the pianist to relax after the complex demands of the preceding movement. Schubert offers a few harmonic surprises, especially in the final line of the minuet, jolting performer and listener alike out of euphoric tonal complacency.

Tempo: Allegretto

Length: 66 measures

Technique: dotted rhythms, sustained and moving notes, changing clefs

**Allegro moderato**

This dance-like movement in 6/8 offers numerous complexities in form and construction. Somewhat reminiscent of a Viennese waltz, short sections of loosely-related material are strung together like beads on a necklace. The composition of these brief segments displays an instrumental quality, with multiple voices intertwining in finger-tripping patterns. The sequential treatment of the thematic ideas allows Schubert to indulge in rather exotic tonal modulations. These fascinating twists and turns prevent a total redundancy in material that displays a disturbing "sameness" of sound.

> Length: 223 measures
>
> Technique: 16th note passage work, sustained and moving notes, melody and accompaniment in same hand, clef changes, important rests and accents, ornamentation, wide dynamic range (ff-ppp)

This appealing sonata was written in 1817 and published in 1829, one year after the composer's death. It was originally in the key of Db, but Schubert transposed it to Eb, probably to meet the wishes of the publisher. According to Kathleen Dale, "the original key of Db made possible the writing of the slow movement in the enharmonic tonic minor (C#), a key more effective for the purpose than the higher G Minor of the Eb version. The minuet and trio were not included in the original Db scheme, but Schubert added them to the Eb version, borrowing the trio from the Scherzo in Db (D.593)."

The influence of the Viennese dance form is readily apparent in this sonata, giving it a nationalistic flavor of cheerful ebullience. Its nature seems to call for a happy, unsophisticated approach.

**SONATA,** B Major, D. 575, Op.147 <u>Advanced</u>

BUONAMICI, G: Schubert--Ten Sonatas for Piano (G. Schirmer).
KALMUS PIANO SERIES: Franz Schubert--Sonatas for Piano, Part I.
MIES, Paul: Schubert--Klaviesonaten, Band I (G. Henle Verlag 146).
PETERS (Publisher): Schubert Sonaten, Band I (No. 487).

**Allegro, ma non troppo**

A fanfare on the tonic triad leads into the introductory bars of this movement. The dotted eighth/sixteenth note rhythm predominates, but abrupt changes in dynamic levels and tonal centers produce an intensely dramatic effect. The whisper-soft ending of the introduction on a D seventh chord ushers in the haunting G Major theme, which is quiet but tension-filled with the pull of dissonant passing tones. An inventive modulation to E Major leads into a brief, dance-like bridge, utilizing the dotted rhythms of the introduction. The song-like secondary theme in F# Minor is carried in the left hand, accompanied by rippling sixteenth note broken chords and a countermelody in the right hand.

The development opens with a restatement of the fanfare. The short dotted note pattern becomes the motif, and its dramatic effect is intensified by sharpened rhythms (double-dotted eighth and thirty-second notes), widened interval leaps, and shifting tonal centers. Hand-crosses and unexpected dynamic changes offer considerable challenge to the performer. Another short bridging section leads to the recapitulation. The fanfare introduction appears in E Major, the primary theme in C Major, and the secondary theme in B Major.

Length: 146 measures

Technique: octaves and octave chords, broken chords, sustained and moving notes, double-dotted notes, 16th note passage work

**Andante** (E Major)

The vigorous martial air, implied by detached chords, dotted patterns, and dramatic rests, contrasts this movement effectively within the sonata as a whole. The homophonic theme and a secondary idea, built around sixteenth notes tossed conversationally between hands, are interwoven to produce a complex tapestry of pianistic effect. A brief section of brilliant left hand octaves offers the performer a virtuosic opportunity.

Length: 82 measures

Technique: octaves and octave chords, rolled and repeated chords, 16th note passage work, sustained and moving notes, double-dotted notes

**Scherzo** (G Major)

The unassuming unison theme of this scherzo evolves into clever cascades of short phrases, scored in multiple voices and tossed to and fro between the hands. The trio smooths out into longer phrases, accompanied by murmuring eighth notes in constant motion. The abrupt dynamic changes dramatically intensify the phrases in this movement, but the overall soft dynamics produce a roguish, tongue-in-cheek effect that is tremendously appealing.

Tempo: Allegretto
Length: 111 measures
Technique: sustained and moving notes, 3rds, 6ths, and octaves, 8th note passage work

**Allegro giusto**

Joyous good humor bubbles out of every measure of this final movement in 3/8. It is playful, vivacious, and full of unexpected effects, achieved by uneven phrase lengths, surprising tonal alterations, and abrupt dynamic changes. Innovative manipulation of the sequential phrases causes most of the twists and turns of tonality. Sudden rests frequently interrupt the musical ideas. The effect is like a wild abandoned game of tag, with total fun for everyone.

Length: 316 measures
Technique: octaves and octave chords, wide interval leaps, sustained and moving notes

According to Paul Mies, editor of the G. Henle Verlag edition of the Schubert sonatas, the composer sketched out this sonata in 1817 and probably abandoned it. This early version differs greatly from the first published edition of 1844. The radical alterations suggest that Schubert himself wrote a later version which was the source of the posthumous first edition.

This exceptional sonata is unjustly neglected. It expresses a youthful exuberance and gaiety that will appeal to both performer and audience.

**SONATA,** A Major, D. 664 (Op. 120) Advanced

BUONAMICI, G: Schubert--Ten Sonatas for Piano (G. Schirmer).
KALMUS PIANO SERIES: Franz Schubert--Sonatas for Piano, Part I.
MIES, Paul: Schubert--Klaviersonaten, Band I (G. Henle Verlag 146).
PETERS (Publisher): Schubert Sonaten, Band I (No. 487).

**Allegro moderato**

Unlike Schubert's earlier efforts in the sonata/allegro genre, there is no experimentation with form in the first movement of this sonata. Its construction is compact and concise, making it an easily assimilated work of enchanting loveliness. Although totally pianistic, its lyrical character is undeniable. The principal theme is carried in the right hand, with a haunting single-line melody over sustaining chords and subdued left hand broken triad eighth notes. The compelling secondary theme, stated in both hands, gains in complexity with its scoring in eighths and triplet eighths against rippling triplet broken chords.

The development section deals briefly with the principal theme, and moves into challenging triplet octave scales, catapulted between the hands and offering the only forte dynamics in the composition. A straightforward recapitulation presents both subjects in the tonic, and ends with a brief coda-like restatement of the principal theme. The quiet serenity of this music is beautifully winsome, and a wonderful study in expressive nuance.

Length: 133 measures
Technique: octaves and octave chords, 8th note scalar and arpeggiated patterns, broken chords, sustained and moving notes, wide dynamic range (f-pp)

**Andante** (D Major)

This Andante offers little contrast in mood to the Allegro moderato, but its beauty is inspirational. The homophonic theme is expressed in the simplest rhythmic terms, with a tension inherent in the harmonic suspensions within the chordal structure. The form of this movement is built around varying treatments of this simple melodic idea, including a single-line statement over broken chords, conversational whisperings between hands, and intensity-building triplet rhythms. The expression of this unassuming melody in such creative ways surely reveals Schubert's genius.

Length: 75 measures
Technique: repeated chords, melody and accompaniment in same hand, broken chords, sustained and moving notes, octaves and 9th chords

**Allegro**

Refreshing tunes and buoyant rhythms, interspersed with bursts of virtuosic passagework, form the basis of contrast in this dance-like movement in A Major. The performer is challenged by widely leaping chords, abrupt dynamic changes, and fast scales and arpeggios in each hand and in unison. The drive of the 6/8 meter and unexpected effects of uneven phrase lengths add zesty exuberance to this finale.

Length: 216 measures
Technique: 16th note scales, arpeggios and passage work, octaves, wide leaps, sustained and moving notes, ornamentation, important rests and dynamics

This is one of the most frequently performed of Schubert's sonatas, probably because of its poetic expressiveness and its compact, concise economy of thematic treatment. It was written in 1819 and published in 1829. M.J.E. Brown calls it a "short, sparkling graceful work." Kathleen Dale says it is "enchanting, summing up the most attractive features of Schubert's youthful production, while at the same time promising the splendors of his later works."

**SONATA**, A Minor, D. 784 (Op. Post. 143) <u>Difficult</u>

BUONAMICI, G: Schubert--Ten Sonatas for Piano (G. Schirmer).
KALMUS PIANO SERIES: Franz Schubert--Sonatas for Piano, Part I.
MIES, Paul: Schubert--Klaviersonaten, Band I (G. Henle Verlag 146).
PETERS (Publisher): Schubert Sonaten, Band I (No. 487)

**Allegro giusto**

This tightly drawn movement contrasts themes of lyrical beauty with stark, explosive outbursts of technical virtuosity. The use of the thematic material is economical and imaginative, displaying the composer's firm grasp of formal development. The logic is readily assimilated and aids the performer in understanding the depth and dramatic intensity of the work.

There are fascinating details that are intriguing and fresh. The quiet introduction, presented in unison between hands, has fragments of its idea utilized in several places. The opening motif becomes the basis for the secondary subject; its statement is enlarged upon in the initial bars of the development. The closing two-note phrase of the introduction receives many rhythmic reiterations throughout the movement, the last time in a whispered final coda. The driving dotted eighth/sixteenth idea, originally integrated within the principal theme of the exposition, becomes the tool of the most dramatic intensity in the lengthy development, and is subjected to highly creative variations within its rhythmic parameters. A final innovation occurs in the restatement of the secondary subject, cleverly altered by the use of quarter note triplets on a theme originally built around even quarter note chords.

Length: 291 measures

Technique: octaves, broken octaves and octave chords, tremolo intervals, wide and abrupt dynamic contrasts

**Andante** (F Major)

The utilization of the three thematic ideas in this movement is a study of fascinating depth as the music develops. The first opens with quiet dignity in unison between hands, thickening to octaves and octave chords as the uneven phrases build in intensity. Between these phrases are small fragments of hushed dotted eighth/thirty-second notes, also in unison between hands. This diminutive motif is expanded upon later in the movement. The third theme, consisting of triplet repeated chords, opens at a forte level, but drops in dynamics and thins in texture to become the accompanying force behind the restatement of the original theme. Imaginative treatment of the dotted note motif leads to a "pp" coda that restates the opening melody.

This movement is highly original and was praised in the nineteenth century for its Beethovenesque qualities. It shows great mastery in tonal color and keyboard effect.

Length: 66 measures

Technique: octaves and octave chords, wide interval leaps, complex rhythmic subdivision, ornamentation, sustained and moving notes, wide dynamic contrast (f-pp)

**Allegro Vivace**

The finale of this sonata is bold and tactilely exciting. The triplet theme receives delightful fugal treatment that has the hands cavorting in parallel and contrary motion. A short brisk octave pattern, alternating with whirlwind scales, arpeggios, and broken chords, builds to periods of dramatic intensity. A contrasting quiet song appears, its simplicity relieved by piquant harmonic alterations and uneven phrase lengths.

These phrase ideas form the structure of this movement, that could perhaps be classified as an elongated rondo. There are three repetitions, with the key changes providing the variations within the material. The unusual twist comes in the last repetition, presenting the quiet song in the middle and ending with the octave fireworks. The last ten bars of canonic octaves are "formidable," to quote Maurice Hinson, and will dictate the tempo of the entire movement.

Length: 269 measures

Technique: 8th and 16th note passage work in parallel and contrary motion, abrupt dynamic contrasts, octave chords, broken chords, octaves

Most scholars tend to regard this as the first of Schubert's mature sonatas, as it breaks with his earlier ornamental style and reflects innovative and original concepts of composition. It was written in 1823, the first year of his illness, and was published in 1839. The recent discovery of the manuscript shows its being subjected to unusually careful revisions. The resulting composition is restrained and economical, yet dramatic and large in scale. Robert Schumann greatly admired Schubert's works, but singled out D. 784 as the composer's greatest sonata.

SONATA, A Minor, D. 845 (Op. 42) <u>Difficult</u>

BUONAMICI, G: Schubert--Ten Sonatas for Piano (G. Schirmer).
KALMUS PIANO SERIES: Franz Schubert--Sonatas for Piano, Part I.
MIES, Paul: Schubert--Klaviersonaten, Band I (G. Henle Verlag 146).
PETERS (Publisher): Schubert Sonaten, Band I (No. 487).

**Moderato**

Two highly contrasting themes appear in this movement. The first is quiet and dreamy and the second harsh and militant, but it is the first that receives the focus of the composer's attention. It appears twice in the exposition, with the key changed and statement broadened in its repetition. In the development section, its possibilities are explored to the fullest, almost in theme and variation style. A filigreed arpeggio replaces the chordal ending. A right hand tremolo supports the melody in the left hand, with further development of the ending fragment of the theme. A canonic interplay between hands leads into a lush crescendo of sound, produced by thick syncopated chords.

The percussive secondary theme also appears twice in the exposition and is reprised in the closing measures of the development. The recapitulation compresses both ideas into short fragments that almost interrupt each other as they appear in brief cameos of sound. The militant theme gains final ascendancy as it drives to a "ff" conclusion.

This movement has a broad, dramatic intensity. There is such logic in the thematic development that each new treatment seems inevitable. The mood builds from a brooding sense of foreboding to a climactic crisis, leaving the audience limp with wonder.

Length: 311 measures

Technique: octaves, broken octaves and octave chords, ornamentation, 8th and 16th note passage work, sustained and moving notes, hand-crosses, wide interval leaps

**Andante, poco mosso** (C Major)

This elegant theme and variation in 3/8 is described by M.J.E. Brown as "one of the most successful of (Schubert's) essays in this genre." It moves from crystalline simplicity to formidable complexity, exploring many colors and textures of sound as it evolves. The opening C Major statement is presented in three voices, with the folk-like tune in the alto, while the soprano holds a pedal point in light suspension above it. As the tune moves along there is an ebb and flow of additional voices and increasing dynamics, but it ends in a subdued "pp." The variations become increasingly difficult. The first pairs the melody with murmuring sixteenth notes that outline the chord structures while adding colorful passing tones. The second presents the melody in two-note phrases of thirty-second notes that trip up the fingers of the unwary. The third variation opens with the three voice texture of the theme, but in the tonic minor and with the pedal point in the alto; the duet between the soprano and tenor rapidly becomes a shouting match of dotted note octaves. Variation four, in Eb Major, features cascades of sound, with thirty-second note passage work in both hands. The ending variation returns to C Major, but heightens the drama with sixteenth note triplets driving the melodic idea forward. Octaves and octave chords force the dramatic climax, and a coda, still in the triplet scoring, winds down to a quiet chordal ending.

Length: 181 measures

Technique: complex rhythmic subdivision, rapid passage work, sustained and moving notes, octaves and octave chords, 2-note phrases, ornamentation, repeated notes and chords, broken chords and octaves

**Scherzo** (A Major)

Heightened by accentuated syncopated chords, the rhythmic drive of the theme provides tremendous tension and excitement in one of the best of the sonata scherzi. Comprised of two upbeat eighths and a half note, the unifying motif is subjected to every imaginable twist and turn of innovative treatment. Interspersed outlining of chords, either in sturdy octaves or tripping two-note phrases, offers rich and varied contrasts. Analyzing the frequent modulations of tonality and modality is a mind-boggling exercise, but to the ear they offer an immutable progression of tonal color.

The pulsing animation of the scherzo is relieved by the flowing graceful lines of the F Major trio, marked "un poco piu lento." The octave two-note phrase of an upbeat quarter and half note recalls the motif of the scherzo, although in a lyrical, relaxed setting. This phrase receives its most complex statement in the closing bars as the right hand repeats it in high and low registers, crossing over the left hand chords in the process.

Tempo: Allegro vivace
Length: 174 measures
Technique: short phrases, detached chords, octaves, sustained and moving notes, double 3rds, expanding and contracting intervals

**Rondo**

The finale of this work is a sonata rondo that returns to the key of A Minor. Its theme is a "perpetual motion" exercise for the right hand, although the left hand has its opportunity as the movement develops. A second idea appears in Schubert's often-used unison between hands. Repeated octave chords provide stunning percussive accents. A third thematic fragment of slow scalar octaves is introduced. The creative intertwining of these three ideas is a wonder of compositional economy, challenging the performer mentally with the innovative thematic development, and physically with finger-crunching technical demands.

Tempo: Allegro vivace
Length: 549 measures
Technique: 8th note passage work, wide interval leaps, sustained and moving notes, octaves and octave chords, 2-note phrases, ornamentation, high leger lines in both clefs, abrupt dynamic changes

Large and dramatic in scale, this sonata established Schubert's status as a composer for piano. It was written in 1825 and published by Pennhauer in 1825/26; it received favorable reviews in Leipzig and Frankfort, widening the scope of the composer's influence beyond Vienna.

The four movements offer wide diversity of mood. The contrasts allow ample opportunity for the skillful pianist, challenging both the technical and expressive expertise in performance.

SONATA, D Major, D. 850, Op. 53 Difficult

BUONAMICI, G: Schubert--Ten Sonatas for Piano (G. Schirmer).
KALMUS PIANO SERIES: Franz Schubert--Sonatas for Piano, Part I.
MIES, Paul: Schubert--Klaviersonaten, Band I (G. Henle Verlag 146).
PETERS (Publisher): Schubert Sonaten, Band I (No. 487).

**Allegro**

Two musical ideas stand out in this movement. The first is a vigorous chordal statement of even eighth and quarter notes. The second has its dramatic effect heightened with triplets in unison between the hands. These themes are extended, contracted, and manipulated in every imaginable fashion, but the general effect is a grinding sameness of often repeated material. On the positive side, this allegro displays a good-humored vitality; its wealth of lightning-fast scales, arpeggios, and turning patterns provides a vehicle for technical brilliance.

There may be discrepancies in tempo markings between editions. Schubert's autograph is in 2/2 with an "Allegro" indication. The first printed edition reads 4/4, marked "Allegro Vivace."

Length: 267 measures
Technique: 8th note triplet pasasage work, repeated chords and octaves, hand-crosses, clef changes, 2 vs. 3, wide interval and keyboard range

**Con Moto** (A Major)

A melody of great beauty, couched in rich textures of orchestral-like color, reveals Schubert's great genius with lyrical expression. A second theme shares almost equal importance within the rondo scheme. Its shorter phrase lengths and quicker notes in syncopated rhythms provide exquisite moments of contrast. Challenges to the performer are formidable. The thickness of chord structures, with important ideas often submerged in sound, dictates absolute control of dynamic balance. The inordinate length of the movement causes almost insurmountable problems in sustained and concentrated momentum. M.J.E. Brown describes it succinctly, saying it is a "lush melody (that) runs to extravagent lengths."

Length: 196 measures
Technique: octaves and octave chords, wide keyboard range, sustained and moving notes, varied articulations, wide dynamic range (fff-ppp), complex rhythmic subdivisions, ornamentation

**Scherzo**

Hans Gal, a biographer of Schubert, perhaps pinpoints the charm of this movement, as revealing "freshness of local color, and not without a touch of tipsiness." It is vivacious and playful, with unmistakeable touches of comedy and exaggerated Viennese "schmaltz."

There is a brisk, bravura motif in dotted-eighth and sixteenth notes that unifies the movement, interrupted by dazzling filigrees of ornamented single notes. The trio, written in the subdominant, is a subtle tune with uneven phrases that melt into each other. Its even rhythms and homophonic textures provide remarkably effective contrast to the robust exuberance of the scherzo.

Tempo: Allegro vivace
Length: 330 measures
Technique: repeated chords and octaves, double 3rds, syncopations, abrupt dynamics, extended broken chords, ornamented passage work, sustained and moving notes

**Rondo**

The folk-like good humor of the scherzo continues in this elongated rondo; there is a graceful tune above a brisk, marching accompaniment that evolves into flurries of passage work. Hans Gal best sums up the mood of this movement: "The relaxed way in which the melody strolls along, the way the local idiom turns pensive in a quieter episode, and the march tune finally dissolves into a rosy cloud of happiness - all this reflects a day of undisturbed contentment."

Tempo: Allegro Moderato
Length: 211 measures
Technique: 8th and 16th note passage work, Alberti patterns, octave and octave chords, changing clefs, wide keyboard range, wide dynamic range (ff-pp)

Of the eight mature Schubert sonatas, this is probably the least effective. It was written in the spring and summer of 1825, as the composer toured northern Austria, and seems to reflect his carefree happiness. It was published by Artaria in 1826 and dedicated to the pianist Karl von Bocklet.

The rather trivial theme of the finale was chosen as a representative theme in the saccharine operetta based on Schubert's life, called "Lilac Time." Unfortunately, the myth presented in that production, picturing Schubert as a penniless, bohemiam light-weight, still colors the perceptions of many people.

As a whole, this work exhibits an exaggerated romanticism. Its ideas are likeable but lack the depth of creativity found in the other sonatas. The rather trite material, compounded by the lengthy statements and restatements, could make the study and performance of this sonata a frustrating exercise.

**SONATA**, G Major, D. 894 (Op. 78) <u>Difficult</u>

KALMUS PIANO SERIES: Franz Schubert--
Sonatas for Piano, Part II.
MIES, Paul: Schubert--Klaviersonaten, Band II
(G. Henle Verlag 148).
PETERS (Publisher): Schubert Sonaten, Band II
(No. 488).

**Molto e cantabile**

The principal theme of this 12/8 movement is introduced in a hushed state of expectancy. Its serenity is belied by the undercurrents of tension in the sixteenth note chords that lead rhythmically and harmonically into the sustained chords on strong beats of the measures. The dichotomy of dissonance within the harmonic framework gives a momentum that climaxes in the thundering "ff" and "fff" restatements in the development section.

The secondary theme lightens the intensity of mood with its quick dance-like elegance. The lighthearted octave melody trips along, but as in the first theme, there is an edge of disquiet produced by the harmonic suspensions. These somber elements remain, even as the melody is restated and embellished with festoons of high register sixteenth notes.

Schubert built this entire movement around these two ideas. His statement does not conform to our preconceived ideas of sonata/allegro construction, but the unpredictable structure reinforces the dramatic intensity of the music, revealing an undeniable inner logic. His mastery of lyric expression, supported by colorful and dramatic effects of orchestral-like richness, produced music of profound depth and beauty. The performer's expressive capabilities will be challenged by this movement; it will be necessary to project moments of sunny optimism, abruptly dispelled by periods of dark despair.

Length: 174 measures

Technique: octaves and octave chords, 16th note scales and passage work, sustained and moving notes, changing clefs, repeated notes and chords, ppp-fff

**Andante** (D Major)

As in the first movement, this Andante has two contrasting ideas. The first is a song-like tune of considerable grace and elegance, supported by voices that double in octaves or harmonize in thirds or sixths. The second opens in a bold, bombastic chordal statement that suddenly melts into a quiet octave melody over murmuring broken chords. Both themes are treated to variation through rhythmic elaboration, with ensuing complexities of beat division within the 3/8 meter. An astounding variety of pianistic effects is projected in this short movement. Contrasts of mood are achieved through major vs. minor tonalities, soothing quiescence vs. biting dynamism, and pounding "ff" vs. hushed "ppp." Tranquility wins out, as the first theme is repeated in its initial simplicity. A brief coda of almost Mozartian classicism ends the piece.

Length: 180 measures
Technique: complex rhythmic subdivision, octaves, broken chords, ornamentation, wide interval leaps, ff-ppp

**Menuetto** (B Minor)

GEEHL, Henry: Schubert--Compositions of Moderate Difficulty (Ashdown).

A stately dignity characterizes this minuet, with thick repeated chords pairing with an octave melody as a thematic statement. The appoggiaturas and harmonic suspensions that embellish these chords add a strident touch as the music develops. This abrasive flavor enhances the contrasting B Major trio, a whispered folk song carried in the alto register of the four voice theme, with sustaining pedal points in the soprano and tenor. The quiet beauty of this trio and the militant stiffness of its companion combine in a movement of unusual freshness. M.J.E. Brown describes it as "one of the most lovable passages Schubert ever penned."

Tempo: Allegro moderato
Length: 83 measures
Technique: repeated chords, octaves, sustained and moving notes, ornamentation, ff-ppp

**Allegretto**

The finale of this sonata is a long rondo in G Major, with key signature changes to Eb Major, C Major, and reversing to Eb Major and back to G Major. The mood is consistently cheerful and good-humored, with a distinct air of Viennese ebullience. The opening theme is the most attractive, with piquant uneven phrases and a rat-a-tat motif of repeated chords interspersed or accompanying the bright tune. The second theme opens at a "pp" level and succeeds in sending each hand scurrying in varying patterns of quick passagework. The C Major melody (appearing only once) is a short, lyrical song accompanied by quiet broken chords. Overall this gay, unsophisticated whirlwind offers a variety of pianistic effects that will challenge the performer's technical skills. It contrasts well with the preceding movements and provides a stunning ending to this superb sonata.

Length: 410 measures
Technique: wide interval chords, repeated intervals and chords, double 3rds, 8th note passage work, changing clefs, wide interval leaps

Schubert composed this sonata in 1826, dedicating it to his friend, Josef Spaun. There are conflicting dates as to its publication, but the first edition was produced in 1826 or 1827 by Haslinger, who gave the separate movements the spurious titles of "Fantasia," "Andante," "Minuetto," und "Allegretto." Unfortunately, his labels are still retained in some editions, and many do not include them as a grouping entitled "Sonata".

This sonata received favorable reviews at the time of publication. Robert Schumann enthusiastically called it "Schubert's most perfect in form and in spirit." There is a record of the performance of this work in Paris in 1875, but its was pronounced "too orchestral and too long." Hopefully, today's pianists will recognize this sonata as one of Schubert's best; it merits careful study and enthusiastic performance.

**SONATA,** C Minor, D. 958 <u>Difficult</u>

BUONAMICI, G: Schubert--Ten Sonatas for Piano (G. Schirmer).
KALMUS PIANO SERIES: Franz Schubert-- Sonatas for Piano, Part II.
MIES, Paul: Schubert--Klaviersonaten, Band II (G. Henle Verlag 148).
PETERS (Publisher): Schubert Sonaten, Band II (No. 488)

**Allegro**

As a young musician, Schubert lived under the shadow of Beethoven, and was properly awed and inspired by the compositions of the great master. He served as a torchbearer at Beethoven's funeral. Whether consciously or unconsciously, the opening movement of D. 958 reflects Beethoven's influence in its first theme and ensuing treatment, which is rich in tonal color and pianistic effect. It is somber and brooding, with dramatic climaxes approached through ascending sequential patterns and supported by intense dynamic escalations.

The secondary theme reveals a more familiar Schubert, of lyrical expressiveness heightened by the innovative harmonic treatments so much his own. The phrases of this idea meld into one another, producing a short song of poignant beauty. The composer subjects this tune to three statements, each surrounded by increasingly complex textures, culminating in a sweep of intense chords and passage work that fade into a haunting, wistful coda.

A crashing "ffz" chord shatters the quiet, opening a "Pandora's box" of disquieting turmoil. The abrupt dynamic contrasts and violent crescendos give physical expression to the twisting chromatic dissonances that spread their pervasive ominous character throughout the development section. These tensions provide an undercurrent of unrest, as the dynamics lessen to whisper soft chords rumbling under "ppp" chromatic scales.

The recapitulation follows the pattern of the exposition, winding down into the same quiet coda. A dramatic pause prepares for a restatement of the development material, building from a "pp" to a tumultuous climax. Descending broken octaves over thick broken chords plunge to the quiet depths, with a murmuring left hand rumble dying away into oblivion.

Length: 274 measures

Technique: octaves, broken octaves, and octave chords, 16th note scales, arpeggios and passagework, wide interval leaps, abrupt dynamic changes (ff-ppp), hand-crosses, clef changes

**Adagio** (Ab Major)

This rondo takes the form of a richly accompanied song, opening and closing in serenity, but interrupted by a dynamic middle section. Kathleen Dale comments that its "refrain recalls Beethoven's cantabiles, but couched in Schubert's own rhythmic shape."

The opening statement in Ab Major attains a quiet dignity through its four voice structure. Its straightforward declamation is halted by two fermatas, and its cadence almost crowded out by the appearance of the second idea, opening in a plaintive Db Minor. After a momentary shifting to major, this statement settles into an uneasy octave melody over repeated triplets. The chromatically expanding and contracting intervals of these left hand triplets produce a tension that mushrooms dramatically as the right hand octaves join in the drive towards the "ff" climax. The climb to intensity is rather rapid, and the fall to a whispering "pp" even faster, as the momentum dies briefly before the whole process is repeated.

The opening song reappears in the same key, but with added rhythmic complexity in accompanying patterns. The secondary theme surfaces as before, but is cut short by percussive octave triplets opening into an extended section of bravura keyboard effects, fluctuating wildly in dynamic levels. Again the driving triplets die away into the song, accompanied by exceedingly difficult wide interval broken chords. The hesitancy of the final phrases, produced by fermatas and rests, heightens the sense of loss as this beautiful work ends.

Length: 115 measures
Technique: octaves and octave chords, complex rhythmic subdivisions, sustained and moving notes, expanding and contracting intervals, 2 vs. 3

**Menuetto**

Undoubtedly the shortest of Schubert's sonata movements, this minuet and trio is unusually brief, probably intended to balance out the inordinately long Allegro to follow. It is a curious amalgam of uneven phrases, abrupt dynamic shifts, and sudden silences. The Ab Major trio contrasts in key with the C Major minuet, but both are unified by common rhythmic and melodic motifs into a clever, subtle piece with great appeal and charm.

Tempo: Allegro moderato
Length: 77 measures
Technique: octaves, 8th note passage work, wide interval leaps, sustained and moving notes

**Allegro**

The infectious gaiety of the tarantella dominates this Allegro, with patterns that skitter all over the keyboard. The formidable length of the movement is a test of endurance for the performer, who must deal with whirlwind triplets, hand-crosses, explosive dynamics, and thirteen key signature changes. The quality of thematic material is uneven, pairing sections of aural and tactile excitement with long statements of curiously flat redundancy.

The sketch of this sonata reveals many revisions, and a major expansion by a later addition of the B Major episode. The changes did not alleviate the problems presented by seven hundred-plus measures of non-stop "noodling."

Length: 717 measures
Technique: 8th note passage work, hand-crosses, high leger lines, wide interval leaps, key changes, clef changes, repeated chords, abrupt dynamics (ff-pp)

This sonata is the first of three written within a four-week period in 1828, the year of Schubert's death. It was published in 1838. Major differences between the original sketch and the first edition suggest that Schubert completely rewrote it, making the most extensive revisions in the last movement.

The first three movements are strong and dramatic, with an undercurrent of somberness and pathos. The ending Allegro has moments of clever appeal, but lacks strength of purpose as a final statement.

**SONATA,** A Major, D. 959 <u>Difficult</u>

BUONAMICI, G: Schubert--Ten Sonatas for Piano (G. Schirmer).
KALMUS PIANO SERIES: Franz Schubert--Sonatas for Piano, Part II.
MIES, Paul: Schubert--Klaviersonaten, Band II (G. Henle Verlag 148).
PETERS (Publisher): Schubert Sonaten, Band II (No. 488).

**Allegro**

Sustaining pedal points in high and low registers give surprising tension to the ascending double thirds in the opening measures of this movement. These somber chords are frequently interrupted by rippling triplet patterns that finally explode into a driving "ff" climax. The fury is short-lived, as the triplets begin to fade in volume; the ebbing momentum is aided by the notated ritardando of triplets melting into the duple eighths that introduce the secondary theme. The ethereal simplicity of this lovely melody evokes an unexpected serenity of woefully short duration. A forte transition sees the return of the triplets, ascending in short chromatic volleys between hands to harried divided octaves. A dramatic silence brings this ferocity to an abrupt halt, and a quiet repetition of the song restores an air of calmness.

A brief scalar motif that ornaments the ending song of the exposition becomes the thematic basis for the extended development section. The complex and colorful pianistic effect offer shimmering waves of sound, ebbing and flowing in dynamics to the "ff" of rich chords marking the recapitulation. The scalar theme of the development makes a final reappearance as the movement ends; it quietly opens a coda built around whispered allusions to the thematic idea that opened this magnificent allegro.

Length: 357 measures

Technique: octaves and octave chords, 8th and 16th note passage work, wide interval leaps, sustained and moving notes, clef changes, double 3rds, hand-crosses

**Andantino**

The bittersweet melody of this 3/8 movement appears and reappears, as if the composer hates to let go of its pensive beauty. Each repetition offers slight variations in ornamented patterns or expanded voicing, but the subtle, unbalanced melody and harmony remain unchanged. A flurry of quick notes, increasing in rapidity and complexity of subdivision, introduces a colorfully dramatic middle section. The technical demands called for in this onward rush of notes will challenge the pianist, and wake up those listeners lulled to sleep by the lullaby of the opening section. Thundering broken octaves add a final crescendo of sound; a sudden "ffz" chord seemingly ends the furor, but curious bursts of quick dynamic expansions keep the drama alive until the reappearance of the lovely song, accompanied by soft rumblings of wide broken chords. Whispering rolled chords spell out the cadence, and the movement ends on a unison tonic note.

Length: 202 measures

Technique: complex rhythmic subdivision, wide interval leaps, octaves and octave chords, ornamentation, tremolandos, hand-crosses, melody and accompaniment in the same hand, changing clefs

**Allegro vivace**

This short A Major scherzo delights in its playful exuberance. The flippant chords of the opening theme jump in quick register changes and evolve into high register eighth note passage work. The secondary theme expands upon the eighth note patterns, as bursts of long uneven phrases flow over accompanying chords and sustaining bass pedal points. A series of these patterns in abbreviated lengths lead into a repetition of the primary theme.

The D Major trio slows slightly, but the frivolous good humor continues as the left hand leaps in wide register changes over a more sustained right hand melody. This is begun at a "pp" dynamic level that escalates through the second section to a "ff" climax. An abrupt return to the pianissimo material calls for even further decreases of sound into a whispered transition before the scherzo is repeated.

Length: 113 measures
Technique: quick hand position shifts, high leger lines, 8th and 16th note passagework, sustained and moving notes, hand-crosses

**Allegretto**

The principal theme of this A Major rondo seems to be derived from the slow movement of D. 537. Its setting in this sonata contains curious rests that seemingly stop a phrase only to begin the next, in a continuous melding of melodic ideas. This lovely tune is stated in each hand, with accompanying patterns that augment from broken chord eighth notes to rippling triplet passage work. A climactic flurry of broken octaves leads to a broad secondary theme that marches in steady even notes over the continuing triplet broken triads. This is given extensive treatment, becoming a "perpetual motion" of quick patterns for both hands. A presto section opens with a new left hand melody accompanied by the now familiar triplets, building in intensity to abrupt chords and a grand pause. A clever coda repeats the ending phrase of the initial melody and explodes into wild arpeggios and vigorous pedal point chords, ending this captivating movement in a totally dramatic fashion.

Length: 392 measures
Technique: sustained and moving notes, octaves, broken octaves and octave chords, 8th and 16th note passage work, duple vs. triple rhythms, wide interval leaps, hand-crosses, clef changes

This sonata was composed in September of 1828 and published in 1838; the autograph and first edition are both available for study. Schubert's biographer, Marek, calls it a "vessel of beautiful tunes." These melodies are couched in dramatic settings, expressied through volatile and often abrupt change of mood. Technical and expressive demands on the performer are substantial. Marek expresses the view that this sonata is a "taxing work which few pianists play and fewer still play well"; one who does is Alfred Brendel, who claims that "Schubert leads us into regions of wonderment, terror, and awe."

**SONATA**, Bb Major, D. 960 <u>Difficult</u>

BUONAMICI, G: Schubert--Ten Sonatas for Piano (G. Schirmer).
KALMUS PIANO SERIES: Franz Schubert--Sonatas for Piano, Part II.
MIES, Paul: Schubert--Klaviersonaten, Band II (G. Henle Verlag 148).
PETERS (Publisher): Schubert Sonaten, Band II (No. 488).

**Molto moderato**

The intensely lyrical themes of this movement will sing under the hands of an expressive performer, providing moments of sheer beauty that reveal Schubert's undeniable genius. The primary statement opens in a whispered undertone, with the warm octaves supported by inner voice eighth notes that harmonize in their own quiet fashion. The phrase endings that sustain over the rumbling low register trills produce a breathless sense of expectancy, which is especially effective as the second strain brightens into Gb Major and evolves into hushed filigrees of quick sixteenth notes. Triplet octave chords crescendo into an urgent restatement of the octave melody, ending in a breathtaking modulation to the F# Major secondary idea. Extensive treatment of this melody and the lengthy coda-like section that follows provide some of the loveliest moments in the work, with constantly fresh insights melding together in incessant revelation.

A seemingly insignificant pattern of accompaying triplets within the coda becomes an important thematic motif of the development section which, like the material before it, teems with the creative flow of lyricism and innovative harmonic treatment.

The recapitulation follows the pattern of the exposition, but with occasional extraordinary changes in minute details. The secondary theme opens in a surprising B Minor and undergoes a creative modulation to B Major. The ending coda has moments of tentative searching before the final measures of the tenderly restated opening melody melt into stillness.

Length: 357 measures
Technique: octaves and octave chords, trills, sustained and moving notes, wide broken chords, wide interval leaps, 8th and 16th note passage work, changing clefs, melody and accompaniment in the same hand, repeated notes, duplet vs. triplet rhythms

**Andante sostenuto** (C# Minor)

The quiet intensity of the first movement is echoed in this C# Minor Andante, although its mood is more somber and introspective. The theme is focused in the middle register of the piano, with pedal point notes of changing register riding below and above it. The harmonic pull of these sustaining notes against the consonant thirds and sixths of the duet-like melody is intensely beautiful. As the chord textures thicken, the tensions are heightened by pointed suspensions, accented by their stressed position on the first beat of the measure.

A second theme in A Major seems to counteract the opening pathos with a mood of hopeful dignity. The pedal point remains in the repeating bass figures as the homophonic chords move, first in hymn-like solemnity, and then evolving into rippling broken chords under the sustained single note melody. Reflecting a sense of optimism, this section does not end in a final cadence, but is interrupted by a measure of silence and the return to the poignant C# Minor melody. The pedal points are intensified with additional ornamental patterns and register extensions. The movement ends with a "ppp" statement of the song in the tonic major, as if sadness were being replaced with serene acceptance and repose.

Length: 138 measures
Technique: hand-crosses, broken chords, melody and accompaniment in the same hand, broken octaves, changing clefs

**Scherzo**

The sunshine breaks through the clouds as this happy, buoyant scherzo sparkles into life. The quick patterns, with leaping octaves, give physical expression to the light-hearted gaiety, but remain elegantly understated, shy of any boisterous exuberance. Melodic ideas are tossed conversationally between the hands, with accompanying divided chords supporting the clever harmonic progressions, and intensified by bold chromaticism. The far-ranging harmonies resolve back to the original Bb Major key as the theme receives its final left hand statement.

The trio opens abruptly in Bb Minor and provides effective contrast, with slow notes spiced by syncopations. Three voices carry the thematic idea, with a cleverly off-beat bass line adding subtle rhythmic accents. As in the scherzo, the material is quiet and understated, with narrow dynamic ranges indicating tightly controlled nuances. The trio ends as abruptly as it began, and the scherzo is repeated with an added whisper soft coda.

Tempo: Allegro vivace con delicatezza
Length: 124 measures
Technique: divided chords, 8th note scalar patterns, ornamentation, clef changes, ties over the bar line

**Allegro, ma non troppo**

This lengthy rondo intensifies the mood of the preceding movement, as the Andante did to that of the opening Moderato. The light-hearted gaiety of the Scherzo becomes bold, tongue-in-cheek good humor, expressed in unexpected silences, abrupt accents, and passionate crescendos of sound. The unwary performer may be tripped up by unending patterns of quick turns, repeated notes, and sustaining melodies over broken chords within one hand. The off-beat left hand line in the second theme is particularly troublesome. These challenges are alleviated by the sheer fun of the tarantella idea that rollicks along, providing great tactile zest. This wonderful piece ends in a presto whirlwind based on the opening thematic motif, first hammered out in octaves and climaxes in a duple vs. triple rhythm that expands to a crashing "ff" ending.

Length: 540 measures
Technique: 8th and 16th note passage work, octaves and broken octaves, repeated notes, broken chords, melody and accompaniment in same hand, duple vs. triple rhythms

One of Schubert's best-known and greatest sonatas was written a few months before the composer's death and published in 1838. The first two movements are especially beautiful and seem to reflect a calm resignation and serene acceptance, overshadowing all the turmoil and trouble life can offer. A quote from Music in History by McKinney and Anderson says it best, "There is something in this music beyond the pure quality of sensuous beauty in which ‚Schubert. delighted; it seems to have been written by a man, as someone has said, who had looked into Hell and was newly seeing God."

## SONATAS—INCOMPLETE

Schubert left ten unfinished sonatas, with fragments ranging from a few bars to almost complete works, such as the "Relique" Sonata in C Major, D. 840. Many of these partial manuscripts contain passages that are characteristic of the composer, but they are uneven in inspiration and were probably discarded for that reason. Most fragments bear early composition dates, so were not unfinished due to Schubert's untimely death.

In the Henle edition, the source used for this section, there are inclusions designated as sonata movements, of short works that have been previously published under other designations. These changes have been made as the result of recent scholarship and represent the most up-to-date information available. Specific changes are enumerated in the foreword to the chapter on "Shorter Works" in this volume.

Erroneous groupings or titles in earlier editions may have been the result of unilateral decisions made by publishers, who placed salability over accuracy. In some instances, proper groupings are difficult to discern because of Schubert's penchant for writing separate sonata movements on unused staves of manuscripts containing other compositions.

There are two works contained in the Henle edition of sonata fragments that we have chosen to treat as complete works and have included in the chapter on Sonatas. The first is the Sonata in E Major, D. 459, that has been titled "Five Pieces for Pianofirte" in earlier editions. The second is the Sonata in E Minor, D. 566, originally published as four separate pieces. They were published as a whole sonata for the first time in 1948, edited by Kathleen Dale.

Note: All of these incomplete sonatas may be found in:

BADURA-SKODA, Paul: Schubert Klaviersonaten, Band III (G. Henle Verlag 150).

## SONATA, E Major, D. 157

**Allegro**

Composed in 1815, this movement was published in a supplementary volume of "Gesamtausgabe" by Brietkopf and Hartel in 1897 and preserved in an autograph.

Length: 251 measures

**Andante** (E Minor)

Length: 112 measures

**Menuetto and trio** (B Major)

Length: 90 measures

## SONATA, C Major, D. 279

**Allegro moderato**

Length: 211 measures

**Andante** (F Major)

Length: 80 measures

**Menuetto and trio** (A Minor)

Composed in 1815, this sonata is preserved in an autograph that suggests there is a lost fourth movement. It was published by Rehberg in 1927, with an undated Allegretto in C Major (D. 346) used as a fourth movement.

Length: 88 measures

**SONATA,** C Major, D. 346

Allegretto

This fragment breaks off after the restatement of the principal theme in the recapituation. A completion has been composed by Paul Badura-Skoda.

Length: 371 measures

## SONATA, Ab Major, D. 557

### Allegro moderato

Length: 99 measures

### Andante (Eb Major)

Length: 96 measures

### Allegro (Eb Major)

This sonata was written in 1817. There is an autograph of only the 3rd movement. All three movements were published in 1888; this early edition is the source of the first and second movements.

Length: 133 measures

## SONATA, Db Major, D. 567 (Op.122)

### Allegro moderato

Length: 238 measures

**Andante molto** (C# Minor)

Length: 122 measures

**Allegretto** (Db Major)

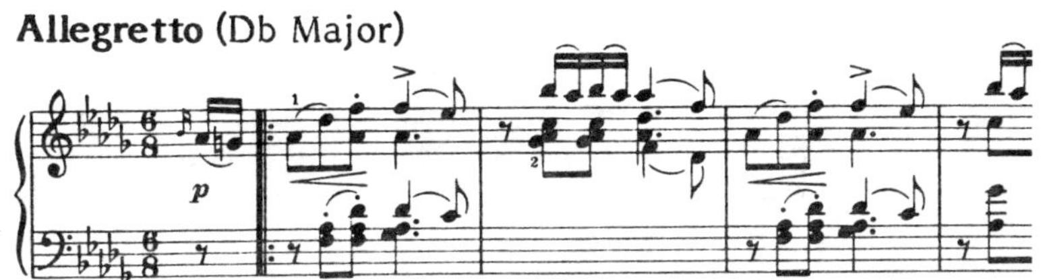

This sonata was composed in 1817; Schubert later transposed the work, setting the Allegro in Eb Major, the Andante in G Minor, the Allegretto in Eb Major, and added the Minuet and trio in Eb Major. The autograph of the sonata in the original key of Db Major contains the first three movements with the last page of the Allegretto missing. It has been completed by Paul Bedura-Skoda.

Length: 184 measures

**SONATA,** F# Minor, D. 571

**Allegro**

This is a fragment only, completed in this volume by Paul Badura-Skoda. Schubert's composition includes exposition and development.

Length: 252 measures

**(Klavierstucke),** D. 604

EPSTEIN, Julius: Franz Schubert--Shorter Works (Dover).

This lovely cantabile movement, composed in 1818, has no tempo marking, but the G. Henle editor suggests an Andante. The song-like melody and the increasingly florid variations within its outlines presages the slow movements in Schuberts's later works. The expressive pianist will find this work a joy to perform.

Length: 63 measures

Technique: complex rhythmic subdivision, sustained and moving notes, expanding and contracting intervals

**Scherzo and trio,** D Major, D. 570

Length: 71 measures

Allegro, F# Minor, D. 570

Length: 302 measures

These four movements seem to share a close relationship; they are all written on the back of sketches dating from 1815-1816. The Allegros, D. 571 and D. 570, are fragments only and are completed by Paul Badura-Skoda in the G. Henle edition; D. 571 was composed in 1817. D. 604 was composed in 1818, and the Scherzo, D. 570, in 1817.

**SONATA,** C Major, D. 613

**Moderato**

Length: 214 measures (complete)

**Adagio,** E Major, D. 612

EPSTEIN, Julius: Franz Schubert--Shorter Works (Dover).

Both movements of this sonata are fragments, completed in the G. Henle edition by Paul Badura-Skoda. D. 613 was composed in 1818. Twenty-one measures of the Adagio (D. 612) were combined with the Rondo from Sonata in E Minor (D. 566) as a pair of pieces known as Op. 145 Nos. 1 and 2.

Length: 256 measures (complete)

**SONATA,** F Minor, D. 625

**Allegro**

Length: 198 measures (complete)

**Scherzo and trio** (E Major)

Length: 150 measures

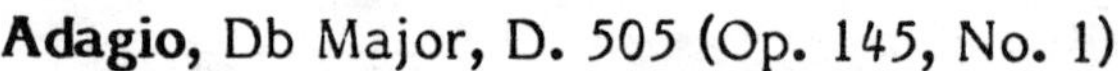
**Adagio,** Db Major, D. 505 (Op. 145, No. 1)

EPSTEIN, Julius: Franz Schubert--Shorter Works (Dover).

Length: 49 measures

**Allegro** (F Minor)

The first and last movements of this sonata are fragments, completed by Paul Badura-Skoda in the G. Henle edition. The adagio and final allegro were paired with the Rondo D. 506 and published separately in 1847 as Op. 145. Examination of a manuscript catalogue made by Ferdinand Schubert lists them as movements of the F Minor Sonata, written in 1818.

Length: 283 measures (complete)

**SONATA,** C Major (Relique), D. 840

**Moderato**

BISHOP, Stephen: Oxford Keyboard Classics--Schubert.

Length: 318 measures

**Andante** (C Minor)

Length: 121 measures

**Minuet and trio** (Ab Major)

Length: 123 measures (complete)

**Rondo** (C Major)

This sonata, composed in 1825, has only the first two movements completed. It is considered the most important of the unfinished sonatas; the two fragmentary movements have been completed by Armin Knab, Ernst Krenek, Walter Rehberg, and, in the Henle edition, Paul Badura-Skoda.

The manuscript of this sonata was given to Robert Schumann by Ferdinand Schubert, Franz's brother. The slow movement was published by Schumann in "Neue Zeitschrift fur Music" in December, 1839.

Length: 555 measures (complete)

**Allegro,** E Major, D. 154

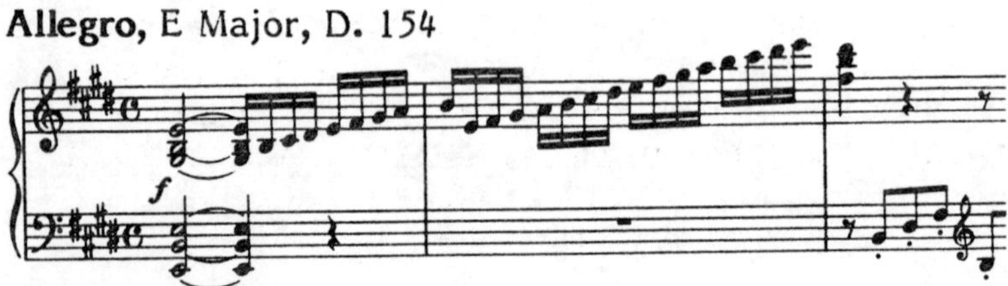

This fragment, found in an autograph, is an earlier version of the first movement of the sonata in E Major, D. 157.

**Allegro,** A Minor, D. 279

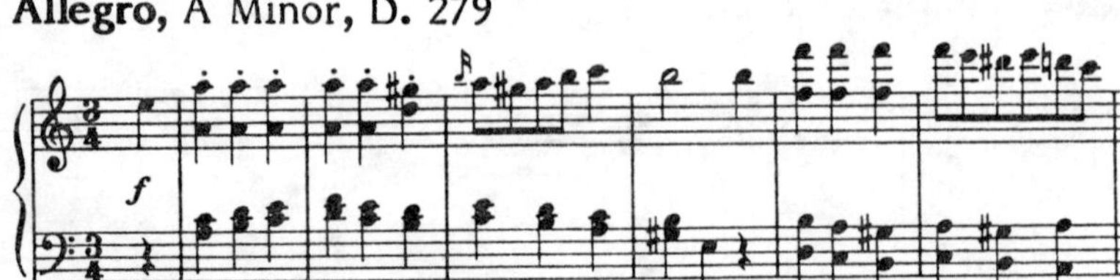

This is an alternative version of the third movement of the Sonata in C Major D. 279: it comes from a Schubert autograph.

**Adagio,** G Major, D. 178, 82 measures

This unfinished movement, and the accompanying sketch D. 178b, were probably composed in April of 1815. Both incomplete works were published by Brietkopf and Hartel in 1897.

**Adagio,** G Major, D. 178b

In the opinion of Paul Badura-Skoda, this unfinished work may have been intended as the slow movement of a sonata. Although it is incomplete in the manuscript, it could be played by repeating bars three through twenty-four. It is an alternative for or a second version of D. 178, and is sketched in the same autograph.

Length: 60 measures

## OTHER WORKS

**WANDERER FANTASY,** C Major, D. 760, Op. 15 — Very Difficult

**Allegro con fuoco ma non troppo**

EPSTEIN, Julius: Schubert--Shorter Works (Dover).
KALMUS PIANO SERIES: Schubert--Impromptus (Belwin-Mills).

This very difficult movement is characterized by repeated chords, arpeggios, broken chords, scale passages, tremolos, and hand-cross leaps. The melody is often played by the thumb within 16th note figurations. The second theme is beautiful in a typical Schubertian graceful way. The sense of energetic drive is continued throughout the entire movement regardless of melodic or harmonic material. Expressive aspects result from quick-changing dynamic extremes and delightful harmonic surprises.

Length: 189 measures
Technique: various articulations, triplets, scales, large chords, repeated chords, arpeggios, octaves, chromatic figures, broken chords and intervals, sustained and moving notes, tremolos

**Adagio** (C# Minor)

This movement is a direct quote from Schubert's well-known song "Das Wanderer." The lied is stated in a beautiful set of theme and variations. The theme is a simple 8-measure chordal melody in C# Minor which moves to E Major. In the first variation it returns to the minor tonality, while the melody remains a simplistic single line. The accompaniment becomes increasingly complex. The subsequent variations are based on harmonic implications, using rapid repeated octave and chordal figures in one case and tremolo and rapid scale passages in the other. The transition between this movement and the Presto is rather ingenious. Schubert ends the movement in E Major while using the G# enharmonically, thus enabling him to start the next movement in Ab Major.

Length: 57 measures

Technique: octaves and octave chords, sustained and moving notes, 16th, 32nd, and 64th note passage work, wide leaps, broken chords, rapidly alternating hands, 2 vs. 3, tremolando

**Presto** (Ab Major)

Thematic material from the first movement is used enjoyably and cleverly, employing the first movement's characteristic broken chord figures. The variation is in the form of a waltz with surprising hand interaction and phrase groupings.

Length: 353 measures
Technique: octaves and broken octaves, chromatic scales, arpeggios

**Allegro**

This movement is in a way a shorter and more concise version of the first, using fugal techniques. Similar themes are employed and each contain the same virtuosic technical devices such as octaves, arpeggios, and tremolos.

Length: 123 measures
Technique: 16th note passage work, octaves, arpeggios, broken chords, leaps, tremolando

This four-movement composition is one of Schubert's few truly virtuosic works. It's title and unifying rhythmic patterns are derived from Schubert's song "Das Wanderer." The Wanderer Fantasy is perhaps most famous for being so incredibly taxing to the performer's stamina and endurance. Strong fingers, flexible arms and wrists and good muscular control are necessities.

**GERMAN GALOP,** C Major, D. 925, Op. 171, or "Grazer Galop" <u>Intermediate</u>

MIES, Paul: Schubert--Samtliche Tanze, Band II (G. Henle Verlag 76).
SHEALY, Alexander: Schubert--his greatest Piano Solos (Ashley).

Along with the Twelve Waltzes, D. 924 (Op. 91), this Galop was composed while Schubert vacationed in Graz in September of 1827. The vibrant good humor evident in this sturdy piece gives no hint of his ill health and impending death less than a year later. The A sections of the ABA form are exactly alike, scored in vigorous dotted note chords paired with a jump bass or occasional octave doublings. The G Major trio has a lighter more graceful quality, with a single-line melody in even eighths and sixteenths. the trio opens and closes in G Major, although its second strain moves to D Major through accidental alterations.

Length: 72 measures
Technique: 16th note scalar patterns, triads and octave chords, jump bass, important accents and dynamic contrasts

**COTILLON,** Eb Major, D. 976 <u>Early Intermediate</u>

MIES, Paul: Schubert--Samtliche Tanze, Band II (G. Henle Verlag 76).
SHEALY, Alexander: Schubert--his greatest Piano Solos (Ashley).

All the elegance and grace of the waltz is embodied in this short piece, but the piquant harmonics add an additional element of surprise and delight. The simple melody, doubled at the octave for emphasis, is accompanied by a straightforward waltz bass. The simplicity of construction makes the beautifully creative writing especially appealing.

Length: 24 measures
Technique: waltz bass, octaves

# BIBLIOGRAPHY

Abraham, Gerald: The Music of Schubert--an Anthology. New York: W.W. Norton, 1947. Article on "The Piano Music," Kathleen Dale.

Badura-Skoda, Eva and Branscombe, Peter: Schubert Studies, Problems of Style and Chronology. Cambridge: Cambridge University Press, 1982. Article on "The Chronology of Schubert's Fragments and Sketches," Reinhard Van Hoorichx.

Brown, Maurice J.E.: Schubert, A Critical Biography. New York: Macmillan/St. Martins Press, 1966.

Deutsch, Otto E: Schubert: Thematic Catalogue of All His Works. London: J.M. Dent & Sons, 1951.

Foss, H.J.: Heritage of Music, Volume I. London: Oxford University Press, 1928. Article, "Franz Schubert," Sir D.F. Tovey.

Gal, Hans: Franz Schubert and the Essence of Melody. New York: Crescendo Publishing, 1977.

Gillespie, John: Five Centuries of Keyboard Music. New York: Dover Publications, 1965.

Hinson, Maurice: Guide to the Pianist's Repertoire: Edited by Irwin Freundlich. Indiana University Press, 1973.

Marek, George R.: Schubert. New York: Viking Penguin Inc. 1985.

McKinney, Howard and Anderson, W.R.: Music in History. New York: American Book Co., 1949

Sachs, Curt. Our Musical Heritage. New York: Prentice Hall Inc., 1948.

Wechsberg, Joseph: Schubert: His Life, His Works, His Time. New York: Rizzoli International Publications, 1977

The New Groves Dictionary of Music and Musicians Edited by Stanley Sadie. Washington, D.C.: Macmillan Publishers Limited, 1980. Articles on Ecossaise, Landler, Minuet, Schubert and Suites.

The New Groves. Schubert. Maurice J.E. Brown with Eric Sams. New York: Norton & Co. 1980

## GRADE LEVELING

Graded levels are included for every composition, and are determined by technical, rhythmical, and musical content. The following levels are suggestions only.

|  |  |
|---|---|
| Elementary<br>Advancing Elementary | -Elementary School |
| Early Intermediate<br>Intermediate<br>Advancing Intermediate | -Junior High School |
| Advancing Intermediate<br>Early Advanced<br>Advanced | -High School |
| Advanced<br>Difficult<br>Very Difficult | -University or Artist |

## GLOSSARY

Note: We are providing incipits that illustrate terms used in the "Technique" sections rather than giving written definitions. They are as follows:

SCALAR PATTERNS
ff
SUSTAINED and MOVING NOTES
pp
TREMOLANDO
f
p
WALTZ BASS
p
cresc.
WIDE INTERVAL LEAPS
pp

## SOURCES--SCHUBERT BOOKS

Alfred (Publisher): Schubert--21 of his Easiest Piano Pieces (465).

Alfred (Publisher): Schubert--17 of his Most Popular Piano Solos (398).

Badura-Skoda, Paul: Schubert--Klaviersonaten, Band III (G. Henley Verlag 150).

Beringer, Oscar: Beringer's School of Easy Classics--Schubert (Augener Edition, Galliard/Galaxy No.5138).

Bishop, Stephen: Oxford Keyboard Classics--Schubert (Oxford University Press).

Buonamici, G.: Schubert--Fantasias, Impromptus, Moments Musicals (G. Schirmer, Vol.75).

Buonamici, G.: Schubert--10 Sonatas for the Piano, (G. Schirmer, Vol.837).

Dexter, Harry: Selected Piano Works--Schubert (Hansen T366).

Epstein, Julius: Franz Schubert Shorter Works for Pianoforte Solo--"Wanderer" Fantasy, Impromptus, Moments Musicals and Twelve Other Works (Dover 22648-4).

Geehl, Henry: Schubert--Selected Compositions of Moderate Difficulty (Edwin Ashdown Limited, London NW2 6QR).

Halford, Margery: Schubert--The First Book for Young Pianists (Alfred).

Halford, Margery: Schubert--An Introduction to his Piano Works (Alfred).

Hansen (Publisher): Franz Schubert--A Highlight Collection Of His Best-Loved Original Works (M444).

Heinrichshofen Edition: Schubert--Easier Favorites Urtext (Peters N. 4051).

Herrmann, Kurt: Easy Schubert, Schumann and Weber (Kalmus Piano Series, 9541/Belwin-Mills).

Hughes, Edwin: Schubert--Master Series for the Young (G. Schirmer, 1113).

Kalmus Piano Series, 3886: Franz Schubert--Impromptus, Op.90-Op.142, Moments Musicaux, Op. 94, Phantasies, Op.15-Op.78, Allegretto, Andante, March, Scherzos (Belwin-Mills).

Kalmus Piano Series, 3876: Schubert--An Easy Album for Piano Solo (Belwin-Mills).

Kalmus PIano Series, 9547: Masters for the Young, Weber and Schubert (Belwin-Mills).

Mies, Paul: Schubert--Samtliche Tanze, Band I (G. Henle Verlag, 74).

Mies, Paul: Schubert--Samtliche Tanze, Band II (G. Henle Verlag 76).

Mies, Paul: Schubert--Klaviersonaten, Band I (G. Henle Verlag 146).

Mies, Paul: Schubert--Klaviersonaten, Band II (G. Henle Verlag 148).

Niemann, Walter: Schubert Dances (Peters, No. 150).

Rowley, Alec: The Easiest Original Schubert Pieces for the Piano (Hinrichsen, No.6/Peters).

Schirmer (G.) (Publisher): Schubert Dances for the Piano (Vol. 1537).

Shealy, Alexander: Schubert--his greatest Piano Solos (Ashley).

Small, Allan: Schubert Waltz Sampler (Alfred).

Volger, Heinz: Schubert--Easiest Piano Pieces (Peters, No. 5015).

Weinmann, Alexander and Kann, Hans: Schubert--Walzer und Deutsche Tanze (Wiener Urtext, UT 50063).

Weinmann, Alexander and Kann, Hans: Schubert--Landler, Ecossaisen, Menuette (Wiener Urtert, UT 50064).

Zeitlin, Poldi: Composers for the Keyboard--Schubert Dances For Piano (Presser, 410-41211).

# TITLE INDEX

## DANCES

Ecossaise



German Dances

# DEUTSCH INDEX

# KEY INDEX

## DANCES

**C# MINOR**



**D MAJOR**



**D MINOR**



**Db MAJOR**

# NOTES